GIANTS OF THE
MONSOON FOREST

GIANTS OF THE MONSOON FOREST

Living and Working with Elephants

JACOB SHELL

W. W. NORTON & COMPANY

Independent Publishers Since 1923

NEW YORK • LONDON

Copyright © 2019 by Jacob Shell

For information about permission to reproduce selections from this book,
write to Permissions, W. W. Norton & Company, Inc.,
500 Fifth Avenue, New York, NY 10110

For information about special discounts for bulk purchases, please contact
W. W. Norton Special Sales at specialsales@wwnorton.com or 800-233-4830

Manufacturing by Sheridan
Book design by Lovedog Studio
Production manager: Lauren Abbate

Library of Congress Cataloging-in-Publication Data

Names: Shell, Jacob, 1983– author.
Title: Giants of the monsoon forest : living and working
with elephants / Jacob Shell.
Description: First edition. | New York : W. W. Norton & Company,
[2019] | Includes bibliographical references and index.
Identifiers: LCCN 2018058217 | ISBN 9780393247763 (hardcover)
Subjects: LCSH: Elephants. | Human-animal relationships.
Classification: LCC QL795.E4 S525 2019 | DDC 599.67—dc23
LC record available at https://lccn.loc.gov/2018058217

W. W. Norton & Company, Inc., 500 Fifth Avenue, New York, N.Y. 10110
www.wwnorton.com

W. W. Norton & Company Ltd., 15 Carlisle Street, London W1D 3BS

For my grandparents

CONTENTS

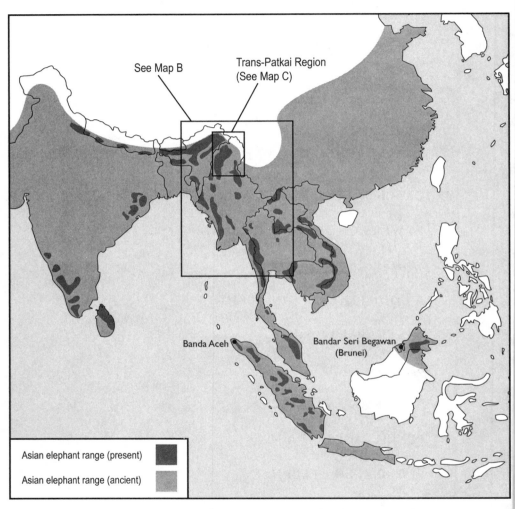

Map A. Present and ancient ranges of the Asian elephant
(*Elephas maximus*) in South and Southeast Asia.
Cartography by Jacob Shell.

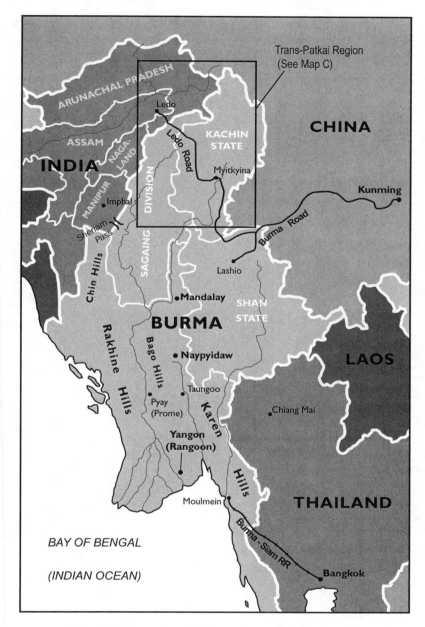

Map B. Central and Upper Burma (Myanmar).
Cartography by Jacob Shell.

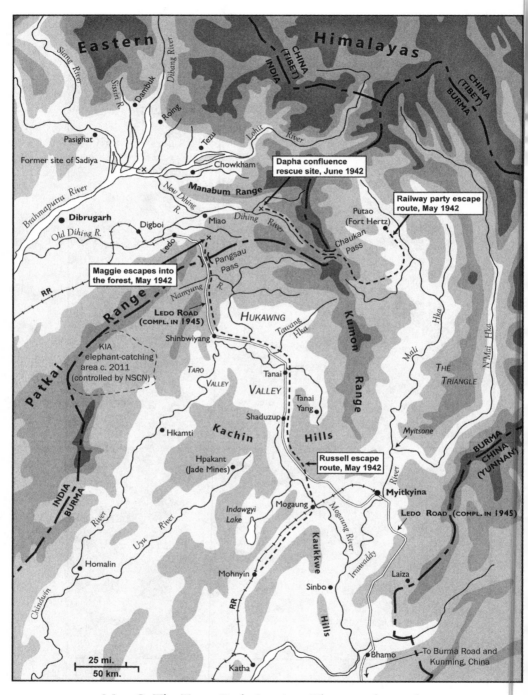

Map C. The Trans-Patkai region. The map shows the
railway party and Russell party escape routes during
World War II. *Cartography by Jacob Shell.*

INTRODUCTION

I AM A GEOGRAPHER BY TRAINING; THIS MEANS, SO I persuade myself, that I should pay close attention to those places that do not show up in today's atlases and maps. Among these places are the tangles of elephant trails that wind their way through the remote forestlands between India and Burma. Pensive giants traverse these trails with humans perched on their broad necks and backs. The routes they follow have a secluded and untraceable quality—shifting their position in seasonal cycles, inaccessible for motor vehicles, hidden from satellite view by tree canopy and monsoon clouds. If contemporary maps are to be believed, the elephant trails stopped existing once modern cartographers traded in their boots and mosquito nets for software manuals and subscriptions to satellite imagery databases. But contemporary maps are not always to be believed. The trails are still there. So are the trained elephants who tread these paths, carrying their riders, who are called *mahouts* in English (a loanword from Hindi) and *oozies* in Burmese.

I visited that sylvan country, in the shadow of the peaks where the green Patkai Mountains meet the precipitous white blockade of the eastern Himalayas, over the course of several trips during the mid-2010s. I always went to meet the working elephants and the mahouts who know them best, and to learn about the trails

that elephant and mahout follow into the obscurities of the forest. On my first trip like this, in 2013, I visited a hillside village in
Burma (also known as Myanmar) whose human inhabitants lived
in bamboo huts, their work elephants thundering about the jungle
by night and hauling great teak logs by day. The monsoon season
was just breaking, and the tropical landscape teemed with creatures who dwell in some intermediate state of matter, something
between water, air, and earth. One day I was coming down a rain-
soaked path by the village and my boots became stuck in the thick,
viscous mud. As I paused to poke the sludge away with a stick,
I was startled by a strange "skipping" snake that hopped by like
a rabbit, bouncing from the ground into the air in fast three-foot
hurdles, then gliding back into the mud from whence it came. At
night torqueing clouds of white flying insects arose from the spongy
earth, seemingly hatched by the pattering of the constant rain.
Some swirled through the falling droplets with goblin-like delight,
while others crawled frantically along the solid matter of the bamboo human shelters, determined to get inside. During another trip,
in a village at the base of the eastern Himalayas, I saw frogs hop
along water surfaces like skimming stones. They went eight, ten
hops at a time as if the liquid surface of a river were sturdy as rock,
submerging only when they felt provoked into aquatic hiding.

From this green backcountry, where earthly elements blend
together during monsoon, emerge the headwaters of the Irrawaddy
River, Burma's largest watercourse, as well as the upper reaches of
the Brahmaputra, the Mekong, and the Yangtze—the great river
systems of India, Southeast Asia, and China. These uplands have
traditionally been a kind of no-man's-land at the outermost margins of the various kingdoms and empires that dominate the fertile
river valleys. The discharge of monsoon rains helps hold the lowland powers at bay, combining with glacial melt from the Himalayas to inundate mountain vales, rearrange local watercourses,

obliterate bridges, and obstruct highways with sudden landslides. Wheeled vehicles of all kinds become stuck fast in the mud and mire, as do the hooves of horses and mules. Boats and river rafts, though sometimes useful, are blocked by debris: felled trees, boulders, and silt.

The elephants, by contrast, thrive in these dynamic conditions— in the constant flux between sand, mud, and mist. At certain times of year, and for people doing certain kinds of work, the elephants are the best way of getting around. Trained elephants have comprised the centerpiece of the Burmese teak-logging industry up through the 2010s. At the turn of the millennium, this industry produced nearly 70 percent of the world's internationally traded teak wood—much of it felled, skidded, and then carefully arranged into neat piles by elephants ridden by their mahouts in the Burmese jungle.[1]

The elephants go where the roads cannot. The ease and skill with which they move across monsoon-soaked landscapes has made them optimal transportation during floods. In one famous incident during World War II, elephant convoys from Assam, a state in northeastern India near Burma, rescued hundreds of Indian, Burmese, and British refugees trapped at an upland river confluence near the Burma-India border. The area had flooded during heavy rains and was unreachable by boat, train, or truck. The British officers charged with running the operation took movie cameras with them; footage of the remarkable "emergency relief elephants" shows the animals and their mahouts fording a torrent of white-capped floodwaters on the approach to the refugees' camp. More recently, following the 2004 Indian Ocean tsunami, elephants assisted in cleanup efforts in northern Sumatra and southwestern Thailand, where the damage to local road infrastructure was so severe that jeeps and trucks could not be used.

Elephants appear in more routine circumstances as well. In 2017

I visited a river at the far northeastern tip of India, called the Sissiri. Scattered along its rocky floodplain are the ruins of makeshift log bridges from dry seasons past. Locals design these temporary bridges to wash away with the first intense summer storms in May. Once the bridge has gone, one can use a floating raft or a canoe to ferry people across. But by the time of high monsoon, in late summer, the river landscape is simply too unsteady for such floating craft. A good crossing point for a boatman in the morning might become obstructed with boulders, silt, and runoff forest debris by afternoon. So by late summer and early autumn, the crossing belongs to elephant and mahout.

Spending several August afternoons at this crossing spot, I watched from the shadows of a bridge ruin as an elephant named Burmay-Moti, a powerful female with a gentle expression, waded back and forth with passengers and bags of rice on her back. Her mahout, Pradip, was shouting commands from her neck and tapping his foot onto her ear. Some locals in the area, mostly members of a hill tribe called the Adis, refer to the elephant crossing as the elephant *ghat*—a Hindi word that intriguingly carries the double meaning of "riverbank" and "mountain range." Throughout the crossing (which can swell to a mile wide after very bad storms, though it was only a hundred feet or so when I was there), Burmay-Moti displayed the sublime combination of power and sensitivity in her trunk, purposing the snakelike mass of intricate muscle to help passengers climb onto her back, or to check river fathoms for unstable boulders, or to hoist obstacles out of the way—or, when she was beyond the shallows, to breathe through a natural upturned snorkel. Under normal monsoon conditions, she could carry five or six human passengers on her back at once or, alternatively, several well-fastened motorcycles. Once, during an especially severe monsoon storm, she carried even more passengers than that: a dozen people in one trip. The diligent giant was needed for the rescue of

a large group of fishermen who had become stranded on a flooding midriver island. During this urgent operation, Burmay-Moti
was working alongside her mother, Sesta-Moti (and Sesta-Moti's
mahout), who also carried many people away to safety.[2] It's often
the case that elephants involved in these sorts of operations in the
forest work alongside their own family members.

The Sissiri River has a strong personality. For humans seeking
passage across this dramatic and confounding landscape, elephants
can be essential. During a monsoon storm, the Sissiri thunders,
froths, and fans, hydra-like, five new broad courses born out of
one, and these snake their way through great white boulders down
to the Brahmaputra valley below. Every new week the monsoon
brings a new and unfamiliar Sissiri to behold. New spates of rainfall, or breached mountain ice dams, engorge the valley with water
and rearrange its riparian mess of channels, rapids, and shoals. Forest debris afloat on the current scours the landscape. The maintenance of permanent roads here is a Sisyphean task; meanwhile,
elephants calmly traverse the beds of mud and winding streams,
carrying passengers and cargo on their reliable backs.

Elephants have participated not only in everyday crossings
through such seasonally flooded landscapes, but also in more clandestine, or subversive, pursuits. An elephant who can go where the
roads cannot is an elephant who can move people and supplies in
secret across wet, mountainous borders, beyond the view of military patrols or modern surveillance. For millennia throughout
South and Southeast Asia—and more briefly in the sphere of the
ancient Mediterranean—trained elephants were used for combat.
But in this remote hill country of the Southeast Asian and northeastern Indian uplands, "war" elephants have served not as cavalry
but rather as facilitators of secret human movements. Examples
of this sort of thing are surprisingly recent. In the Burma theater
of World War II, the British rode elephants across the Patkais to

escape the Japanese invasion, and the Japanese employed elephants in the construction of their Burma-Siam Railway (a project made famous in the film *Bridge on the River Kwai*). The conflict between the Allies and the Japanese over Upper Burma was brutal, the "Stalingrad of the East," as some in the wartime press called it. As the region's natural "transport vehicles," the elephants became objects of intense struggle. Some memoirists who survived wartime operations in the region suggest that elephants were the key to controlling not just Upper Burma but also its pathways between India and China—and thus by extension the key to the entire Asian theater of the war.

The postwar period, despite its increased mechanization, did not render the transport elephant obsolete. During the Vietnam War, Vietcong mahouts rode elephants along the famous Ho Chi Minh Trail, under cover of the forest canopy, so as to keep the flow of supplies hidden from American reconnaissance planes. Elephants have similarly proved instrumental in Burma's numerous insurgencies over the past half century, especially in Kachin State, in Burma's far north. Here an armed ethnic organization called the Kachin Independence Army, or KIA, utilizes some fifty to sixty elephants for moving goods about the jungle. These clandestine "elephant brigades," the last of their kind in the world, were still very much active in the 2010s. The elephants carry passengers and goods—jade, gold, food, medicine, and arms—across river courses similar to the Sissiri, across remote hill ranges, and through secret mountain passes. The militia soldiers prefer these elephant-mounted convoys in order to avoid the better-equipped Burmese army, whose patrol trucks and jeeps are confined to the region's sparse network of all-weather roads. Traversing the refuge of the Kachin forest, the KIA elephants sometimes cross paths with wild elephants, with whom they mate; elephant pregnancies are inconvenient but happy occasions for the brigade.

South of the hilly forests of Kachin State stretches the wide val-ley of the Irrawaddy River. In the roadless hill ranges along the sides of this great channel, there are yet more trained forest ele-phants who drag timber by chain or carry them upon their tusks. In these Burmese timber forests, as in the secret KIA elephant trails of the Burmese far north, as at the fords across the remote Sissiri River, the elephants work as partners with humans. Everywhere the two adjoined figures, elephant and mahout, are furtive and elu-sive: the taciturn giant trying to survive in an increasingly crowded and inhospitable world; the chattier hominid perched above, seek-ing passage across one of that world's last great "shadowy" spaces, the Asian monsoon forest. They share a mysterious bond and a unique, codeveloped understanding of the sylvan country on which both of them, for distinct but overlapping reasons, depend. This book explores that relationship's surprising persistence through modern times.

ASIAN ELEPHANTS are the world's second largest land animal species, behind African elephants. They live in the forests and grass-lands of the South and Southeast Asian tropics. There are many more African elephants remaining in the world today than Asian elephants: some half a million African elephants survive, in con-trast to only forty or fifty thousand Asian elephants. Unlike Afri-can elephants, a large percentage of the world's remaining Asian elephants—between a quarter and a third—are trained for work. Some of these "work elephants" give rides to tourists, or march in parades, or perform tricks. Most of them, though, probably around nine thousand elephants overall, are engaged in labor, especially transportation and logging, which is well beyond the view of most tourists.[3]

It should not surprise us that humans work with elephant partners. After all, over the millennia, we have developed complex working relationships with other large or midsize mammals, such as horses, cattle, or dogs. Among these animals, though, Asian elephants are highly unusual. Humans have selectively bred these other species around specialized practical tasks. Domesticated dogs have been bred into many varieties for hunting, digging, retrieving, guarding, attacking, pulling sleds, rounding up sheep, and so on. Similarly, horses have been bred for racing, cavalry warfare, or hauling heavy wagons. Cattle have been bred for dragging plows, in addition to producing milk or meat. Camels have been bred for racing, or for carrying people and baggage across arid regions. And of course, humans have bred a number of other animals (cats, sheep, chickens, and so on) who don't "work" in the sense of performing imposed tasks separate from their natural inclinations but nonetheless provide benefit for people.

But humans have never selectively bred elephants.[4] Elephant generations take too long—usually two decades, or ten times longer than a dog generation. (The specialization that a dog breeder achieves over fifty years would take an elephant breeder half a millennium.) Furthermore, elephants resist mating in micromanaged, human-controlled environments, preferring the relative freedom of the forest. How is it possible that elephants, despite having never been selectively bred by humans, have nonetheless proved to be indispensable work partners for humans in the forest? The work can be complex and cognitively demanding. Sometimes the tasks that the elephants perform have incredibly high stakes: rescuing people stranded during a flood, for example. And yet elephants weren't selectively bred to do this. To appreciate how extraordinary this outcome is, where the elephants just "happen" to be good at these sorts of urgent and complex jobs, it's helpful to further pursue an analogy with dogs. Imagine if, instead of using a Saint Bernard as a mountain rescue dog, or a Belgian Malinois as a bomb sniffer, humans attempted these same tasks with wolves—wild animals captured directly from their natural habitat and then trained for a few years—and that it *worked*. That is in effect the situation of Asian work elephants.[5]

Giants of the Monsoon Forest goes to a remote part of the world to understand how people live and work with elephants in the forest, and why they've done so for millennia. People in these remote areas haven't been selectively breeding the elephants, in the sense that a dog breeder breeds dogs or a horse breeder breeds horses. But they have been employing the elephants in tasks that give the elephants substantial periods of time in the forest every day to roam and mate with a considerable degree of freedom. In fact, these work elephants' daily pattern might sound familiar to anyone with a nine-to-five job. They do transportation or logging by day. Then, in the late afternoon or early evening, they are released into the surrounding forest to wander, sleep, forage for food, and mate with each other and with wild elephant herds passing by. The next morning the mahout comes to "fetch" the elephant, to return it to its daily work site, a logging tract or a cross-forest trail. An elephant employed under these conditions has a much better chance of reproducing than an elephant trapped in a spatially enclosed environment like a zoo.[6] With access to fresh vegetation and room for plenty of exercise, work elephants in the forest tend to live much longer than the elephants in zoo compounds: one scientific study suggests over *twice* as long.[7]

In this book I argue that Asian elephants have in effect formed a kind of interspecies "alliance" with humans who seek to go where roads and wheeled vehicles cannot. Perhaps these humans covet resources in areas where topography or weather conditions hinder the construction and maintenance of permanent roads. Perhaps, for political reasons, they're trying to avoid other groups of humans who are "road-bound": military patrols, for instance.

Perhaps they're trying to harvest a crop that grows best in quiet, roadless forests. Humans with any of these compulsions or motivations are of special interest to Asian elephants, from the standpoint of elephants' survival. And over hundreds of generations, Asian elephants have in effect cultivated skills that make them useful to those humans. While it's important not to naïvely romanticize this relationship (a relationship that can sometimes be harsh or even abusive), the dynamic between elephants and humans presents clues about how the giants have survived for so long and how they might survive in the future.

In exploring this argument, we'll enter the shared world of forest elephants and their mahouts. We'll see how mahouts catch elephants in the forest and train them, and how these elephants balance the duality in their lives, where they are both working animals and "wild" ones free to mate with passing herds. We'll watch these elephants perform complicated work, even devising their own ingenious solutions to urgent problems like river logjams, rescue operations, and emergency construction projects. The elephants' intelligence and acute situational awareness have often made them brilliant co-workers for humans. We'll look at examples of intense wartime escapes on elephant-back from the combat zones of World War II, the Vietnam War, and the ongoing Kachin conflict in Burma's far north. The elephants possess unique evasive or "fugitive" skills, and we'll examine how their partnership with humans may have resulted from gradual historical and geographic processes involving co-species migration and escape—processes that never affected or shaped the Asian elephants' more numerous cousins in Africa. In Africa, as we'll see, the history of elephant domestication presents a different sort of drama.

An important aim of the book is to give readers a sense of what might be "done" with Asian elephants during the remainder of the twenty-first century. Today the demographic trendlines for Asian elephants are very grim. By this century's end, the species seems likely to succumb to what some paleontologists are calling the "sixth great extinction," the tsunami wave of species extinguished by the activities of humankind.[8] Are there promising strategies of avoiding this outcome for the Asian elephants—of saving the species? On a continent whose human population is in the billions and will certainly continue to grow, is it nonetheless possible to set aside sufficient forest ranges for Asian elephants to become a completely and sustainably wild species as they were millennia ago? Alternatively, are there favorable future roles for the elephants as work animals, roles that can still keep these amazing creatures happy and help them flourish once again? In the book's final chapter, I propose one such possible role: elephants as helpers in flood relief operations. This could ally Asian elephants with a human need that seems likely to expand in future years, as a growing human population finds itself, increasingly, on flood-prone terrain.

Some might find it helpful to think of this book as a kind of "ethno-elephantology"—a term coined in recent years to describe new research, among anthropologists, geographers, historians, biologists, and others, aimed at better understanding the complex relationship between elephants and people.[9] Much of the research done in this area has focused on elephants in tourist parks, government-managed wildlife preserves, and religious festivals. Mostly omitted have been the domesticated elephants of the frontier forest zones, where elephants are released into the forest each night and fetched each morning.[10] *Giants of the Monsoon Forest* looks to this frontier.

Throughout the book I refer to a wide array of ethnic groups from which forest mahouts tend to hail: Kachin, Hkamti, Karen, ethnic Burmese (Bamar), Assamese, Moran, Adi, and others. Many of these groups are small ethnic minorities, and a reader can be forgiven for finding this whirlwind of ethnic names a bit bewildering. The involvement of so many minority peoples in forest-based mahoutship is no coincidence. Elephants are most useful as labor where an infrastructure-building state is weakest. The groups likeliest to be living in such areas are so-called "hill tribe" minorities. Indeed, keeping the state at arm's length was often the reason these groups took to the geographic margins in the first place. The use of elephants for everyday work helps such groups derive wealth from their forest surroundings and in turn consolidate power—a power connected directly to the continued existence of this canopied hinterland. The elephants get something from this arrangement too. By associating themselves with these humans and their forest-based economy, Asian elephants boost their own likelihood of inhabiting the sort of landscape in which they tend to be healthiest and happiest: a large forested area, buffered from the "normal" human world of huge cities, farms, and motor traffic along busy roads.

During the mid-2010s, I traveled to two regions where mahouts work with elephants in the forest. One region was central Burma. Here I visited teak forests where the Burmese government uses elephants to drag valuable timber. This elephant logging system follows the synchronous life cycles of humans, elephants, and teak trees. In the government's teak-logging villages, a mahout and an elephant may grow up together as children, reach peak work age at the same time, and enjoy retirement side by side. The teak wood is harvested in maturation cycles lasting between three and eight decades, depending on the desired wood quality. Though this would be a rare event, the same elephant-mahout pair could conceivably harvest a single timber tract twice: once as teenagers and again in their fifties, each time replacing mature trees with saplings.[11]

Another area I visited I'm calling the Trans-Patkai region, a tribal area straddling the Indian-Burmese border, encompassing Burma's Kachin State, parts of Burma's Sagaing Division, and the eastern part of the Indian state of Arunachal Pradesh. Unlike central Burma, this is an area of relatively weak state control over forest territory and over the elephant-riding peoples therein. The huge crescent formed by the Patkai Mountains bisects this region. I use the odd term *Trans-Patkai* partly to emphasize commonalities in the elephant cultures on both sides of the mountains, and partly to obscure the precise location of certain politically sensitive activities practiced by some of the mahouts, whether on the Indian or the Burmese side of the international border.[12]

For a Western visitor raised on Conrad and Kipling, the Trans-Patkai can seem a land from the recesses of some dark and vivid imagination. Here is a land of tigers and great hornbills, of tribes that hunted heads until just a generation or two ago, where animist worship of forest spirits is widespread and many communities have their own "deathly priest"—their shaman who prays to the forest spirits in incantations of obscure origin. Meadows of opium dot the hills, and militant rebels cross jungle streams on elephant-back. Camp life is everywhere: the camps of hunters, elephant mahouts, and panners for gold. People's houses here are made of bamboo and cane, fetched from the surrounding woods. For much of the year the region is blanketed in the thick clouds of monsoon that obstruct the watchful eyes of modern satellites passing overhead.

In part, such romantic impressions can be misleading. People here drive cars and motorcycles and talk on cell phones and read the internet for news. The wage economy has eclipsed alternative economies almost everywhere, and the formal industrial sector here is not so different from that of the United States a few generations ago: mining, oil, coal, and sugar all loom large. One will pass a crater that used to be a hill, that once had monkeys, hawks' nests, and jungle cats: now the hill is a pile of gravel that will become a road to provide access to another hill full of potential gravel.

And yet one's initial romantic sense that danger, beauty, and mystery lurk beyond each mountain ridge would not have been entirely wrong. Beyond the gravel roads lies a hidden world of work camps and communities linked by elephants. Here the typhonic force of geographic elements reigns, especially during the monsoon season, as windy storms beat upon the mountainsides and huge flows of rainwater, mud, and uprooted trees block the advance of wheeled vehicles. When mudslides and floodwaters swamp the roads' uppermost reaches, a different logic of movement necessarily emerges.

The normal world, the "exposed" one to which we're accustomed, has not been good to the elephants. It builds endless roads and replaces forestlands with cities, towns, and farms. Sometimes the exposed world will put elephants in zoos or in gated park compounds. The people of the exposed world often mean well when they do this. But it's ample forestlands, with plenty of room to migrate and eat bamboo and wade through running water, that these giants need most of all. Zoos and fenced parks cannot replicate such conditions. By contrast, the setting of this book is among the least deforested areas remaining in South and Southeast Asia, despite this setting's position directly between two areas of incredible human density, India and China. The unique partnership here between elephants and humans has been a major factor in this remarkable geographic outcome and has helped resist the forces of deforestation.

FORTUITOUS TIMING made this book possible. Some two-thirds of the world's domesticated elephants who are released into the forest at night are in Burma. Since the 1960s, Burma's main experience has been one of military rule, economic isolation, and instability due to interethnic civil wars and ethnic cleansing campaigns directed against minority peoples. A study like this one would have been far more difficult, perhaps impossible, to undertake at any point from the 1960s through the 2000s, especially for an outsider. The mid-2010s, though, were a period of relative liberalization and democratization for the country. During my first few trips, optimism seemed to be in the air, among nearly everyone I spoke with: in Yangon, in the central Burmese upcountry, in the eastern hills and in Kachin State.

Sadly, during the last year or so of the research, the military began to reassert its control over the country's fragile parliamentary system. Potential peace deals in the far-north Kachin conflict stalled or collapsed. And by 2017 the military regime and some sympathetic militias were conducting a full-blown ethnic cleansing campaign against the Rohingya minority people along Burma's Bangladeshi border. Hopefully these recent conflagrations of violence, oppression, and military authoritarianism will rapidly extinguish themselves. Perhaps they'll prove to have been merely the final death throes of a fading repressive regime. But I cannot help but anticipate that, in a few decades' time, the mid-2010s—the period when I was able to speak with many Burmese forest mahouts about their lives, their work, and their unique knowledge about elephants— will seem to be a historic exception.

It also would have been impossible for me to do this research alone. In addition to knowing how to ride an elephant, the "perfect" researcher for this kind of work would have to know the Burmese, Assamese, Hkamti, Jinghpaw (Kachin), and Karen languages. I had just English and beginner's-level Burmese and Jinghpaw. Everywhere I went, I had guides who were multilingual and consistently brilliant. In the chapters that follow, I refer to them by their first initials or by altered names. Nor are all the mahouts we interviewed fully named. I took such precautions to protect the identities of several participants in the research. These people's time, energy, attention, and resourcefulness made the book possible. I will have to find ways to express my gratitude to them other than by naming them. At times I felt the guides, along with a number of the interviewed mahouts, understood my research and research questions far better than I did.

We have very little "hard data" pertaining to Asian elephants who live deep in the forest, in areas with relatively weak state presence. The topic is necessarily composed of the impressions formed by people who have lived and worked with these giants in such remote places. More often than not, such people articulate the complexity of their impressions and experiences through the vivid stories they tell about their lives in the forest and about the elephants they've known.

Chapter 1

CATCHING
ELEPHANTS

I WAS IN THE REGION I'LL CALL THE "TRANS-PATKAI."
Fifty million years before, the Indian continental plate had col-
lided with Eurasia, scraping along a head of land to the east that
formed the green march of the Patkai Mountains. It rammed with
far greater violence to the north, to force up gargantuan masses of
rock: the Himalayas. These two mountain ranges merge in a kind
of topographic eddy that swirls across a series of high passes: the
Pangsau, the Chaukan, the Phungan. During the epoch of human
history, the mountains have divided powerful kingdoms and states:
the Patkais separate India from Burma; beyond the Himalayas lie
Tibet and China. Yet the passes through these mountains, though
high and remote, compose regional entities in their own right. The
Kachin, Hkamti, Lisu, and Naga peoples all have populations on
both sides of the Patkais, linked by the passes.

I arrived in that transmontane region when the mustard flowers
were in full bloom. The landscape was awash in yellow, broken by
the greenery of nearby tree groves and undulations of dark mountainous forest. Vistas of distant snowy peaks occasionally emerged
between the trees. I was with a local guide, whom I'll call Sang,
on the sandy bank of a river. The spot was tranquil except for the
occasional braying of black and brown goats who grazed on a steep

grassy slope behind us. The slope led upward toward a lonely bamboo hut on a high crest, with yellow fields beyond.

The drive here from the main road followed what was barely a dirt track and took nearly an hour. At one place, the track was obstructed by a swampy pool, filled with the overflow from an adjacent stream. Scattered messily across the pool were planks of wood. "Ah," said the guide. "We'll have to get out for a moment." He and the driver set about retrieving the planks from the reachable margins of the water. Having collected a dozen or so, they carefully arranged the pieces in a tracklike pattern, engineering a temporary causeway. This was what the wooden planks were for, but they'd been dispersed by the previous week's hard rains. The next such rainfall would scatter the planks again, and the next motor traveler down this quiet path would have to repeat the process. "Why does no one build a permanent bridge?" I asked.

"No point," replied Sang. "In the really dry season, it's so dry that you don't need any bridge. In the really wet season, it's so wet that a bridge would wash away, even a very good one that was bolted down. And anyway, this whole road from start to finish can't be used at all during the rainiest time of year; you'd walk—or with heavy cargo, you'd use an elephant."[1]

At the end of this drive, we stood at the remote riverbank, with the group of goats and the vast yellow mustard fields up the hill. The guide gestured across the river to the opposite shore. "Jacob— here they are!" Three massive elephants emerged from the forest and stepped into the reeds. They were carrying two men each, one perched on the neck and the other sprawled across the arched back. The three elephants waded toward us, the men smiling and waving. The guide spoke with them in the local language. The men were friendly but could not help but overawe. The three sitting on the aft hips of the elephants were armed, with rifles slung across their backs. Everyone wore scabbards that held long machetes. Huge coils of heavy ropes and dark chains were piled up like pythons on the elephants' backs. The elephants themselves were enormous, some of the largest I'd seen in Asia, around nine feet at the shoulder. It was as if the men were riding on houses.

"*Khoonkie* elephants," Sang pronounced with satisfaction. This was what he and his partner the driver had brought me, across the swampy dirt track and the endless mustard fields to this riverbank, to see. These were elephants that I'd only read about in books. Khoonkie elephants (called *pansein* by some people in central Burma) were, from the standpoint of the local elephant people, the smartest and bravest of the tamed elephants, the ones with the strongest instincts for protecting the humans riding on their huge bodies.[2] Their job, during this time of year, was to help humans catch wild elephants. It was not the most difficult job an elephant could get, necessarily—that distinction likely goes to the work performed by the Burmese logging elephants whose specialty is clearing midriver logjams. But it was certainly the most dangerous job for the *humans* involved. Only a special group of elephants was selected.[3]

The three men riding on the necks of the khoonkie elephants were called *fandis*: master elephant catchers.[4] The three armed men riding on the elephants' backs were their assistants. Fandis have three methods of catching wild elephants. In the pit method, they dig a hole and cover it with branches and leaves. Then, riding their khoonkie elephants, they chase a wild elephant into the hole. Skilled fandis disdain this method, as the wild elephant usually injures himself or herself in the fall and thus makes a poor work elephant in the long run.[5]

In the second method, sometimes called *kheddah*, or *gor shekar*, a huge stockade is built in the forest, made of wooden pikes strapped together with strong bark rope. From the air, the stockade resembles a symbol for gamma, a huge V with a tiny circle at the point (γ).

Elephants are chased into a broad opening in the stockade that gradually narrows until reaching a passageway, through which the stockade opens again into a circular compartment reinforced with the strongest pikes. The narrow passage is then barricaded behind the elephants.[6] These stockades require much time, planning, and investment to build, but they have the advantage of being able to trap many elephants at once.

Guy Tachard, a French Jesuit visitor to the Ayutthaya kingdom in Siam in the seventeenth century, described a kheddah of breathtaking scale. The Jesuit, a sometime astronomer, was there to observe a lunar eclipse, but since this astronomical event was still several nights away, the Ayutthaya king offered to take him to see the elephant hunt occurring in the nearby hills. The king had employed tens of thousands of royal subjects in the construction of a vast stockade, whose open section, the Jesuit tells us, extended outward for ten leagues: over twenty miles. The hunt took place at night. A long row of thousands of men swept through the forest, carrying torches and beating drums, frightening many hundreds of wild elephants into a retreat that would take them into the stockade opening. The Jesuit wrote of the spectacle of the torches: "it seemed to me in the dark the finest sight and loveliest illumination I ever saw."[7] One might dismiss Tachard's story as hyperbole, but a separate account by an ambassador from Persia supports his estimate of the operation's mind-boggling scale.[8] The Ayutthaya kings, skilled in hospitality and diplomacy, seemed to enjoy showing off this incredible procedure to emissaries from abroad.

Today the stockade method typically occurs on a much smaller scale, with the open section extending outward for several hundred yards and the elephants captured in groups of five or six rather than hundreds at a time. Burma's government-run timber industry, which employs elephants to haul teak timber out of the forest, was running these smaller kheddah operations as recently as the 1990s.[9]

But these six fandis sitting atop their huge khoonkies were engaged in a third method of elephant capture, known as *mela shekar* (also called *kyaw hpan* by some masters in central Burma): the lasso or rope method.[10] In this method, the lead fandi, riding his khoonkie elephant, swoops in on the flank of a wild elephant in the forest; if the fandi is right-handed, he and his khoonkie approach from the right. In the meantime, the two secondary khoonkies encroach from the left. If all goes well, the wild elephant freezes, unnerved by this unexpected behavior from the three khoonkie elephants. The lead fandi tosses a huge rope around the wild elephant's head. The noose of this lasso is much larger than that of a typical cattle rope and must be tossed with two hands at once. With both hands occupied, the lead fandi can't balance himself on his khoonkie elephant, who is likely pivoting and maneuvering to control the movements of the targeted wild elephant.

To keep himself in place, the lead fandi wears thick pants made of fibrous canvas that are fastened to ropes around elephant's chest and neck. These pants are sometimes painted in a striking rainbow scheme, which helps the other fandis and khoonkies to keep watch on the lead fandi during the commotion. The lead fandi also has an assistant behind him, who is ready to cut the ropes if the lead man's life seems to be in danger—or to use his rifle if need be, though this is exceedingly rare. If the lead fandi succeeds with his rope, then the fandis on the other elephants throw additional ropes. Once lassoed by multiple lines, the wild elephant, grasping the severity of what has occurred, may crash into the forest in an attempt to escape, and the khoonkies all give chase. Usually this results in the ropes becoming entangled around several trees. The wild elephant at this point might put up a fight, but its struggles are controlled by the ropes and the intimidating presence of the three khoonkie elephants.[11]

The most acute danger in the mela shekar process arises when the fandis have chosen to capture a wild elephant calf. Calves offer clear advantages for capture: they are easier to lasso and train, and they can provide more decades of service as work animals than a captured adult. But the mother of the calf is usually nearby, and faced with the prospect of losing her offspring, she fights more fiercely than would a huge male tusker who finds himself ensnared in rope. Multiple fandis I spoke with in this region recounted incidents where their khoonkies fought off enraged mother elephants, thus saving the fandis' lives. Others spoke of fellow fandis—friends, brothers, uncles—who'd died this way. The breaking up of elephant families, and the subsequent aftermath, is in fact the major disadvantage of the mela shekar capturing method. The fandis worry less about the potential loss of human life due to the rage of the protective mother elephant—such deaths are rather rare—than about the trauma experienced by the captured calf, which tends to subtract from its psychological reliability and work potential. Fandis get better results if the mother and calf can be captured together, as often happens in the stockade method.[12]

Nonetheless, mela shekar also has some clear advantages over the stockade method. The stockade method involves a huge outlay of human labor. Usually whole bureaucracies have to be involved. It also leaves a significant mark in the forest landscape, as trees must be felled to make pikes, and the pikes, unless removed, obstruct the movement of other forest animals. The mela shekar method is flexible, requiring relatively little advance planning (though years and years of training are needed) and only a small handful of humans and elephants. It also leaves virtually no visible mark on the forest— which, if the magistrates in some far-off capital city have passed ordinances against elephant capture, might be the most important advantage of all.

At the riverbank with the three khoonkies, the mood was cheerful. The three fandis and their assistants had recently caught an elephant calf. Apparently the operation had gone very smoothly, with no violent attacks from a mother elephant. The calf was tied up deep in the forest country across the river, and the fandis were checking on it daily, initiating the training process. They brought bamboo shoots and rice treats for the calf to munch on while they chanted words into his ear. Soon the training process would turn grimmer, mixing negative with positive reinforcement. Eventually, the elephant would likely be sold to nearby mahouts in the region, to do transportation work during the monsoon season, and to work in forest tracts moving valuable pieces of felled timber.

The fandis insisted I climb onto one of the big khoonkies and ride with them up the hill toward the sprawling fields above, where we would have lunch and talk. I hesitated. Up close the elephants' size was daunting. The biggest was the largest contiguous mass of living flesh I'd ever beheld. Growing up in New England, I'd seen humpback whales in the Gulf of Maine, but I'd never seen more than a few sections of these mammals at once, as they remained largely submerged. I'd seen African savanna elephants in zoos— but those were simply not this big. Or perhaps the big khoonkie before me simply *seemed* bigger than an African savanna elephant, because he was carrying two people and a large jumble of heavy forest equipment, and because I knew, from my books and interviews, what this elephant could do.

I was especially intimidated by the big one. The fandis were amused: "*Borsat. Bat! Bat bat bat* . . ." The huge elephant, Borsat, sat down. "You will ride Borsat," the guide informed me.

Tungpa, Borsat's fandi, retreated onto the elephant's back and helped me climb to his abandoned perch on the pachyderm's nape. From behind me, the fandi gestured to a rope slung around Borsat's neck. The rope had a loop on each end, into which I ought to place my feet. Looking at these loops, and also at my feet, Tungpa and I both realized that he and I were really very different sizes. The loops barely made it past my knees. I looked at the knot on the midsection of the rope that shortened or lengthened it. Fumbling with the knot seemed risky, as it required both hands, and Borsat could stand up at any moment and send me flying. The elephant, however, seemed to grasp that some adjustments to the ropework on his neck were needed, in order to transport this awkwardly pro-portioned human who'd suddenly been added to his burden. He stayed very still. Eventually I got the foot loops to the appropriate length, and Borsat stood up.

Encouraged by Tungpa, I attempted to give some commands. I tried a term for "get up, go." Borsat seemed uninterested in my voice.

"Tap his ear with your foot! That's how you tell him to turn!" the guide Sang shouted up to me. I tried this too. Borsat snorted scornfully out of his trunk, and the fandis laughed. Borsat remained stationary.

Behind us, the fandis' assistants were in the river, washing off the mela shekar equipment. A fisherman drifted by on a bamboo raft. Finally, the other two khoonkie elephants set off up the hill through the grass and brush, scattering the braying goats. Borsat, motivated more by interest in his elephant friends than by my clumsy com-mands, followed the other two. I leaned in toward the giant's great domed head, to keep my balance as we made the ascent. Borsat tilted leftward and rightward navigating the slope, my spot on his neck swaying like a small boat riding an ocean swell. The path became gentler, and we made our way across the rippling yellow fields in the direction of the Patkai foothills.

LATER I WAS eating a meal at the house of Vithaya, one of the three fandis. Vithaya lived with his wife and daughter in a bamboo house with a thatched roof. It stood a mile or so from the spot where he and the other fandis had emerged from the forest with the titan Borsat and the other two khoonkies. By this point in the day, the three khoonkie elephants had been released to roam freely in the forest nearby, where they'd remain until the next morning. Then they'd be fetched, and the whole team—the six humans and the three elephants—would go back to the captured calf.

The main room of Vithaya's bamboo house was organized around a fireplace. There was no chimney, as such a contraption would have let in too much water during the rainy season. Instead a large multileveled smoking rack, also made of bamboo, dangled from the ceiling. Here pieces of pork and deer were left to char for months on end, a method of preserving them as jerky. Above, the underside of the thatched roof was stained black from smoke. We were eating pork that had been roasted over the fire, along with a salad made of fresh ginger and herbs picked from Vithaya's garden. There was also a kind of bitter fruit, similar to gooseberries, that turned sweet with a sip of water. One of Vithaya's fandi friends fidgeted with a bamboo opium pipe in the corner of the room.

"We have some important rituals for mela shekar," Vithaya explained in his own language, and Sang translated. I was scribbling notes. "Some are secret things—"

Vithaya's friend in the corner cut in to say something I did not understand. There was laughter. The guide smiled and explained, "They're joking that you don't look like a professor." After a pause, he added, "I think the fandis here are wondering about you and about why you are interested in mela shekar. They can understand that a Westerner would want to see wild elephants or maybe go on a safari ride. But why would you want to know about what they do, the catching elephants part?"

I'd explained this many times in all the places I'd conducted my field research, in as many ways as I could think of. But I could never succinctly explain my whole jumble of thoughts. "I'm here to learn about people who work with elephants in the forest," I began, "and who permit the work elephants to roam in the forest at night, so they can eat there and mate with wild herds. Very few people where I'm from know these practices exist. I'm not comparing these work elephants with elephants who live in the wild their whole lives; I'm comparing them with captive elephants elsewhere: in zoos, at tourist parks, in stables—places where the elephants don't have the ability to roam the forest." I was already making this too long-winded and complicated and cut myself short.

The guide rephrased what I'd said in the local language. There was more chatter, and smoking. "They are saying that with your beard and unkempt hair, you maybe look like an 'activist' and not a professor," Sang mused. But by this time he and the fandis had relaxed and were discussing what an American geography professor is "supposed" to look like. More chatter and chuckling. Vithaya, apparently satisfied, gestured to his friends to quiet down. He returned to the spiritual rituals: "For mela shekar, the main ritual is to sacrifice one farm bird at home, then bring a second bird with us into the forest. This forest sacrifice is for the wild elephant's own ghost rider, or spirit-mahout." The pipe was passed from fandi to fandi. "You see, every wild elephant in the forest has its own spirit-mahout. As fandis, we are taking this spirit's elephant away. So we must bring the spirit something as compensation. And if we don't, then the spirit-mahout will interfere with the whole mela shekar process. The spirit will conjure up bad luck and cause bad things to happen."[13]

Fandis throughout the Trans-Patkai region follow something

like the ritual Vithaya described, for appeasing "spirit-mahouts" associated with the wild elephant herds. The commonality is somewhat surprising, since Trans-Patkai fandis hail from at least three ethnic groups, the Kachin, the Hkamti, and the Moran—groups that differ in many respects, including religion. The Kachins are mostly Buddhist on the Indian side of the mountains and Christian on the Burmese side; the Hkamtis on both sides are Buddhist; and the Morans are Hindus. But all three groups retain varying degrees of local animist practices: the worship of the local forest spirits, including those who ride wild elephants.

A Moran fandi from the region, now in his eighties, told me a remarkable story involving these "spirit-mahouts." The fandi, Miloswar, used to have an elephant named Sokona. Sokona was a fabulous khoonkie, highly intelligent and attuned to his fandis' needs. He had naturally small tusks that limited his usefulness for logging (logging tuskers can hoist huge logs up by balancing them on their tusks) but were a good feature for a khoonkie. Without large tusks, the khoonkie was less likely to accidentally gore the captured elephant during the commotion of mela shekar. Furthermore, male elephants' facial muscles tend to grow larger and stronger when they don't have to spend a lifetime counterbalancing long tusks. The added size and strength are advantages for khoonkies as well.[14]

Earlier in his life, Miloswar recalled, he and his fellow fandis received word that a new group of wild elephants was in the nearby woods. The migrating herd had descended from the mountains in search of fresh bamboo shoots and water. In his haste to get into the jungle, Miloswar rushed the spiritual ceremonies. He was the group's lead fandi, and Sokona the lead khoonkie. Approaching the wild herd in the woods, the team came upon a mother elephant and her calf. Sokona approached the two, and Miloswar threw his rope, aiming for the baby. But he missed, and freakishly, the loop wound up around the mother elephant's head instead. At this point

Miloswar shouted to the other fandis, "We'll catch the big one!" since his line was attached to her. But she was an especially powerful elephant, and the other fandis could not land their ropes. She charged through the forest. Sokona, with Miloswar and Miloswar's assistant riding on his back, chased after her, trailing by a rope taut as a harpoon line. The rope never tangled in tree branches as was usual. After several intense minutes of pursuit, Miloswar and his assistant realized the chase was hopeless: she was too strong and fast and was having too much odd luck with the rope and the trees. Miloswar took out his machete to cut the rope, but in the tumult the machete slipped from his hand.

Sokona meanwhile was still barreling after the wild female and pulsating with exhaustion. The assistant tried to loosen the knot that fastened the lasso line to Sokona's rear belt, but with the speed of the chase and no hands free for balance, he was thrown from the elephant. The other fandis found the assistant on the forest floor with a broken leg. Miloswar, seeing how dangerous the situation had become for him now, released his canvas pant buckles from Sokona's neck and leaped off. Landing on the forest floor, he was dazed but not as badly injured as the assistant behind him. Sokona and the wild female, still connected by the lasso rope, disappeared into the jungle.

One man stayed with the assistant whose leg was broken, while everyone else climbed onto the remaining khoonkie elephants and followed the trail of broken branches blazed by Sokona and the wild elephant. Much later in the day, they caught up with the elephants. The rope had finally become entangled in some trees. Sokona and the wild elephant did not appear to have fought each other at all during the wait. They were both exhausted and stood there in the shade, eating shrubs and creepers. Miloswar cut the rope, and the wild elephant escaped. He took Sokona home.

From that point forward, though, the khoonkie was never the same. He was never as obedient with Miloswar as he'd been before—as if his mind were always somewhere else. "He just didn't act like a normal khoonkie anymore," Miloswar remembered. "So I always wondered if maybe I did the ceremony beforehand too fast, and this was why this mishap occurred. I wondered if maybe while the two elephants were waiting for us to catch up with them, Sokona was taken, or possessed, by that wild elephant's spirit-mahout."[15]

Miloswar became more and more animated as he told this story. He leaped up from his seat and gestured with his arms to convey the motions of the rope, the chase, the fall. His whole family was gathered around: his wife, his sons, their wives, and several grandchildren. Electricity ran through the room. The audience was transfixed, though perhaps they'd all heard this story before. When it was over, he retreated to his seat: an octogenarian once again.

This belief in spirit-mahouts holds that domestic and wild elephants are like mirror images of each other. From a spirit-mahout's point of view, the wild herd is "domesticated," and the humans' elephants are "wild." Genetically, work elephants are indistinct from wild ones. An individual elephant can go from being wild to being domesticated, and though this is more unusual, it can also go back to being wild. We could think of the sacrificial ritual the fandis perform as a way of compensating for the difference between the number of elephants who go from the wild into domesticity and the number who go from domesticity back into the wild.

Of course, there is another way of looking at the story of Sokona. Something transpired between him and the wild female while they were both tangled up together in the trees, the fandis still hours away. Some idea, or mindset, was communicated between the two giants—something that touched the khoonkie to his core and altered the burden of thoughts that he carried with him during his remaining days. After Sokona's behavior shifted, Miloswar gave the elephant to another mahout and does not know what happened to him.

———

"I DON'T SEE the mark."

I stared at the forest floor. It was a beautiful morning in the low mountains of central Burma, where elephants drag great logs of teak from the forested slopes to roadside timber depots. The sunlight percolated through the trees in brilliant beams. Mists from the nighttime dew rose from the horizon, turning the tall narrow trees in the middle distance into a shadow-theater of silhouettes.

"I still don't see it."

P., the guide, kept pointing. "It's right there." His index finger followed the sylvan floor from the spot beneath me to the mahout walking up ahead. The mahout was named Otou, and he climbed a slope in front of us. "That's the mark the elephant left last night. We'll find Gunjai soon."

I followed P. in Otou's direction. After much studying the ground, I could make out some faint version of what the two Burmese men saw so clearly: a mark left by a long chain that Otou's elephant Gunjai had been dragging during the night. The mark would wander through the forest soils and across piles of fallen leaves. Then a huge fallen log would obstruct our path, and the chain mark would disappear again. "Over there," Otou would say, pointing. We'd walk for several hundred feet—and the mark would suddenly start once more. Here and there Otou would drag his foot perpendicularly across the chain mark, indicating to other mahouts in the area that this trail didn't lead to their elephant.

We climbed hillsides choked in vines and creepers. Otou and the forest guide both seemed sleepily comfortable, but I was already winded and perspiring. It was just after six a.m. Distractedly, Otou removed a machete from a green scabbard at the end of his sash and started thwacking at a baby bamboo shoot. "The baby shoots are very hard," P. explained. "He'll make it into a new handle for his knife." We proceeded through a gully and into an area of low brush. Here at last Otou looked perplexed. "Gunjai the elephant likes to play tricks." The mahout looked at us. "You stay here." Otou jogged up ahead and looked around. "No, no, he didn't go that way. He's clever and naughty." We returned to the gully. "He went down the gully and doubled back," Otou mused. "To confuse me. He's done it before." While climbing along the gully toward a hillcrest above, Otou explained other such elephant tricks. "Sometimes they pick up leaves with their trunk and stuff them into their wooden bell. That way the bell makes no noise and it's harder to find them." This trick might buy an elephant another thirty minutes or an hour before the mahout finally finds him, and the workday begins.[16]

Hearing about such tricks as we followed the elephant's path, I recalled a story I'd read from a British forest officer, Bruce, who was stationed in these jungles in 1903. He once saw a female elephant running away from her mahout. The attendant ran after her, shouting for her to stop and trying to catch the long chain attached to her leg. Seeing that the mahout was getting too close, the elephant picked up the chain with her trunk. She galloped off into the jungle, holding the chain triumphantly overhead; Bruce did not say whether this elephant was ever found.[17]

Evidently the double-back at the gully was the only trick Gunjai had in store for us today, for promptly the air began to fill with the *tink tink tink* of a wooden bell, a sound that could almost be mistaken for the babbling of a stony brook. The bells are carved of teak, and each one produces a slightly different note, identifiable by the mahouts. These elephant bells are a Burmese custom: one tends not to see them in the work elephant areas of northeastern India.

We found Gunjai at a grove of bamboos, munching tall blades of grass. He wasn't a beautiful creature, at least not from the angle we approached. In fact, he looked ridiculous. His belly bulged outward, full of fodder consumed during the night. He was a *mokona* elephant, a male born without tusks. In a normal herd, a certain percentage of the males always carry this trait. Isolated herds adjacent to ivory hunters will sometimes lose all their males with the tusker gene, leaving only mokona males. This seems to have happened in much of Sri Lanka, as well as in a section of the Patkai Mountains called Tirap.

"*Dwa! Dwa!* Come here!" Otou's commanding voice stopped short of a full shout. The elephant looked and snorted. His trick hadn't worked well enough. He stepped toward the mahout and released a quantity of steaming dung, as if to make a point. It was a dreadful display. But his belly looked more elegant now. I forced my way through the bramble to get a better look at Gunjai. He had the nice high forehead typical of mokona elephants. His long trunk ended in a splotch of pink.

A chain connected the elephant's two front legs: the fettering chain. Elephants released into the forest at night almost always wear one. The fetters are slack enough to permit the elephant to walk comfortably but not to run. This way the creature rarely wanders more than a mile or two from the evening release spot. Otou removed Gunjai's nighttime chain.

More often than not, Gunjai would be found close to the base area, usually as little as a half-mile away, but the route of the mark left by his dragging chain, which often wound in confusing patterns through hills and gullies, took Otou on long excursions that sometimes lasted over an hour. This was the morning ritual. It occurred to me that some time could be saved if the elephants were wearing GPS devices. Perhaps the time saved would make it possible to loosen that fettering chain more—or to remove it altogether.

P. interrupted my musings. "Why don't you step back from the elephant, Jacob," he said. "I don't think he likes you."

The guide perhaps had a point. As we followed the elephant, who now had Otou on his neck, the huge animal kept glancing back at me and P. and nervously walking faster. "I spend a lot of time with this elephant, and we always get along. It must be you." P. gave the matter some thought. "It's your trousers!"

He explained. That morning I was wearing beige pants that resembled the trousers that timber industry officials wore when they did surprise inspections. Otou and the guide, by contrast, were wearing traditional Burmese *longyi*: long fabric wrapped around the waist like a skirt. Gunjai knew the mahouts hated surprise inspections from the officials, so he hated them too. My pants and height and my general manner suggested to the elephant that I was an industry official, a member of the Burmese professional class. Not a mahout.

I liked P.'s theory. If it wasn't right, it surely ought to be.

We reached a small watering hole—too small, as the springs in these hills were running dry—and Otou began to wash Gunjai with a brush. The elephant clearly enjoyed the procedure. This relaxing bath was his daily reward for agreeing to exit the forest and begin the workday.

"What do the mahouts here do during *musth*?" I asked Otou as he scrubbed the elephant. Musth (pronounced "must") is a hormonal surge that male elephants experience—and females too, on rare occasion—which causes black tears to flow from glands near their eyes. The black tears are followed by a visceral urge to mate, which is followed by bouts of aggression and violence. A biologically important component of elephants' reproductive behavior, musth places forest mahouts in close proximity with the elephants when they were at their most dangerous. To me, this hormonal surge sounded like a serious impediment to the elephant-based work in the forest.

"It depends a lot on the elephant," Otou explained. "What we usually do here is let him go into the forest for a few days or a week. We try to let him get the musth out of his system. Usually during that first week, he just wants to mate and doesn't feel aggressive at all, and really he isn't so dangerous. But later the aggression sets in, and at this point we have to tie him up. Sometimes we tie him up by the ear. If we just tie him by the legs, he can break free with his strength or even knock down the tree he's tied to. But if we do it by the ear, he knows not to move." Sometimes, Otou went on, mahouts don't immobilize the elephant until after a mishap. The elephant in musth might attack another elephant. Or he might knock over someone's hut or even kill a person. But such events were rare.

Listening to this, I thought back to similar conversations about musth I'd had in the Trans-Patkai area to the north. Two tribal logging mahouts—one Kachin, the other Hkamti—told me their musth strategy was to give the elephant more tasks to do during the day, in the hopes that the extra burden would leave him too exhausted to become aggressive.[18] But a retired commander of the elephant transport brigade of the Kachin Independence Army described an approach similar to what Otou was telling me: during musth, the militia's mahouts give the elephants time off in the forest.[19]

Gunjai's bath was over, and he and Otou came up from the watering hole. P. the guide had found a bush full of sweetflowers and offered me one, demonstrating how to suck out the sugar. Then, as if proving to me that he was indeed old friends with this elephant, so the issue really must have been my pants, he hoisted himself onto Gunjai's neck and set off down the hill.

THE CAPTURE OF wild elephants and the nightly release of work elephants are foundational practices for the human-elephant working relationship in this part of the world. The nightly releases are needed because of the sheer quantity of fodder an elephant requires, which is around six hundred pounds each day.[20] An elephant engaged in cross-forest transportation might require less food at night, since the elephant probably spent much of the day-time munching on shrubs and bamboo shoots along the forest trail. Nonetheless, from the mahout's point of view, the nocturnal roaming period is a required element for keeping the elephant a healthy, happy, and reliable co-worker. A British elephant logging official from the colonial period, James Howard Williams (or "Elephant Bill," as he was nicknamed), remarked that in these forests a work elephant is really domesticated only "eight hours of the twenty-four."[21]

The nighttime wandering period also gives the elephants time to sleep and to mate: either with other domestic elephants or with elephants in wild herds passing through. Domestic female elephants free to wander the forest on a nightly basis leave progeny with far greater frequency than females stuck in enclosed compounds like zoos. Domestic males with this same freedom mate with wild females, which to some extent (but not fully) offsets the reduction in the wild population due to capture.[22]

The capture of wild elephants out of the forest, through methods like mela shekar and kheddah, is similarly vital, as it provides the mahouts with a significant number of their elephants. Though mahouts will often say that the elephants born to domesticated mothers make the best workers, female work elephants are less likely to mate during the night when work areas become isolated from wild elephants' migratory routes. This problem has become especially pronounced with greater forest fragmentation in recent decades.[23] Elephant capture can help offset such losses. A mahout may also turn to capture in order to supplement his herd while one of his females is pregnant or nursing her young. (The pregnancy period lasts around twenty months.) Though fandis sometimes "overcatch" elephants and destroy a wild herd, usually they do so to feed demand for elephants from tourist parks or from religious organizations that need elephants for their parades—not from the logging and transport mahouts. Lacking external demand, the forest population should tend toward an equilibrium, where the number of wild elephants who are caught by fandis and sent to work with forest mahouts is counterbalanced by the wild herd's birthrate, as well as by occasional escaped domestic elephants who rejoin the wild herds.[24]

Agricultural interests consider huge forested areas in the Trans-Patkai region to be cultivable and profitable for staple crops like sugar, wheat, and rice and thus present deforestation pressures. But numerous groups here have a direct stake in the continued existence of the forest, and these groups' mutual interest is the basis of a kind of forest-centered coalition. That coalition consists not only of mahouts and fandis who use elephants for logging and transport, but also poppy growers, gold panners, and hunters, all of whom need the forest as well. Rebel militias in the region (in particular the Kachin Independence Army and the National Socialist Council of Nagaland) depend upon the forest to provide cover for their clandestine operations. The Kachin Independence Army depends not only on the forest canopy but also on the elephants for moving supplies about in secret. Add to these affinities bonds of kinship, clan, and language, and suddenly the forest-centered coalition, with which the caught elephants have managed to align themselves, starts to look very formidable: the strongest network of such forest interests anywhere in the Asian elephant's natural range. But remove the fandis from the picture, as well as the input of trained elephants that they provide, and conditions begin to favor agricultural expansion and consequent deforestation.

One area I visited in the Trans-Patkai revealed what happens when elephant capture is removed from the local picture. In this area, police have been especially aggressive over the past decade in pursuing and arresting local fandis who capture wild elephants.

(Hence my decision not to name this location.) As a result, mela shekar is dying here. This shift has gone hand in hand with a decision among local elites to transition the local economy away from forest resources and toward farming wet rice in paddy fields. However, as the paddy fields spread into former forestland, domesticated elephants have begun wandering into the paddies at night. Consequently, the local elites have told local mahouts to keep their elephants chained to trees during the night. The local elites—who are usually the formal owners of the elephants—have done this reluctantly and unhappily, but the feeling has been that the rice paddies need to be protected, because they are compensating for local economic losses due to cessation of local elephant capture.

Because this village is located in an especially lush jungle zone, the elephants can be confined by 100 to 150 feet of chain at night and still find sufficient fodder. Nonetheless, the chain means the domesticated elephants cannot seek out wild herds and potential mates at night. And so even as the community receives no new elephants from mela shekar, its females are not becoming pregnant. Sometimes mahouts try to conjure pregnancies by leaving their elephants tied up in corridors they think wild herds will pass through; it's not clear yet whether this sort of thing can be effective. Due to these interconnected factors, the political and economic system here is in the process of "tipping" from being forest-oriented toward being farming-oriented, and the long-term situation for both the elephant-keeping culture of the area and the local forestlands looks very uncertain.[25]

This is not to say that, in areas with less police intervention, the elephant-keeping cultures of the Trans-Patkai region have necessarily succeeded in expanding local elephant numbers or even in maintaining a level population. Overall, numbers in the Trans-Patkai have not been definitively tallied by anybody, but they seem likely to have gone down over time.[26] Even so, the pressures against the local elephant population seem to have more to do with deforestation, ivory poaching, and market demand for captured elephants from distant religious organizations and tourist compounds than with mela shekar captures aimed at keeping the elephants situated in these forests. Likely, some captures of elephants have even helped move elephants away from forest areas with ivory poachers and toward safer sections of the forest, since poachers are less likely to encroach upon the forest turf of armed fandis and mahouts. Indeed, some mahouts remarked that the reason they bring their guns into the forest is only secondarily to protect themselves from wild elephants and other dangerous animals; primarily it's to protect their elephants from poachers.[27]

The working relationship between the two species must be understood with open eyes. When talking to the fandis of the region, I usually had to harden myself before listening to certain descriptions of mela shekar—and especially the subsequent training process. In the Trans-Patkai, a captured elephant is usually tied up for months on end in the forest, each leg fastened to a tree. The fandis will deny food to the elephant at first, then gradually bring more and more fodder, and eventually rice and salt treats, to reward the elephant for learning the command terms and developing desirable human-friendly behavior. Sometimes the relationship can retain this abusive dynamic long after the training period is over. The working relationship can sometimes be complicated and cruel, a topic we'll return to in Chapter 6.

Yet even with these troubling aspects of the relationship between forest mahouts and their work elephants, the mahouts' communities have proven more adept at resisting the economic pressures associated with deforestation than have areas elsewhere in the Asian elephant's natural range. And elephants require that forest cover, to eat, to mate, and to be happy. Through the unique combination of elephant capture, elephant employment, and nightly elephant release, such communities have been able to meet this requirement of forest access in a way that no one else in the world has.

Some indignant outside observers might assert that all these elephants should be left in the wild, and that the remaining forestlands should receive sufficient investment and protection to safeguard the wild elephants' migration corridors. In reality, such indignation has not been effective at stopping deforestation in this part of the world. While a number of practices among some fandis and mahouts here cannot be defended from a conservationist standpoint, overall fandis and mahouts have a great deal to teach concerned outsiders about how human beings, as morally imperfect creatures, can act as guardians rather than destroyers of the forest's last giants.

Chapter 2

POWERS OF TRUNK
AND MIND

LET US RETURN TO THE SCENE OF THAT HUGE ELEPHANT-
catching stockade of the Ayutthaya king in the seventeenth century.
The stockade was the size of a geoglyph, and within its wide opening, which was many miles across, stood a particularly steep mountain. This mountain had no stockade wall. Nor was it secured by
any of the royal elephant hunters carrying torches and drums. The
Jesuit priest visiting this royal Siamese kheddah asked his hosts
why the escape path had been left exposed. Because, he was told,
the mountain's slopes were so steep that they were insurmountable
even for the elephants. The mountain was a natural barrier aiding
the king's titanic stockade.

Soon the mass capture began. The long front line proceeded
toward the kheddah's narrowest point, carrying torches and drums
and lighting firecrackers. But as many wild elephants in the forest
retreated farther into the trap, the Jesuit priest kept his eyes on the
steep mountain. He made note of what he saw:

> Ten or twelve of them escaped that way, and for that purpose
> made use of a very surprising expedient; fastening themselves
> by their trunks to one of the trees that were upon the side of
> that very steep mountain, they made a skip to the root of the

next, and in the same manner clambered from tree to tree with incredible efforts, until they got to the top of the mountain, from whence they saved themselves in the woods.[1]

Some twenty elephant generations later, in the teak-logging area of central Burma, I witnessed something that reminded me of the Jesuit's extraordinary account. An elephant had been asked by her mahout to retrieve a log at the pinnacle of a steep hill. The log was an awkwardly shaped piece. Instead of going to the timber company's main depot, it would likely become construction material for the mahout's own family hut a mile down the stream from this prominence.

At the top of the hill, the mahout strapped a chain to the end of the log. He fastened the other end of the chain to an X-shaped wooden apparatus resting on two cushions along the sides of the elephant's spine. The duo dragged the slightly contorted piece of red timber along the crest of the hill, until they reached a spot where the bluff below them had no trees in the way. The mahout climbed down from the elephant and unfastened the chain. The elephant, without being prompted, kicked the log into place, so that its narrow point now faced the bluff. *"Tih!"* cried the mahout, and with a great heave of her forehead, the young elephant pushed the log over the precipice. Down it went! But the slope was so choked with vines that the log became caught about halfway down.

Having watched this process from the top of the bluff, then from the base having scurried down, I thought the log was irretrievable. It dangled in the middle of the cliff, ensnared by roots and vines. But the elephant proceeded to walk, headfirst, down a nearly vertical decline. She kept her hind legs at a crawl and her forelegs fully and muscularly extended at an angle against the bluff face. While the rear of her body slithered along very close to the bluff's surface, her head was hoisted away from it and leaned at a purposeful angle to create counterweight. As they proceeded, the mahout on her neck leaned farther back to add ballast. But it was really the elephant's trunk that permitted this extraordinary assemblage to make progress down the cliff.

An elephant's trunk, or proboscis, is a sublimely powerful, precise, and versatile instrument. It contains nearly 150,000 muscle subunits, or fascicles, which are linked by several long probiscidean nerves that swoop down from the elephant's dome and face, making their way in sensitive twists and turns to ultimately bifurcate across a series of tactile bristles, or feelers, at the trunk's tip.[2] These bristles are covered in dermal flaps that can perform surgically sensitive actions like cracking open a nut or retrieving a bill from a wallet. At the same time, the trunk can lift objects weighing many hundreds of pounds or break a person's spine in a few seconds. For millions of years, the trunk was the *Elephantidae* family's evolutionary analog, or retort, to *Hominidae*'s digits. An elephant "gathers in" much of its perceptual world, and makes sense of that world's possibilities, through the interface of the trunk. This elephant before me, along the cliff of the central Burmese teak hill, was using her trunk as a buttress, brake, steering mechanism, and feeler all at once.

At last the elephant-mahout pair came upon the log, and the elephant used an impeccably timed step forward with her left foreleg to give the upper end of it a swift kick. The log shot forward and crashed down the bluff, landing on the dirt path at the bottom with a tidy thud. Elephant and mahout followed downward, her trunk at times seeming to support their entire combined weight, like a metal spring. At last they reached the bottom. I was stunned by the display, but they were unfazed, apparently having done this many times before.

The creative dexterity of Burma and northeastern India's work elephants in facilitating movement across difficult forest terrain or forest channels comes up again and again in their recent history. Miloswar, the elderly Moran fandi who told the story of Sokona's "possession" by a spirit-mahout, told me another story in which he and an assistant were crossing a swift mountain stream during monsoon, atop a female elephant. With them was a young calf, her offspring. The two had been caught in tandem during mela shekar, a difficult feat.

Coming to the rushing channel, the mother hoisted the baby upward with her trunk and rested him so that his legpits were carried by her lower jaw and two small tusks. The female, now carrying a smaller elephant with her trunk and two humans on her back, proceeded into the river. The current was very rough, and the fandi assistant on the elephant's back lost his footing and fell into the water. He was a poor swimmer, and Miloswar thought he would likely drown. But the mother elephant, despite being freshly caught and still "raw," grabbed the assistant with her trunk, while keeping the baby pressed against her mouth. She proceeded to complete the ford with the assistant clinging to her trunk, the calf pressed firmly between her tusks and upper jaw, and Miloswar watching from above, amazed. She was only half trained at this time; the old fandi said she was just naturally compassionate. Over the ages, such dexterity and empathy have allowed elephant men like Miloswar to build and maintain relationships with the elephants as work partners in the forest.[3]

I saw another display of these work elephants' incredible dexterity along a muddy trail. I was in the Manabum hill range in Arunachal Pradesh, in a logging area the local mahouts call Mithong. Here several powerful local Hkamti and Singpho tribal families held great forest tracts.[4] To get to the area, I had ridden in a jeep for an hour past the town of Chowkham, until the road became a dirt track. This track had ended at a sawmill in the forest, and the mill workers were mostly young Adivasi men. The Adivasis had come to this area from central India during the nineteenth century, to work in northeastern India's expanding tea plantations. Harvesting tea was still their main type of work, but some were out here in the forest frontier for the superior wages offered in the timber industry.

From the sawmill, I climbed into a flatbed truck with massive thick wheels. The truck belched diesel smoke and proceeded along a dry riverbed, the "road" nothing but terrible bumpy boulders. An elephant had set out from the mill with us, a tall mokona male (that is, a male lacking the tusker gene). Like many mokonas, this male had an especially high forehead, which sloped upward and even somewhat forward. He was ridden by a Nepali, another ethnic group associated with elephant work in this area. The mokona and Nepali were making better time along the rocky dry riverbed than the truck. As the motor vehicle bounced and jolted, I watched the elephant disappear up the path in front of us and regretted not having asked to go that way. Eventually the truck reached a muddy path, which split off from the dry riverbed and snaked its way into the forest. Here the truck stopped. I walked with a guide and several lumbermen up this path, stopping on occasion to poke the mud off the soles of my boots. The lumbermen were Hkamti, and their machete scabbards were adorned in elegant carvings. After some twenty minutes, we came upon the front end of another truck, smaller and painted green and yellow. It was tipped at a steep angle: half the vehicle had sunk into the thick black mire that was everywhere along this trail. Beyond the awkward and precarious truck was a massive log, and an elephant.

It wasn't the mokona elephant from before—that one had proceeded past this site, to a loggers' camp up the path. This elephant, though also a huge male, was squat and broad. He was a natural tusker, rather than a mokona, but his tusks had been trimmed so that they were barely noticeable. He belonged to the main Hkamti logger who'd brought me here, a long-haired young man named

Tenam. "This is Air Singh," Tenam declared with some pride. "You'll watch what he can do." The mahout on Air Singh was Gam, a teenage Singpho-Kachin. With Gam calling a few commands, Air Singh pushed the truck about ten feet with his huge forehead, so the flatbed now faced the log. The truck's engine was plainly useless for this task—if anything, spinning the axles with the diesel power would just cause the wheels to sink further. At this point I still didn't see how the elephant was going to get the huge log, from a hollong tree, onto the truck. The flatbed was four or five feet higher than the log, which was fifteen feet long and nearly four feet in diameter and must have weighed well over a thousand pounds.

Air Singh set to work. His first step was to grab a different log with his trunk—a much narrower and lighter log—and carefully lean it against the edge of the flatbed. He did the same with another narrow log, placing it nine or ten feet farther down the long side of the truck's rear platform. It was a makeshift ramp. Air Singh and Gam studied the two ramp beams' placement for a moment, and after several seconds, Gam murmured some command term I could not make out. Air Singh adjusted one of the ramp beams. The pair seemed satisfied and turned their attention to the much larger and more valuable piece of timber.

Watching this spectacle, I still didn't understand how they were going to push the huge log up the incline. It seemed too big ever to move without a huge bulldozer or a powerful crane. Moreover, on the opposite side of the log was nothing but thick forest; Air Singh had nowhere to stand to get a head start.

Nevertheless, the elephant walked delicately into the narrow opening between the hollong log and the forest edge. As I expected, he couldn't face the log head on, but then, he didn't have to. He simply turned and leaned his head into it, gradually creating space for himself, so that eventually he could indeed face the log with his full force. By this point, the constant pivoting had jerked the two makeshift ramp beams out of place. One in particular was now off at a worrisome angle. Several of the lumbermen jumped onto the flatbed and attempted to straighten the beam but it proved too heavy. Gam shouted at them to get out of the way.

With a few quick, skilled motions, Air Singh hoisted the huge hollong log a few inches upward with his trunk and tapped the off-kilter beam back into place with his foot. It was a bit like watching a waiter wipe down a table with one hand while balancing a tray of champagne glasses with the other. The elephant was satisfied that the ramp was ready now. So was Gam. *"Agat!"* Go for it! The elephant began pushing into the log with his forehead, and Gam, to keep his own balance, leaned back so far that he was nearly lying on the animal's back.

"My god," I said, as I know from the sound recording I was making.

"Jesus." My guide, Kagung, was also taken aback. He was not from an elephant area and had never seen anything quite like this.

Air Singh rolled the huge wooden mass high, high up the ramp. Near the very top, he let out an enormous breathy *whoooooooshh*! from his trunk, from the sheer exertion. And then—*boom!*—the great log finally landed onto the truck bed, the suspension coils creaking with surprise. Air Singh calmly removed the two ramp beams out of the way. Once again he and Gam studied the position of the log. Evidently it wasn't perfectly centered. The elephant gave the log one last push, this time with his trunk. Then several lumbermen strapped the log down with chains, and a driver started the ignition. Air Singh, still not finished, went behind the truck to push it out of the sinkhole. Dislodged from the mire, it gained traction and disappeared down the muddy trail with its log, leaving a large wet pit where it had been stuck. Air Singh cooled himself down by looping his trunk into his mouth and sucking on the trunk cavity's moisture—a common elephant trick.[5]

Air Singh was one of the Mithong logging area's finest work elephants, a favorite of Tenam's. Back at the sawmill, over a lunch
of stewed chicken with potatoes, Tenam told me more about Air
Singh's life. He was named Air Singh, which means something like
"Lord of the Air," because he was born at the Tezu airfield on the
other side of the Lohit Valley—a military landing strip that had
been cleared by local work elephants during the 1962 border war
between India and China. Air Singh's mother was called Pagli, an
Indian term meaning something like "the crazy one." Pagli had been
a wild elephant in the forests beyond the Tezu airfield. But unlike
most wild elephants, she liked to come very close to the mahouts'
camp, to help herself to the rice treats left out for the domestic elephants. She would show up during both day and night, spurning
her own wild herd, and the mahouts grew accustomed to her. Eventually she mated with a domestic male and gave birth to Air Singh.
When the airfield work was completed, Pagli followed the Hkamti
mahouts back to their usual woodlands south of the Lohit River,
by the Manabum hill range. She couldn't be trained for work tasks,
but she also didn't want to follow the wild herd. She was a *pagli*.
The mahouts liked her, bringing her treats through her old age.
She'd paid them back by producing one of the logging area's best
elephants, after all.[6]

More often than not, the best logging elephants do not have
"pagli" mothers. Rather, they gain their skills during childhood
by watching their domesticated mothers at work. Farther up the
muddy trail from the spot where Air Singh loaded the massive hollong log lay the forest mahouts' main camp, and here a mother elephant passed by on her way to some task deeper in the hills. With
her was her mahout and also her calf. This is also common at the
government-owned logging areas in Burma. The mother does relatively light tasks—hauling smaller logs, carrying supplies, and so
forth—and takes frequent breaks to tend to her young. The calf

observes his or her mother doing the work tasks and responding to the human command terms, and this supplements the separate training that the calf receives from human masters.

Nonetheless, mothers like Pagli, who show little interest in doing the work tasks, are important for understanding how these elephant-centered forest practices emerged in the first place. Pagli was abnormally friendly toward humans, as compared with the rest of her wild herd. Perhaps unsurprisingly, this unorthodox attitude on her part went hand in hand with a certain antiauthoritarian streak: she spurned the authority not only of her own wild herd but also of the mahouts who wished to train her for work. Pagli elephants are likely an important source of human-friendly traits for the population of work elephants, though they don't always produce offspring that make fine workers like Air Singh. Tenam pointed out that Air Singh has a brother who ran away from the camp years ago and who becomes belligerent whenever he sees humans approach.[7]

The dexterity of the work elephants in moving massive logs also finds expression in the water: in particular, in the clearing of river logjams. This dangerous activity has been an especially important component of the government-managed Burmese teak-logging industry, where, in some areas (but fewer and fewer after the 1990s), elephants drag logs not only to trucks but also to rivers. The logs are then floated downstream to waterside depots or mills. Since teak is naturally water resistant, being immersed does not damage the wood's quality. This method of log transport remains relatively common in Burma's upper Chindwin Valley. The flaw in the method is that oftentimes the logs get jammed at sharp turns of the river. During the monsoon season, debris, such as fallen branches with leaves, plug the spaces between the jammed logs, and the jam becomes a huge dam. This not only entraps hundreds of valuable teak logs, it also causes dangerous flooding upstream and eventually downstream too. The logjams need to be broken up to prevent danger. This job goes to the most capable elephants.[8]

U Toke Gale, a Burmese elephant official, saw an elephant perform this dangerous, dramatic work in 1939. Gale was in a northern teak forest that boasted two especially memorable elephants, both tuskers. Swai-gyo, so called because he'd broken his left tusk in an accident, was unbeatable when it came to "handling teak in difficult terrain, like those stranded high and dry on the edge of rocky cliffs, or wedged in between two large boulders." And Pegu, named for the city near Burma's coast, was a maestro at breaking up logjams in a jungle stream. Gale remembered how both displayed so much efficiency at his particular branch of work that a local mahout coined a couplet:

On land, it is Swai-gyo,
In water, always Pe-goo.

One day during monsoon, the logging mahouts came upon a narrow bend in the river and found there a confused tangle of logs and debris spanning the eighty-foot breadth of the stream. The jam contained hundreds of tons of floating teak. No mahout in his right mind would go into the jam, Gale noted, due "to the danger of being swept away and crushed to death between the logs" at the moment of the dam's release.

Pegu was fetched, relieved of his harness, and sent into the water. "Pegu swam cautiously towards the center of the logjam—the muddy waters surging and swirling furiously around him, sometimes submerging him altogether, leaving only his trunk above the water," Gale recalled. The tusker placed his head against a large log, but the mahout back on shore was not satisfied that it was the "key" log that would break the jam, and he yelled at Pegu to keep looking. Finally the elephant placed his trunk on a log that the mahout thought looked promising. *"Hti like, maung gyi! Hti like!"* shouted the elephant man above the noise of the current. "Push it over, big brother! Push it over!" The words reached the elephant's great ears "above the din of incessant rain and the roar and rumble of a river in spate. Pegu heaved, loosened, pulled, lifted the offending log between his tusks and the trunk."

When the jam broke, the pile of timber that had stood still a moment earlier "now trembled, creaked, and then moved down the stream with a tremendous force." Pegu, sensing the danger and knowing he hadn't a moment to lose, trumpeted and turned around sharply, swimming athletically toward the bank. The procession of logs shooting out from the growing breakage in the jam was catching up with him, but he brushed them aside with his legs and trunk as best he could. The bank was steep, and Pegu couldn't gain a foothold to hoist himself out. So he went on swimming, hugging the bank, as logs floated past him and hit him on the rump. Eventually he found a small upward protrusion of the river bottom, a boulder or submerged shoal, barely large enough to accommodate his four feet. He was trapped. Etched on his face was "fear, desperation, anger, as log after log raced towards him." He continued to push them away with his trunk, forelegs, or tusks. Eventually he climbed the steep muddy embankment, to escape the river, the same way the wild elephants witnessed by the Jesuit priest in the seventeenth century ascended the steep mountain slope to escape the king's kheddah: he got out "using his trunk like a man his hands."

Now that Pegu was on dry land, his proud head hung low with exhaustion. He was bruised and bloodied on his knees and his trunk. The mahout waited for many minutes for Pegu to grow tranquil, knowing that the elephant, still furious and excited from the river, might charge anyone who dared approach. Eventually he softly encouraged Pegu to come with him, promising boiled paddy and salt back at the camp.[9]

The clearing of logjams obviously places elephants in tremendous danger. And for anyone concerned for the individual elephant's immediate welfare, it's hard to defend the practice. Perhaps the only positive thing one can say is that it keeps the elephants at work sites in the forest rather than in zoos.

In the tribal areas of the Trans-Patkai region, most logging occurs during the dry season, when river levels are low, so mahouts rarely ask their elephants to clear logjams. During the wet season, the elephants are needed to transport goods to places that have become isolated by the monsoon inundation of roads. In Burma's government-run logging industry, by contrast, most of the heavy-duty logging occurs during the wettest months, when the animals are most in their element and can work the hardest. The dry months, officially, are a "rest" period for the elephants, though in reality during this time the mahouts have the elephants retrieve forest materials (mostly bamboo and ironwood) for the use of the mahouts' own families. The contrast reveals the different priorities in the two situations. Whereas the Trans-Patkai mahouts would rather use the elephants' best work months for transporting passengers and everyday goods, the Burmese government's timber enterprise prefers to use that period for dragging its major commodity, teak.

THE SKILLS DISPLAYED by mighty logjam-clearing elephants like Pegu, or cliff-descending elephants like the one I saw in central Burma, or timber-handling elephants like Air Singh, are in large part the same as the skills of river-fording "ferry" elephants like Burmay-Moti, the elephant we met in the Introduction, who carries passengers and goods across the Sissiri River during monsoon. Pegu's tale gives us a good sense of these elephants' ability to yank, hoist, and sweep aside huge midriver obstacles. Burmay-Moti is

frequently asked to perform comparable but less dangerous maneuvers while fording the Sissiri, where floating logs or tangles of forest
debris can impede the crossing.[10]

During my travels, Burmay-Moti was the only elephant I saw use
her trunk to assist passengers in climbing onto her back. Usually the
method of mounting an elephant is an awkward but reliable procedure where the elephant kneels down and the passenger climbs up
one of her rear hamstrings onto her back. Sometimes the elephant
offers a helpful boost by slowly elevating the hindleg. This poste-
rior route was the one I used to mount elephants in the forest camps
of the Trans-Patkai and central Burma. Tourist parks I visited in
Thailand and Sumatra offer an easier way: they've built elevated
platforms at the level of the standing elephant's back. Mounting
these creatures reminded me of stepping off a station platform into
a metro train.

But a number of Burmay-Moti's regular passengers across the Sissiri preferred a far more graceful and acrobatic method. I was never
able to do it myself, so I had to appreciate it simply as an observer.
One afternoon, an ethnic Adi passenger arrived at the Sissiri crossing point by motorbike. The river conditions that day were mild,
and the Adi man was able to shout across the river to a friend, who
was waiting there at the opposite bank in a pickup truck. The Adi
man then turned to Burmay-Moti's mahout, Pradip, who was sitting on the elephant's neck, and they began chatting in Assamese
and some Adi. Pradip is not himself an ethnic Adi, but rather an
Adivasi. Regardless of this ethnic difference, though, the two men
seemed to have a good, friendly rapport. I later learned that Pradip,
in addition to being the main mahout in the area, is also the local
ringleader for afternoon river fishing, an activity in which many
local Adis, Assamese, Nepalis, Adivasis, and Mishmis like to
participate.

After Pradip and the Adi man finished talking, the female pachyderm lowered her trunk down to the ground and curled the end of it upward. The Adi stepped onto the serpentine appendage. Burmay-Moti folded her big ears inward toward him, and the man grabbed both of her ears with his hands, balancing on the trunk with his feet. At first the display perplexed me, but then Burmay-Moti gently lifted her trunk upwards, maintaining a sensitive curvature to protect the Adi man's footing, while he used her two great ears for balance. Upward he ascended, as if riding an elevator. When he reached the crown of her head, he released her ears and climbed past Pradip to the elephant's back.

The current at the Sissiri River can be powerful, and when it is, Pradip and Burmay-Moti wade across at a forty-five-degree angle against the current. The elephant seems to have greater dexterity and control pushing upstream than she would if she were allowing herself to be swept along with the current. Even at deep spots in the river, where Burmay-Moti must swim with her trunk upturned for air, she paddles at an upstream angle. One evening I was in the village of Dambuk, on the "monsoon island" side of the Sissiri, speaking with Pradip and some of his mahout friends who work the Sissiri crossing. They recalled an incident from a monsoon season some years back, when other mahouts had attempted to ford the river head-on. These other mahouts hailed from a village called Mebu on the busier, "mainland" side of the Sissiri, and they were experienced with using their elephants for logging but not for cross-river transport.

The decision to cross head-on was disastrous—several elephants lost their footing and in effect "capsized." A number of people were killed, and one of the elephants disappeared completely, swept away in the current. Pradip and an older Assamese mahout named Sikya recalled that, upon hearing of this disaster, they fetched their own elephants and headed to the river to help. Far downstream from the crossing point, at a rocky bend in the river, they were able to locate the lost Mebu elephant. Her foot had become trapped in the rocks.

Burmay-Moti's mother, Sesta-Moti, was sent into service. She used her body as a natural breakwater to relieve the hapless Mebu elephant, then gave a firm shove with her head to dislodge her from the rocks. The two elephants used their trunks to climb out of the water together.

Burmay-Moti and Sesta-Moti (which translate to "Sister Diamond" and "Mother Diamond" respectively) seem to be Dambuk's two most skilled fording elephants, as of the 2010s. Until very recently a third elephant, an extremely skilled male, could even give rides across the Dibang River, a much larger watercourse on Dambuk's east side. Unfortunately, this male was killed by a hunter some years ago who mistook him for a wild elephant.[11]

The largest rescue operation Burmay-Moti and Sesta-Moti were involved in occurred during the 2000s, when some two dozen local river fishermen became trapped on a midriver island during a monsoon storm. The water was rising rapidly and would soon overflow the island. Sister and Mother Diamond and their neck-mounted pilots carried all the humans to safety in a single crossing—meaning each elephant took about eleven or twelve humans on her back at the same time, the most I have ever heard of an elephant carrying. For more routine, lower-urgency crossings, five or six humans (or two tied-up motorcycles) would be considered a "full" load.

Mother and daughter do not see each other very frequently: Burmay is usually brought into the forest ranges south of Dambuk, while Sesta is sent to the north. Nonetheless, when they do see each other for joint operations like the rescues, or when they pass each other in a forest trail, they become excited, trumpet at each other, and touch trunks.[12]

THE ELEPHANTS are adept at learning multiple languages—or rather, different groupings of command terms pulled from different human languages. This in turn enables a trade in elephants among forest peoples, which in turn helps circulate a single elephant through multiple zones of fragmented forest. Such circulation is significant for the elephants' health, reducing the likelihood of inbreeding within isolated forest pockets. On their own, elephants cannot easily walk across corridors of agricultural and urban development, from one forest to the next, seeking new mates—not without provoking conflicts with farmers, townspeople, drivers along highways, and so on. In southern India, wildlife parks contain many thousands of elephants, but the parklands are also highly noncontiguous. Elephant "corridors" between the reserves exist but mostly only in theory.

By contrast, when the mahouts of the Trans-Patkai move their elephants from forest to forest by selling their elephants to each other (or by embarking on long-range transport operations, or by moving forest camps in search of new work), they provide a kind of "bridge" permitting elephant genes to hop across these agricultural and urban barriers. Elephants' ability to learn multiple command systems creates more opportunities for such "bridges," expanding the number of ethnolinguistic areas a mahout can trade with. On the Indian side of the Trans-Patkai, mahouts' terms are mostly derived from Assamese or Hkamti (the latter being a Tai language, related to Thai and Lao). Kachin mahouts on the Burmese side mainly use terms from their own language. South of here, mahouts in the Burmese government's teak forests use Burmese words. Karen mahouts have their own set of terms as well.[13]

A trade of elephants across the Patkai Mountains, between Burma's Hukawng Valley and India's Lohit and Dihing valleys, was relatively common until just a few decades ago, when border controls tightened.[14] If traded from the Hukawng into India, these elephants would learn new terms with an Assamese linguistic basis. If traded in the other direction, they had to be able to learn new terms with a Burmese or Kachin linguistic basis. In central Burma, I encountered several elephants who spent the first decades of their working lives in the upper Chindwin Valley, where the command terms had been mostly Hkamti. Later they were moved to the central hills, where the terms became mostly Burmese.[15] Mong Cho, a Hkamti mahout in the southwestern Kachin Hills, explained to me that in his region the Kachin and Hkamti elephant command systems are really quite distinct, but that elephants learn them both with ease and thus can be traded easily between the two communities. He told me of elephants who mastered Kachin-dominated, Hkamti-dominated, and Burmese-dominated command systems simultaneously and were able to switch from one to the other to the next depending on their current mahout.[16]

The command systems usually consist of around thirty-five words, though some mahouts said very smart elephants can learn closer to one hundred terms.[17] No mahout I spoke with recalled an elephant ever forgetting a command term learned earlier in life. Typically, it takes the elephants a few months to learn a new command system, as the mahouts introduce a few new words at a time. The terms range in significance from the simple—*go, stop, sit, get up*—to the remarkably complex. One command means "Clear that grass out of our way with your foot." (The Hkamti mahouts would say, *"Thal dob! Dob, dob . . ."*)[18] Another means something like "Stick your leg out so the passengers can climb down your leg." (Here the Hkamtis would say *"Pish kuhl!"*) Mahouts can gain a more refined set of meanings by combining the terms or by adding tactile signals like tapping the elephant's forehead or ear. A skilled Hkamti mahout might say *"Pish kuhl!"* and *"Bichu!"* ("Back!") in succession, then touch the elephant's right ear: "Right hind leg out! The passengers will climb down that way."[19]

The elephants possess other fascinating cognitive traits. Their mnemonic and geographic cognition of the wider landscape makes them useful as guides. One mahout recalled an episode where his elephant refused to pass in the shadow of large slope. The duo found another route. Later that day the slope collapsed into a violent landslide.[20]

Similarly, I heard several stories of elephants carrying mahouts extraordinary distances when the mahouts were unable to direct the way. Miloswar, the old Moran fandi, told me a story about his father, who had been working for many months in a row with his elephant in a logging area in the Tirap forests, about forty miles from his family's home. He hadn't seen his family since the work season had begun. At last the season was over, the final logging day completed. But it was already late in the day; it would have been prudent to spend one more night at the work camp and begin the journey in the morning.

But Miloswar's father was so eager to get home and see his family that he decided he and his elephant would ride in the moonlight. They proceeded across the Dihing Valley. The sun went down. Almost immediately Miloswar's father fell asleep, while sitting on the elephant's neck. When he awoke, it was morning, and he was somehow at his family's farmhouse, along the New Dihing River. After months of working at the logging site in Tirap, the elephant, without having to be told or directed, intuited that Miloswar's father was trying to get home. The elephant already knew the way, forty miles in the darkness.[21]

A similar but tragic story dates from World War II, when many British and American soldiers were encamped in the Tirap Hills, building the first stretch of the Ledo Road that would be used to carry arms to the Chinese. The soldiers needed rations, especially rice. Some local agents hired Hkamti and Singpho-Kachin mahouts near Chowkham to bring the supplies. It was a huge convoy, roughly one hundred elephants with two mahouts each. But there was a terrible miscommunication. The elephant convoy came to a river, on the other side of which was a large U.S. camp, a construction corps. The convoy crossed the river, and the lead mahout, who never received clear instructions from the go-between agent about how they should announce themselves, thought he should fire a warning shot. The Americans took this as an attack from the Japanese and immediately opened fire. Many of the elephants and mahouts were able to retreat back across the river, or hide behind boulders and trees, but several dozen mahouts and elephants were killed. While the surviving mahouts regrouped and debated what to do, some of the surviving elephants picked up their dead masters and carried them all the way back to the mahouts' families in Chowkham, some sixty miles away.[22]

SINCE ONE CANNOT directly interview the elephants, it is impossible to capture their own inner cognitive relationship with the work they do. Yet in many instances, the giants' heightened situational awareness, adaptability to different human milieus, and creative dexterity in a dynamic landscape seem to point to a working consciousness that goes well beyond being merely reactive and "sensorimotor," to being solution-seeking, contemplative, and mediated through abstract thought. Work elephants can be, at times, remarkably innovative. We've already seen how they invent clever ways to extend their nocturnal roaming time, as when Gunjai doubled back on his own trail to delay the morning fetch. The elephant observed by the forest official Bruce in 1903 picked up her dragging chain with her trunk so it would leave no mark. Other elephants stuff their wooden bells full of dead leaves, so they cannot be heard at a distance. The Kachin Independence Army's elephant battalion adopts this technique too, when it requires stealth.[23] Perhaps the elephants learned the trick from the rebels, or vice versa.

In addition, elephants seem to have invented some original

work methods themselves—methods that impressed the attending humans, who had not thought of the solution on their own. An especially compelling case comes to us from James Howard Williams, a British elephant official in Burma during World War II. The British were overseeing the construction of a teak log bridge in the middle of the jungle, and many elephants with their Burmese mahouts were assisting in the construction. At one point an especially large tusker elephant was asked to heave a massive log onto a platform lying atop one of the bridge foundation's pylons. The log first had to be balanced on the animal's tusks, a job the mahout and elephant had done plenty of times together, the mahout shouting out his commands, the elephant knowing the process but reassured by the sound of his human partner's voice.

The elephant picked up one end of the log with his trunk and eased his tusks underneath it. Then he hoisted the log upward with his tusks, for a few seconds, to check the balance of the load. The log was too heavy on one side, so the elephant put down one corner of the beam, held the other upright with his trunk, and readjusted the position of his tusks. This process was all routine. After the elephant correctly balanced the log, he and the mahout finally approached the bridge and the audience of construction workers (Burmese and Indian) and British officers, all transfixed by the spectacle.

As the elephant approached the pylon, however, the ascent to the high platform was so steep that the log began to roll backward, away from his tusks and onto his head. What's more, it seemed likely to roll further, onto the mahout mounted on his neck. Despite impatient shouts from some other workers, the elephant refused to go forward until this danger was addressed. The onlooking humans, unaccustomed to building wartime bridges in the Burmese jungle, were at a loss as to how to proceed. But the elephant had an idea. Setting the log down, he paced around the nearby brush for a few moments, until he found a short but sturdy club-shaped branch. Urging the mahout to let him balance the log on his tusks yet again, the elephant grabbed the branch with his trunk and pressed it diagonally between his tusks. In effect, he repurposed the branch as a safety lock. The humans, astounded, wondered why they hadn't thought of it themselves. Williams tells us the result:

> This time the club-shaped bit of wood was there . . . so that the log could not roll back over his forehead onto his rider. An oath came from the Major, a murmur of admiration from the Brigadier. I could feel my heart beating, as the animal moved toward the bridge platform, carrying the balanced log. . . . It was one of the most intelligent actions I have seen an elephant perform.[24]

This elephant's intrepid thinking raises an important question: to what extent has it been the *elephants* all along, rather than the humans, who innovated these methods, maneuvers, and tasks? One might suppose that most of the elephants' jobs were concocted by mahouts, perhaps sitting around a campfire discussing the possibilities, and then developing their ideas through trial and error with the elephants. Perhaps in many cases this has been so. But this piece of archival evidence, Williams's account of the ingenious "safety lock" elephant, has the *elephant* as the innovator. Consider, too, the sheer amount of moment-to-moment resourcefulness and improvisation we've seen in many other elephants already: Pegu finding a way out of the log-choked, rushing river, or Burmay-Moti navigating a route across a torrential river full of meandering channels and debris. Consider crazy Pagli, who liked humans well enough but preferred to think on her own rather than follow orders.

If elephants, as much as humans, are devising these tasks, or certain aspects of them, this would support the idea that for the elephants, forest-based work has been a scheme of species survival. All these tasks are keeping elephants in situations where they have wild elephants' access to the forest, but they are also interwoven into working human communities that are invested in guarding them. What's more, some elephants' unique skills and abilities encourage their human partners to mobilize them across agricultural and urban barriers, which in turn allows the elephants to mate with herds in different forests and mitigate inbreeding. Such skills include the elephants' multilingual abilities and their ability to perform cross-forest and cross-mountain transportation.

Furthermore, from the standpoint of humans, the elephants' talent for "escape mobility" makes them useful for unexpected emergency situations: an impromptu bridge that has to be built in the jungle; a drowning mahout who has to be rescued; or (as we'll see in Chapter 3) humans fleeing a military invasion. Such mobilization increases the odds that elephants will enter into new forest areas with new reproductive opportunities. Who, then, is riding whom? By allying themselves with the forest mahouts, elephants are in a way "hitching a ride" across deforested areas that they wouldn't otherwise be able to traverse, thus linking fragmented herds. In the village of Dambuk during monsoon, humans are isolated like elephants who inhabit lone pockets of forest. Corridors of human development obstruct elephants as much as a swollen river restricts the mobility of humans. The two situations mirror each other, with elephant and mahout switching roles on each side.

Chapter 3

MUDDY
EXODUS

IN 1942, THE YEAR THE EMPIRE OF JAPAN INVADED AND
occupied the British colony of Burma, hundreds of thousands of
refugees, mostly British and Indian, fled the country and traveled
west to India, crossing through wild rainforests and difficult mountain ranges. Asian elephants played an indispensable role in many
of these escapes. Trained elephants sent into the highlands carried
evacuees and their possessions across river fords and mountain
passes, terrain that other types of transportation, wheeled or not,
had little or no chance of traversing successfully. It is likely that
thousands of refugees had some experience, during their journey,
of being ferried by elephant.

The stories of three elephants in particular, fortuitously preserved in written memoirs, convey the nerve and resourcefulness
of the tamed giants during this human exodus. These elephants
were Rungdot, who rescued evacuees below a northern mountain
pass called Chaukan; Maggie, who ferried refugees at the nearby
Pangsau Pass; and Bandoola, who led a convoy of rescue elephants
through a southern pass, Shenam. By examining these remarkable
mass escapes and the elephants' often heroic role in aiding them, we
can get a better of sense of an activity where work elephants seem
most to "come into their own": the transportation of human beings

when, due to war or weather or both, the human beings' roads cannot be used.

THE REMOTE AND TREACHEROUS Chaukan Pass is some eight thousand feet above sea level, far above the normal range of wild elephants. Landslides and flooding can be especially severe here, due to a combination of glacial melt and monsoon rains. In late spring of 1942 a group of refugees, several hundred in number, fled from Burma through this pass. Most of them were British and Indian, though some Burmese were in the group too, as well as other Europeans. All the members of the party were from a railway surveying team that had been in Upper Burma plotting a possible route for a Burma-China railway—a British project that never came to fruition. Surveying work had been occurring throughout 1941.[1]

Then came the Japanese invasion, in January 1942. The British colonial government was utterly unprepared. Though rich in timber, minerals, and agricultural land, Burma did not offer a significant resource that the Japanese military and industries desperately needed, such as oil or coal. Japan already controlled the rest of Southeast Asia, including Singapore, along with large swaths of China, especially along the coast and in the northern interior. Much of the Japanese naval fleet was far off in the Pacific, where the Japanese military strategists had ordered an attack on Pearl Harbor the month before. The British high command in India and Burma assumed that the Japanese, having committed themselves to challenging American naval supremacy, were spread thin across three fronts and could be counted on to stay out of Burma.

This proved to be a grave miscalculation. For Japanese imperialists, the value of Burma was not its extractable resources but its location. British Burma was the "back door" to China. It was in effect a wide Sino-British borderland. Chinese laborers had already

built a long, winding, all-weather road—an incredible engineering achievement at the time—that twisted and turned through the
highlands of Yunnan and the Burmese Shan States. Dubbed the
Burma Road, the hairpin thoroughfare linked British Burma to a
large area of southern China beyond the Japanese military's reach.
The British had been sending arms and supplies down this new
road into China from 1938 onward, to Chiang Kai-shek's Nationalist forces. The road was making it impossible for the Japanese to
bury the Chinese resistance and divert field resources elsewhere. By
invading Burma, the Japanese could finally cut off this supply line.

They invaded suddenly, seizing the seaports of Moulmein and Rangoon in January 1942. The occupation of the coast was itself enough
to block British access to the Burma Road, since the only way British
supplies could get to Burma in the first place was by sea. But the Japanese anticipated that the British would attempt a work-around by
building all-weather roads from India across the Patkai Mountains
and into Upper Burma. If built, such roads would create a link to the
Burma Road by land. Aiming to deny the British this potential land
route, the Japanese commanders had their forces push deeper into the
Burmese interior. Supplied by ships from Singapore, as well as through
a mountain pass from Thailand, Japanese forces were able to move up
the three main river valleys of central Burma, the Irrawaddy, Sittaung,
and Salween, during the spring of 1942. By May 1, they had taken the
whole country, except for a tiny, isolated pocket in the far north, an
area at the foothills of the eastern Himalayas called the Putao Plain.
Adjacent to the Putao Plain was the Chaukan Pass.

As the Japanese swept into Burma, the railway surveying party
found themselves part of a mass exodus of Britons, Indians, and
some Burmese out of the country. Hundreds of thousands of refugees had no route to the sea, as the Japanese had control of the
coast. Some were able to exit by air, but there was nowhere near the
air capacity needed to move so many people out of the country in so

short a period of time, especially as the number of British-controlled airfields in Burma shrank with the Japanese's rapid advance north. Most would have to cross the Patkai range to get out.

The British, who'd been in control of Burma since the nineteenth century, had occasionally discussed building roads or railways through the Patkais and the Chin Hills, so as to link Burma with British Assam and with Bengal. But the high costs, due to the engineering challenges posed by monsoon, had always seemed prohibitive. Anyway, the facilitation of Indo-Burmese trade had never really been the point of Britain's Burma colony. The British had conquered the place over the course of three wars, in 1825, 1852, and 1885, and the idea had always been to assume control of the country's resources and funnel them southward through the port of Rangoon to the British commercial empire beyond. For the British, teak was the most prized resource of all; the wood's naturally water-resistant properties made it ideal for British shipbuilding.[2]

With the Japanese occupation of Burma, British colonial officials saw their mistake in never developing transport through the mountains. They dusted off old plans to build roads through the Shenam Pass (which links the Imphal Plain of Manipur with central Burma's Chindwin Valley) and the Pangsau Pass (which links Assam to northern Burma's Hukawng Valley). In May 1942, though, these roads were still just ideas, and monsoon season was about to begin. There would be no fleeing Burma across the Patkais in comfortable motor vehicles. The evacuation would have to occur on foot. At the Shenam and Pangsau passes, hundreds of elephants were put to work carrying the refugees and their food supplies across the mountains, along muddy jungle paths and across dangerous river fords.

The railway surveyors were in Myitkyina (pronounced *MEE-chee-na*), a city in Upper Burma that lay along the upper Irrawaddy River amid the Kachin Hills. The city had a mixed population of Kachins, Shans, Karens, Burmese, Britons, and Indians. When word spread that the Japanese were on the march from the south and rapidly approaching the Kachin Hills, large groups of Indian and British people fled into the surrounding countryside.[3]

British administrators in India were not giving clear evacuation instructions, and communications were generally shaky, as the Japanese had taken the major radio hub in Mandalay the previous month.[4] The railway party's inner circle of leaders debated what to do. One possibility was to head south to the Shenam Pass. To get there they would have to walk westward out of Myitkyina, along the road that went to the Hpakant jade mines. There they'd turn left, or southward, and cross the jade area until they reached the gold-mining region along the Uyu River. They could follow the Uyu to the Chindwin, and then the Chindwin Valley to the base of the Shenam Pass.[5]

The railway party knew there was already a reasonably well-organized evacuation route through the Shenam Pass, which had been taking refugees out of central Burma for months. James Howard Williams, an enterprising British "teak wallah"—a forest manager in the Burmese teak business—had succeeded in mobilizing hundreds of logging elephants out of the Chindwin Valley teak forests and toward the mountains, to assist in the evacuation. These elephants were carrying refugees out of central Burma toward the relative safety of British-held Imphal, in India. Though the railway party wouldn't have been familiar with the details of the Shenam operation, the scene of this southern escape route is worth briefly describing.

In his memoirs, Williams recalled of the Shenam Pass that "in some places it was so steep that the elephants would almost be standing on their hind legs. . . . We were as high as Hannibal when he crossed the Little St. Bernard"—an allusion to Carthaginian general Hannibal Barca's march across the European Alps with thirty-seven war elephants, in the third century B.C.[6] During the initial trek through Shenam, Williams recounted, his elephants—

who were carrying women, children, and the sick, as well as baggage and food supplies—had hesitated when confronted with the intimidating clifflike slopes. He had a team cut a series of steps in the sandstone bluffs, "each just big enough to take an elephant's foot." Once that was done, he sent for his best elephant, Bandoola, who was a huge tusker, and his best mahout, Po Toke, a Burmese. "Don't worry," Po Toke half-joked. "Bandoola knows how to close his one eye on the cliff side of the path." Bandoola and Po Toke inched their way up the ascent. Po Toke was as solemn as a "pallbearer at a village funeral"—that is, until he reached Williams, who was waiting at the crest. At that point Po Toke turned to Williams and, with something of a wink, remarked, "They'll all follow now." Indeed, emboldened by Bandoola, the rest of the elephants went up as well. "I learned more in that one day about what elephants could be got to do than I had in twenty four years," the logging official Williams would later write. Throughout much of the spring of 1942, this elephant stairway through the Shenam Pass was one of the most important evacuation routes out of Burma.[7]

Word of the Shenam Pass escape route had spread throughout the country. But it was mostly being used by refugees from central Burma—from places like Mandalay, Taungoo, and Prome—not those as far north as Myitkyina. If the railway party made the overland trek to Williams's elephant operation at Shenam, the journey would take them far to the south, where their chances of encountering Japanese patrols increased. The party sought other options.

Another possibility was to start out trekking toward Shenam, but then to turn right, or westward, at the Hpakant jade mines. From there, they could cross the Hukawng Valley—a region notorious for intense monsoon flooding and for its mosquitoes and leeches—and attempt to walk through the Pangsau Pass. The hills around this pass were poorly mapped and were reputed to have unfriendly tribes. A sign at the fork in the road near the Hpakant jade mines read, in regard to this rightward path: "This route is a death trap for women and children. Women and children should turn left."[8]

These appeared to be the only two options: Shenam Pass to the south, where encountering Japanese patrols was likely, or Pangsau Pass to the west, where there was dangerous flooding and potentially hostile locals. But one midranking surveyor, Moses, gained the attention of the railway party's core leadership and proposed a third option: they could head north toward the Putao Plain, the one area in Burma the Japanese did not control, then hike across the Chaukan Pass, which would lead to the Dihing River, which they could follow into Assam. Moses explained that several years before, in his personal wanderings through the region, he'd crossed through the Chaukan Pass coming from India into Burma, and the journey had taken him ten days. After some deliberation, the leadership accepted the plan.[9]

In subsequent reports written after the Chaukan affair was over, Moses's colleagues wondered whether he had exaggerated his previous experience with the Chaukan Pass. The railway party's journey through Chaukan began poorly and ended disastrously. Moses tended to get the blame. One gets the sense, from these accounts, that as the journey progressed and the monsoon rains began, the group lost confidence in Moses, who became despondent and isolated. His status as an outsider within the European circles of the railway party—Moses was a Dutch Jew while the others were mostly Anglo and gentile—appears to have contributed to this isolation.[10]

In late May, the huge party of refugees set off from the Putao Plain and into the hills toward Chaukan. A monsoon storm was beginning to break, and the party rushed to traverse the mountains before the heaviest rains hit. Francis Kingdon-Ward, a British botanist and explorer who'd visited the region during the 1920s, provides a stirring description of what these mountain forests could be like during the monsoon floods:

During the rainy season it is, of course, impossible to get along. . . . The swollen river fills its bed and comes galloping madly down from the hills; as it rushes along at the foot of the forest, it plasters the lower branches with flotsam. The stagnant air throbs with the roar of the flood and the rumble of grinding boulders. Pale wisps of clouds writhe through the tree-tops like wet smoke, and the melancholy drip, drip of the rain from the leaves sounds a perpetual dirge. There is a rank odor of decay in the jungle, though life everywhere is triumphant. Scattered over the dark squelchy ground are speckled pilei [mushroom caps] in flaring colors, and horrid fungi scar the bloated tree trunks. Pale, evil-looking saprophytes lurk beneath the creaking bamboos, and queer orchids peep from the bibulous soil. The atmosphere is foul with mold, yet life is at full flood.[11]

There was much confusion in the early days of the trek. One man, Gardiner, had managed to grab a map from the government office in Myitkyina (most of the maps had been destroyed so they would not fall into Japanese hands), but it showed the Chaukan area in considerably less topographic detail than the surrounding regions.[12] No one knew which saddle-shaped passage through the green, gray, and white peaks was actually the Chaukan Pass. Moses seemed disoriented, saying the landscape looked completely different in the rain and mud than it had during his previous journey, which had been at a drier time of year. The path he remembered seemed to have been washed away, and mudslides had altered the terrain, erasing memorable landmarks. The party had no elephants. They were accompanied by local porters, who were mostly Kachins and Lisus. But upon seeing the conditions along the path, many of the porters turned back. The leaders of the party attempted to persuade them to stay, offering large sums of money, but the porters were resolute. Even if the Chaukan Pass could be crossed, they reasoned, by the time they got to Assam, it would be high monsoon, and they'd have no means of returning until the dry season, a half-year away. By this time, the war might have reached the Putao Plain, where they all had families. The prospect of being stranded in India for months on end was unacceptable.[13]

The railway party sadly watched the porters depart. A few stayed, though, mostly Nungs, a clan of the Lisu. The refugees trudged through the long corridor of the pass, still nervous that they were following a "false" pass that led only to more mountains. Their spirits revived when they finally spotted the upper headwaters of an Assamese river, the Dihing—perhaps the worst was over! But just downhill from there, the party found itself blocked by a roaring river confluence, where the Dapha River meets the Dihing. By this point the rains were coming down in full force, and snowmelt from the white-tipped northern Patkais was pouring into these forbidding watercourses. The party of hundreds was deep in the wilderness, where there were no indigenous settlements to be found. Nor was there any hope of a British rescue party. In the confusion of the flight from Myitkyina, and in the party's rush to begin their journey before the monsoon broke, no communication had ever reached British officials in Assam telling them to expect a large party of evacuees near the Chaukan Pass.[14] The party was now starving and exhausted and appeared to be trapped.

JUST THIRTY MILES SOUTH, a similar exodus was unfolding at the Pangsau Pass. By late May, the sign near the Hpakant jade mines urging refugees to avoid the Pangsau had been taken down. The British had lost control of all of central Burma and could no longer advise stranded Europeans and Indians to make their way southward. S. Farrant Russell, the director of a missionary hospital in the railway town of Mohnyin in the Kachin Hills, not far from the jade-mining area, later recalled receiving a leaflet dropped by airplane in mid-May: "A suspension bridge is being built over the Namyung," the major river near the Pangsau Pass.[15] The colonial government was now telling refugees to exit through this westward route after all. The railway party had fled Myitkyina for the Putao Plain mere days before the new message was disseminated.

Russell's memoirs, recalling his own group's journey from Mohnyin through the Pangsau Pass and into safety in India, is a remarkable piece of writing, rich with drama as well as classical and biblical allusion. Entitled *Muddy Exodus*, its references to the ancient Israelites' flight out of Egypt and across the Red Sea loom large. Russell refers to his party's march across the Hukawng Valley toward the Pangsau Pass as a trek "down the old slave road"— for "down this road had come, in past years, the Kachin slaves who had escaped from their masters in the Valley."[16]

Russell's party was small, some half-dozen people who were colleagues from his hospital or evacuees from Myitkyina whom he'd met along the Hukawng Valley trail. Many other parties of evacuees were marching toward the Pangsau Pass as well—on the trail Russell met Karens, Kachins, and Burmese, along with Britons and Indians.[17] The Hukawng Valley itself was something of a terra incognita for colonists. The colonial commercial interests had never considered the area profitable for teak, nor was it along a corridor that naturally linked two railway hubs. The Hukawng Valley was, perhaps, less out of the way than the Putao Plain, but colonial administrators had always given the latter more attention, perhaps because of the way it jumped out on a topographic map of Burma. While the British had developed an important base in Putao Plain, Fort Hertz, there was no similar outpost in the Hukawng Valley. Hukawng was an easy place to overlook. Many people here kept domesticated elephants. There were also large herds of wild elephants and prides of tigers.

Due to its setting, the valley was especially flood-prone. "Before our journey ended," Russell would write, "we were destined to

learn a good deal about mud, of different qualities." During the
torrential downpours,

> the path became a rushing cataract of yellow water, each great
> footprint left by an elephant, a deep puddle. On the slopes, it
> was difficult to stand; one looked desperately for any project-
> ing root or stump, against which to place the foot, or for any
> overhanging branch or bamboo, by which to haul oneself up.

Conditions did not improve during the brief letups between
storms. The mud was so sticky and glutinous that, as Russell put it,
"one learnt to sympathize heartily with a fly on a fly-paper."[18] This
adhesive type mud stuck to the travelers' boots, which took on a
new stratum of mud with each step, until eventually the boots came
off from the sheer weight of the mud. Some tried tying their shoes in
place with string or canvas, but these wraps disintegrated or unrav-
eled from the water and the friction of the march. Others gave up
and went barefoot. But there were leeches, which released antico-
agulants into the skin. This allowed bitemarks to become open
wounds, which led to dangerous infections from dirt and dung.[19]

Another traveler through this pass described the grim milieu:

> As we trudged through the jungle, in dark overgrown places
> which for thousands of years had remained undisturbed, I felt
> a strange feeling of insecurity among those stately, wicked,
> bearded trees which seemed to conspire with their long-clawed
> parasitical creepers to seize our clothing. . . . The rain pattered
> down as hard as ever. . . . The soggy drenched ground was
> churned into numerous muddy pits.[20]

But the transport elephants along the road had no problem with
the mud. Their feet contracted along a complex pattern of muscu-

lature, allowing their legs to sink down several inches through the mire, to a point where it was neither slippery nor sticky. Here the toes would expand for stability. Every elephant performed this maneuver instinctively and automatically with each step. They'd practiced it with every passing generation since being pushed out of the grassy valleys of India and China and into these rainy hills, thousands of years ago.[21] The elephants were a bright spot in an otherwise bleak and frightening march. The Russell party had with them a female elephant named Maggie, or *magwi*, the Kachin word for elephant.[22]

Approaching the Pangsau Pass, Russell passed by morbid scenes. Next to wrecked trucks huddled groups of the injured. Elephants were sometimes employed in turning the trucks upright or in pulling them out of the mud.[23] Mostly the vehicles were abandoned. The track was increasingly less usable for such machines as the journey went on. A recent "cyclonic storm" had torn a narrow lane through the jungle, felling huge timbers and blocking the path.[24] Around this area, the Hukawng Valley's main river, the Tanai, forces its way through a narrow gorge in the Patkai foothills—an obstruction that causes a greater part of the lower valley to flood during the rains, and the rains were already falling heavily.

On the approach to this gorge, the marchers encountered fewer trucks. Russell now saw only other weary refugees, some mules (who like the humans struggled in the mud, their hooved legs sinking into the earth like signposts), and elephants. A group of some thirty timber elephants came up from behind Russell's group on the road and overtook them. They'd been marched to this spot from some timber area to the southeast that had fallen into Japanese hands, Russell supposed. Likely, they were being taken to the Pangsau Pass to assist in evacuations and to carry supplies for the initial stages of the all-weather Ledo Road, whose construction, it was hoped, could help turn the tide of the war. The elephant herd came to a large, rumbling river and waded to a broad sandbank in the middle of the channel. Beyond the sandbank, the current became much swifter. A great tusker led the way, and some of the bolder elephants followed, swimming through the oncoming rush of the current. But many elephants stayed put on the sandbank, some looking back to the east from whence they came. In all, only half completed the crossing. The rest "strode into the further jungles and were seen no more," going over into the wild.[25]

The refugees continued through more Kachin villages where fellow refugees occupied every available foot of space. The mud was worse than ever. Maggie was heavily laden and breathing hard through the ascent through the hills. The Russell party heard rumors (that "curled over the hillsides like the mists") that a recent rainfall had rendered the upcoming Namyung River uncrossable, "a swelling Jordan." This was the river that the airdropped leaflet had promised could be crossed by a suspension bridge. There was none to be found. In a scene mirroring that of the railway party at the confluence of the Dapha and the Dihing, hundreds of people were stranded at the Namyung. Some built makeshift bamboo rafts and tried to get across that way. The rafts capsized or broke apart, and the passengers either struggled back to shore or were lost in the current.[26]

Russell and his fellow travelers arrived at this ford. The place was called Tagap. Upon seeing the condition of the river, Maggie's Kachin mahout refused to go any farther. Like the porters who'd refused to proceed to the Chaukan Pass, this mahout had family back in the Kachin Hills. He saw that crossing through the mountains would strand him in India for many months. Before he left to return back to Burma, he did his best to teach Russell and his colleagues the needed command terms for Maggie. "We were determined to do our best to drive her ourselves," Russell later wrote. "But the real difficulty was the finding of Maggie in the early morning." They considered tying her up at night, against custom, but realized they wouldn't be able to fetch enough food for her. Releasing her at night was the only option, yet the party hadn't any idea how to do it. "The situation seemed hopeless"—when another refugee, an ethnic Burmese, happened to arrive at the Tagap ford. The man had owned and ridden elephants earlier in his life and agreed to drive and ride Maggie into Assam.

Now joined by the Burmese mahout, Russell's small party waited for calm weather and, when it arrived, made the river crossing borne by Maggie. Wishing to help the hundreds of people still stranded on the other bank, Russell and his fellow travelers then spent the day riding Maggie up and down nearby slopes to fetch cane from the surrounding woods. From the gathered cane, they wove a very long rope. Recrossing the Namyung, they linked their rope to trees on both sides of the river, so that other refugees, lacking elephants, could at least have a chance of hoisting themselves across by hand. It was a fine idea, but they could not fully fasten the line, and a group of refugees became stranded midway across the river.[27]

"This was to prove Maggie's finest hour," Russell recalled. The powerful elephant, already exhausted from the climb through the mountains, returned again and again for more passengers and their bags of food and supplies—loading men, women, and children, "ever returning for another burden." Russell described her combination of perseverance and acute situational awareness over the course of these labors. At one point, while stepping down a slope toward the river, she stiffened, refusing to take another step. The Burmese mahout above her, and several other humans, yelled for her to move. She wouldn't budge. Investigating the path, those present realized that it had become dangerously undercut by the water. Another step, and it would collapse under her bulk. Maggie had detected the problem well before the humans did. They found a different path.

At another point, while crossing the river, the mahout noticed a group of women who were stranded midstream. There they huddled together, clearly overwhelmed and exhausted, and the current seemed likely to sweep them off their feet at any moment. The mahout, yelling, steered Maggie in the women's direction. Maggie intuited what was needed. She waded alongside the women, on their upstream side, breaking the current. She then proceeded across the river more slowly than usual, so the women could follow along in this pocket of tranquillity.[28]

Everywhere the scene was full of life and death and mist and mud. There were wounded soldiers on one bank, from the China front, the smell of whose wounds filled the air. Elsewhere a woman was in labor. "The poor family had been on the move from faraway Lashio," Russell would write. "The third member had decided to enter this unfriendly world at a most inopportune time."[29] Grateful for some way to be useful, Russell fetched what medical instruments he could—a knife, a piece of parachute cord, a bottle of rainwater— and assisted in delivering the child, a girl. Russell called the crossing a "jungle Styx," a reference to the river in Greek mythology separating the worlds of the living and the dead.[30]

THE SAME WEEK that Russell and his party finally traversed the Pangsau Pass, the railway party refugees camped beneath Chaukan. Without elephants, the party was trapped at the deluged confluence of the Dihing and Dapha rivers, deep in the Patkai wilderness.

Somehow an SOS would have to reach one of the British stations farther down the Dihing Valley. The Nung porters proposed that somewhere upstream on the Dapha, there was likely still a wadable crossing point. However, as the monsoon worsened, the location of that crossing would surely migrate farther and farther upstream. During the high monsoon months of July and August, it might disappear altogether. A small group of healthy men might be able to "catch" that last crossable point, before it retreated up into the high mountains. Then this group could walk into Assam and deliver the SOS. Two British men, Leyden and Millar, went to find this last crossing, along with a dozen of the Nung porters.

From the records, one gets a strong sense that the real leaders of this SOS mission were the Nungs (none of whose names appear to have been recorded), and Leyden and Millar were sent along simply to give the message a veneer of credibility when, hopefully, they reached a British station down in the valley.[31] And it was indeed one of the Nungs who found that hypothesized last crossable point. The SOS party had already hiked a day's trek from the main camp of refugees, when a Nung who'd run up ahead returned to them with bad news to report. The river ahead was mostly rapids, full of dangerous rocks and debris. There was a waterfall and precipice eventually, and the advance scout thought it likely that above the waterfall the river would be gentle. But it would take another full day's march to get up the precipice and another day to get down, and the SOS party was already exhausted and half-starving.[32]

Suddenly another Nung was at the river below, wading across— barely. For much of the crossing, the man permitted himself to be swept along a bit by the current. But by keeping his feet pressed against the rocks and periodically pushing off at an angle, he made progress and reached the opposite bank. Having achieved this, he made his way back toward the rest of the party, which had been watching him with amazement. The party then formed a human chain and crossed together. This was likely the last day that year that such a crossing over the Dapha River was feasible.[33]

The Leyden and Millar party delivered their SOS at a British sta- tion called Simon in early June. The message was handed off to the British official responsible for organizing work elephants in the area, a tea planter named Gyles Mackrell. During May, Mackrell had coordinated the mobilization of elephants from Assam up toward the Pangsau Pass area. These elephants were there to help Pangsau refugees cross the difficult fords near the pass, especially at the Namyung River. Upon learning of the party trapped at the Dapha-Dihing confluence near the Chaukan Pass, Mackrell organized a rescue convoy of one hundred elephants. The elephants were hired from Kachin and Hkamti chiefs in the Dihing and Lohit valleys.

The rescue party set off toward the Chaukan Pass. The elephants, as usual, were permitted to roam for fodder at night. At one point on their way up the Dihing, the rescue convoy crossed paths with a herd of wild elephants, and a work elephant absconded with the wild group. But mostly the elephants remained focused on the task at hand.[34]

The rescue team reached the river confluence on June 9. A large group of refugees could be seen on the opposite shore, waving, their shouts drowned out by the roar of the river. But this was not the entirety of the railway party. Desperate and starving to death, the group had split into multiple smaller parties, mostly along linguistic lines. Anglos, Sikhs, Gurkas—everybody was spread out in the soggy wet forest, looking for safe passage and for food. None of the splinter parties had found a way across the river.[35] Mackrell's rescue convoy would have to find as many of these lost parties as they could.

But first, the convoy would have to cross the Dapha. The conditions along the river were far worse than when the SOS party had departed two weeks before. The river's white-capped waves produced a deafening roar. Furious collisions between unstable boulders and drifting logs created billowing clouds of white mist. The elephants hesitated. Mackrell demanded that the convoy's best elephant be summoned, a huge tusker named Rungdot. The previous month Mackrell had been with Rungdot in a similar, if less intense, situation at a river called the Namphuk, near Ledo. Here a rainstorm had swept away a cane suspension bridge. The other elephants had followed Rungdot's lead across the ford.[36] Rungdot was now asked to do the same thing, at a much larger river, leading a much bigger group of elephants, with hundreds of human lives at stake.

Mackrell, incredibly, had brought a movie camera with him, and he filmed the efforts of a large tusker, likely Rungdot.[37] In the footage, the tusker and his mahout can be seen stepping into large undulating waves. The elephant leans his head into the current for stability, while the mahout, soaking wet, clings to the elephant's neck, communicating entirely with foot-taps to the ears, as the thundering noise of the rapids must have drowned out speech.[38] Mackrell indicates in his notes that this particular moment caught on film was not a successful crossing, and that the elephant and mahout had to wait until the weather calmed to try the ford again. Rungdot finally got across the next morning, and the other elephants followed, just as Mackrell had anticipated.[39] Soon Rungdot and the elephant convoy ferried dozens of people at the encampment to safety.

The rescue still wasn't over. The many splinter parties that had abandoned the main refugee group still had to be found. Over the remainder of the summer, the site at the river confluence became a sprawling elephant camp, a logistical nerve center for the rescue operation. One wartime writer whimsically called this camp "Paradise Regained."[40] The rescue team needed the elephants not only to ferry people across the rough current of the river but also to carry search parties in the surrounding forest and to retrieve supply crates dropped by plane.[41] These heroic efforts mitigated the scope of the disaster but could not recover everybody. A large fraction of the original railway party—apparently as much as a third—was never accounted for.[42]

THE RECORDS from the Chaukan rescue provide precious little information about Rungdot, and nothing at all about Rungdot's mahout. Mackrell's notes refer in passing to the mahout as an ethnic

Hkamti, but the British tea planter's understanding of tribal affiliations seems blurry. Mackrell sometimes used the ethnonym "Mishmi" as a blanket term for the local porters and trackers, and "Kamti" as a blanket term for the mahouts.[43] He does not mention the Kachins at all (or Singphos, as they likely would be called in that region).

According to tribal elephant mahouts living in the Chaukan region today, the mahouts who went with Mackrell were all Kachin and Hkamti.[44] Furthermore, Rungdot was certainly a Kachin elephant, lent by a Singpho-Kachin chief, Bisa. The Bisa family is still influential in the region. I visited their main house, in the tea gardens beyond Ledo, in January 2016. The Bisa elder who greeted me, Bisa Laknung, was the grandson of Bisa Jonga, the man who lent Rungdot and many other elephants to Mackrell for the huge rescue operation. The Bisas are the kind of powerful local tribal family without whose help the rescue would have been utterly impossible. It's said that the Bisas first attained power in the seventeenth century, by offering refuge to a deposed monarch, Gadadhar, from the Ahom kingdom farther down the Brahmaputra Valley. Gadadhar rebuilt his strength in the Singpho Hills and eventually retook power in the Ahom kingdom. The Bisas were rewarded with royally mandated landlord status in the Singpho Hills. During the nineteenth century, the Bisas reinvigorated their privileged political position in the area by helping the British establish tea plantations along the Old Dihing River. (The river bifurcates into a new and an old branch after it exits the Patkai Mountains at Miao.) Under the British they became formal *majumdars*, tribal leaders responsible for collecting revenues from the surrounding hills.[45]

Bisa Laknung grew up after the war, with many elephants—Rungdot among them. He remembered playing with Rungdot when he was a boy and going on rides with him in the forest. The elephant was especially quick in retrieving items dropped on the forest floor or in the middle of a river.

"He was a really very huge tusker," Bisa Laknung recalled. We were sitting in small plastic chairs outside his house, a sprawling hybrid of modern concrete and traditional Kachin bamboo architecture. Both the concrete and the bamboo wings of the house had steep-pitched rooflines, characteristic of Kachin huts in the hills. "He was nine and a half feet at the shoulder. Like many of the best elephants, he was actually born with us, not in the wild. I grew up with stories about his father, Klangdot, who must have been born in the nineteenth century sometime."

I asked about Rungdot's mahout during the war.

"Rungdot had many mahouts over the years. I don't know which one it was during the war. The elephant rider I remember best from my childhood was named Siong Gam. But he wasn't Rungdot's mahout—he was a fandi, an elephant catcher. His khoonkie was named Grammon." The conversation's turn from mahouts and fording elephants to fandis and khoonkies didn't surprise me. In the Trans-Patkai area, fandis are generally perceived as more prestigious, and therefore more memorable, than mahouts. Nonetheless, I pressed for more information about Rungdot.

Bisa Laknung acquiesced. "He died at around the age of seventy. It was 1972, 1973 maybe. We'd been letting him roam in the forests near Digboi. Sometimes we'd have him do some logging work, or we'd need him for transportation. Even after the war, you really needed elephants for transportation here. Not so much like now. Maybe Rungdot made elephant babies in the Digboi forest, but we'd have no way of knowing that."

Bisa Laknung's son and two grandsons were with us. The family was clearly very proud of its connection to this chapter of the war. They'd lent out elephants not only for the Chaukan Pass rescue but also for rescues at the Pangsau Pass. Later in the war, their elephant teams assisted in the early stages of building the Ledo Road, which starts not far from the Bisas' house and then winds upward through the hills toward the Pangsau Pass. From there, the road crosses the Hukawng Valley and loops through Myitkyina, turning south to finally meet the original Burma Road, which goes into China. With the completion of the Ledo Road in 1945, the British in India were finally able to supply the Chinese resistance by way of an all-land route. By this time the war's tide had already turned. In the 1990s, the Bisas hosted a reunion of American veterans who'd been stationed along the road. The family showed me a home video they'd made: families had come from Texas, Arkansas, and Michigan to the tea gardens of Ledo.[46]

The fading of the mahouts from memory—whether oral or archival—is disappointing. They were, after all, the humans most responsible for the rescues. In the case of Maggie's unnamed Burmese mahout, one wonders whether, for one reason or another, Russell wanted to protect his identity. In the case of the Chaukan episode, author Andrew Martin proposes that a kind of class divide separated the mahouts from everybody else involved in the operation. The mahouts "combined the independence of all taxi drivers with the unionized bolshiness of some train drivers," Martin opines.[47] This coheres with the recollections of James Howard Williams, the official in charge of elephant logistics around the Shenam Pass. In his memoirs, Williams remembered having to deal with strikes and labor agitation among the mahouts of the Burmese teak forests during the 1920s.[48] Martin cites a similar type of incident during the Chaukan rescue, in which Mackrell placed one of the mahouts, Ragoo, under arrest. Ragoo had been organizing his fellow mahouts to demand better pay for their involvement in the rescue. The other mahouts agreed to continue working at existing wages, but only if Ragoo was set free.[49]

Of course, elephants in these situations had their own way of going "on strike." They could refuse to do the tasks before them. They could steal off into the forest at night. But the officials always seemed more eager to remember the names of the elephants than of the mahouts who knew the elephants best, and who represented half of the relationship that made these daring operations possible.

BANDOOLA, MAGGIE, RUNGDOT: these were just a few of the elephants who assisted in the human exodus across the Patkais. They were the ones who happened to cross paths with Westerners, who—armed with cameras or possessed of a desire to pen memoirs—told the evacuation elephants' story after the war. Many other elephants, numbering in the hundreds, were also involved in these operations. Some of them appear in other accounts, though we rarely find such detailed narratives. A British captain, R. H. Gribble, recalled chatting with his Kachin mahout as they approached the Pangsau Pass in 1942. The mahout turned to him and said, "Do you know that elephants used to be men—that is why they have so much intelligence?"

The Kachin looked so serious when he said it that Captain Gribble almost believed him. "Thank god they now have four powerful legs," he replied. "Otherwise our chances of getting out of this jungle would be remote." The two men laughed.[50]

By 1943, the main movement through the Pangsau Pass was by British and American troops coming in the other direction, from India into Burma. The Allied armies were gradually chipping away at the Japanese occupation, and the elephants were still essential. One major recalled that "Shan and Kachin mahouts jabbered at ex-clerks from the North of England on how to handle the mortar-carrying elephants."[51]

Another soldier, Ian Fellowes-Gordon, remembered being assisted by a Hkamti elephant named Ma Gam, during a mission to take supplies from the Putao Plain through the Kachin jungle to the Burma Road. At the southern edge of the Putao Plain, the platoon reached a village where they'd hoped to eat and rest for the night, only to find it abandoned due to the war. One house remained standing, but its roof had collapsed in the storms. The platoon slept there anyway, exposed to the pouring nighttime rain. "Only Ma Gam was happy," recalled Fellowes-Gordon, "thundering about his jungle in search of leaves while the humans soaked slowly indoors."[52]

In 1943 and 1944, as the British moved back into the Chindwin Valley, they repurposed many of the work elephants as "sappers": bridge construction labor. The elephants proved uniquely useful at hauling teak logs from nearby forests to the bridge construction sites and at hoisting the timber upward onto pylons.[53] The ingenious "safety lock" elephant we met in Chapter 2 devised his technique at such a work site.

Throughout their occupation of Burma, the Japanese also employed hundreds of elephants and mahouts, mostly for timber and infrastructure-building projects. While the British had their Bombay-Burma Timber Corporation, the Japanese had their Nippon-Burma Timber Union: both were elephant logging corporations.[54] While the British used elephants to help build teak bridges along the Chindwin Valley and along the northern Ledo Road, the Japanese employed some four hundred elephants in the construction of the Burma-Siam Railway. This Japanese project was designed to link Bangkok to the Burmese seaport and rail terminus at Moulmein, thus hastening the flow of supplies to Japanese-occupied Burma. The Japanese high command hoped this would undercut the Allies' Ledo and Burma road projects in the north. Along the Burma-Siam Railway, elephants crashed paths through the thick jungles of the Karen Hills. They also carried barrels of water, which construction workers needed continuously, not only for themselves but also to wash their boring drills when they clogged with mud.[55] The Japanese also took 350 logistics elephants with them during their foray into Manipur, India, in 1944.[56]

The Japanese were cruel to their elephants, according to Williams, refusing to let them roam in the forest at night, for fear that the mahouts would use the morning fetch as an opportunity to desert.[57] It's hard to know how much credence to give Williams here, in this characterization of the other side. A Burmese teak and elephant official, U Toke Gale, writing after Burmese independence, agreed that the Japanese commanders tended to mistreat and overwork the elephants. But Gale seems to have been close with the British teak wallahs earlier in his life, during the colonial period (Gale makes this clear enough in his book), so his memories of the war might have been colored by those previous friendships.[58]

The later recollections of some Japanese soldiers deployed along the Burma-Siam Railway suggest that in tending to the elephants, the Japanese followed the usual local methods: a nightly roaming period followed by the morning fetch. "Everyone took good care of the elephants," former soldier Abe Hiroshi told an interviewer in the early 1990s. "Even Japanese soldiers who beat up Burmese never took it out on the elephants." Hiroshi described how the Japanese overseers would let the elephants loose in the mountains in the evening:

> They'd search for wild bananas and bamboo overnight and cover themselves with dirt to keep from being eaten up by insects. In the morning the Burmese mahouts would track them down from their footprints. They'd usually be no more than one or two kilometers away. Then they'd get a morning bath in the river. Each mahout would scrub his own elephant with a brush. The elephants looked so comfortable, rolling over and over in the river. It took about thirty minutes. Then they had full stomachs and were clean and in a good mood. Now you could put a saddle mount or pulling chains on them and they'd listen to commands and do a good day's work.[59]

Ian Denys Peek, a British POW who was made to work along the Burma-Siam Railway, would later write that for his Japanese work-masters, a POW was in effect "one fourteenth of an elephant." His account too seems to contradict Williams's impression of how the Japanese treated their elephants.[60]

What's most striking when considering in tandem the British and Japanese experiences working with elephants during the war is the degree to which the elephants became objects of intense struggle— not as symbolic "booty" but as a resource of enormous strategic importance. Simply put, elephants were the key to controlling the rain-soaked Burmese uplands between India and China. The 1942 evacuation from Burma into India, the 1944 Japanese invasion of the British Indian province of Manipur, and the eventual Allied reinvasion of Upper Burma—all these operations made extensive use of trained elephants.

Thus, individual elephants might work for different sides over the course of the war. The most famous example is Lin Wang, a Burmese logging elephant seized by a Japanese platoon during the occupation. Chinese Nationalist soldiers captured Lin Wang from the Japanese in 1943 near the Shweli River on the Shan-Yunnan border, along with several other Japanese elephants. The elephants helped the Chinese soldiers cross rivers and hoist large crates onto trucks. When the war ended, the soldiers wanted to march the elephants triumphantly to the Chinese coast, but the route, going through mostly agricultural territory, didn't have any forestland in which the elephants could feed at night. The elephants rode most of the way in trucks and drew visitors in Guangzhou. When the Nationalists withdrew to Taiwan, Lin Wang went with them. He died at the Taipei Zoo in 2003, at the incredible age of eighty-six.[61]

AND WHAT BECAME of Bandoola and Maggie, the principal elephants of Williams's and Russell's memoirs respectively?

Bandoola's fate was an unhappy one. After the evacuation

operation at the Shenam Pass and the eventual Allied reinvasion
of Burma, Williams had Bandoola and many other elephants sent
to the Chindwin Valley to drag timber and do sapper work such
as bridge or boat building. One morning in 1945, Williams found
Bandoola in the forest—dead. He'd been shot. One tusk was sawed
off, the other intact. Enraged, Williams questioned the whole work
camp for information and discovered that the elephant had been
dead for several days, and that most of the mahouts in the camp
knew about it but didn't inform Williams for fear of upsetting him.

At first, Williams assumed that a tribal Chin hunter must have
come down from the hills and murdered Bandoola for the ivory.
He took several soldiers to the nearest Chin village and placed
many people there under arrest, making angry threats about
what would happen unless a villager came forward and produced
the stolen tusk. But, calming down, Williams reconsidered how
strangely his own mahouts back at the camp had acted—especially
Po Toke, who had been Bandoola's mahout at the ascent up the
elephant stairway at the Shenam Pass and who was now the
manager of the sapper camp. Williams later wrote: "I have often
wondered whether old Po Toke had become so war-weary as to
become slightly deranged in his intellect and whether he had shot
Bandoola, rather than leave him to a successor." Williams further
wondered whether perhaps the one missing tusk hadn't become
a sentimental keepsake for Po Toke—and whether the other one
hadn't been left there for Williams. Reflecting on how much the
mahouts had already suffered and sacrificed through the war, he
decided not to investigate Po Toke and sadly let the matter drop.[62]
A biographer of Williams adds:

> Such was the complicated and often paradoxical relationship
> between the two men that in the agonizing days after the dis-
> covery, Williams was filled with a bitter kind of love for Po

Toke. Here was the man who had taught him everything and shared with him this astonishing creature.[63]

As for Maggie, the elephant who'd ferried so many human beings across the Namyung River by Pangsau Pass: she went with Russell and the others into India as far as a village called Nampong. This was close to the British railhead at Ledo, and the road had become better. The elephants were no longer needed in the journey. There were still many refugees back at Pangsau Pass, and also at Chaukan. The officials at Nampong asked that the refugees leave their elephants behind so the animals could be sent back into the hills to continue the evacuation work. Russell agreed to give Maggie up.

But the next morning, when the Burmese mahout went out to look for Maggie, he found only the remains of a broken chain. Though he trailed her footprints up a hill into the forest, he did not succeed in catching her again. She was gone. "Maggie had faithfully brought us this far," Russell wrote. At the Namyung River, "God provided her to meet our need: at Nampong, her work was finished, and He took her away."[64]

The local elephant fandis in the hills around Nampong might put it a different way: a spirit-mahout had fetched her instead.

THE FATE OF MAGGIE, and its contrast with those of Rungdot and Bandoola, is instructive for thinking about survival among Asian elephants more generally. On the whole, World War II appears to have been disastrous for the work elephants of Burma. On the eve of the Japanese invasion, the colonial Burmese logging industry calculated a population of roughly ten thousand domestic elephants. More work elephants likely lived in the tribal uplands, untallied by the forestry department. At the war's end, though, the number had collapsed to fewer than four thousand.[65] Over the next half-century, the number gradually grew again, as elephant lumbering operations became centralized in the post-independence government, under an entity called the Myanmar Timber Enterprise. The forestry department kept careful annual records of the number of elephants belonging to government timber camps or to licensed ethnic minority owners. The department recorded just over six thousand elephants in the 1970s. Since then, the number has slowly shrunk again, to closer to five thousand.[66]

The war's impact on *wild* elephants, though, is much less clear. It's possible that the violence of the war significantly reduced the wild herds. But a number of details from the narratives given above, and others like them, indicate that something else may have been occurring. Williams, Russell, and Fellowes-Gordon all describe passing through abandoned villages. Areas that during peaceful times had many hunters' and swiddeners' camps became more wilderness-like during wartime. The records from the Chaukan rescue convey a similar landscape: the railway party had hoped to find Lisu villages in the area around the Chaukan Pass but found none. Thus at least in some areas, the war may very well have had the effect of expanding the wild elephants' range into zones normally occupied by humans.

Consider too the scenes of work elephants' crossing paths with wild herds and sometimes absconding with them; or of whole groups of timber elephants' disappearing into the forest; or of Maggie's own disappearance into the jungle beyond Nampong. It's plausible that in the chaos of the war, a great many domesticated elephants went over into the wild, and that some of the herds they joined then migrated into areas beyond the war's reach. Such escapes into the wild might even account for a significant part of the decline in officially tallied work elephant numbers.

This isn't to say that the war was "good" for the elephants over-all. Many wild elephants did not escape the violence. Williams recalls that for a period of the war, the fighter pilots of the Royal Air Force were under orders to open fire on any elephants seen in Japanese territory, since they could potentially be work elephants for the enemy. Some pilots, appalled by the order, asked that it be cancelled, but the requests went unheeded.[67] A similar phenome-non would come up decades later during the Vietnam War, when American pilots were similarly ordered to open fire on elephants, seen by the U.S. command as potential transport vehicles for the Vietcong.[68]

Many other elephants wound up like Bandoola: killed while on the job. The Hkamtis of the Lohit Valley remember two unhappy incidents where Allied troops fired on Hkamti elephant convoys bringing them supplies. Dozens of elephants and men died, and the surviving elephants are remembered for carrying their fallen mahouts through the forest back to their home villages, dozens of miles away.[69] Other elephants wound up like Lin Wang, mobilized away from the Burmese forests to become "compound" elephants in zoos or in tourist camps—with good food, perhaps, but few opportunities to mate. Many wound up more like Rungdot: they went back to the logging and transport work they had done before the war, and for the remainder of their days they had the freedom to forage in the forest at night and to mate—perhaps with wild ele-phants like Maggie.

What we might consider, from these fragmentary insights into the elephants' collective wartime experience, is that just as Asian elephants have developed a set of everyday work skills that keep them adjacent to the monsoon forest—skills in handling timber and performing transport across muddy forest terrain—they also seem to have skills that are especially useful for certain kinds of human emergency situations. Such skills, if understood and appreciated by the elephants' human handlers, can increase the odds of work elephants' being moved into settings where they can commingle with wild herds they would not ordinarily encounter. The emergency mobilization of elephants—into forested areas, anyway—can open up new opportunities for species reproduction.

Such emergency situations also provide the elephants with improved odds of escape. But the elephants do not always seize the opportunity. Perhaps this hesitancy is force of habit, or perhaps the elephants sometimes feel a genuine sense of responsibility and loyalty to the humans in plight. An elephant who went over into the wild would more likely be a female, like Maggie, than a male. While a male work elephant at an emergency work site can mate with wild females in the forest and return unburdened each morning to his labors, a pregnant female ought to avoid strenuous work. Better to be pregnant in the forest. Elephant experts in the Burmese logging industry, as well as tribal mahouts in the Trans-Patkai area, agree that female work elephants are likelier to join wild herds than males are.[70]

Thus, at any given time, a nonnegligible number of wild-born elephants have mothers who knew domesticity with humans. At a collective level, elephants have experiences of both wilderness and domesticity that circulate among the broader elephant population through this process of capture and escape. With such patterns and dynamics in mind, we might begin to think of the elephants' emergency evacuation skills as a kind of subtly coevolved trait—developed both through elephants' interactions among each other and through their cooperation with humans in distress.

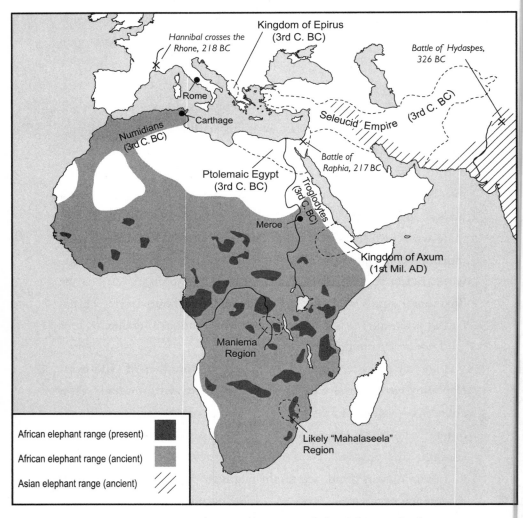

Map D. Present and ancient ranges of the African elephant (*Loxodonta africana*). *Cartography by Jacob Shell.*

Chapter 4

A COUNTERPOINT
IN AFRICA

IMAGES OF ELEPHANTS PERMEATE GLOBAL POPULAR
and consumer culture in the twenty-first century, turning up not
just in nature documentaries but also in advertising, company
logos, children's books, cartoons, and all manner of decorated consumer goods. Almost always this popular, globally commercialized
image is of an African elephant, not an Asian one.

There are an array of aesthetic explanations for this tendency.
The African elephant is taller—or at least the savanna subspecies
is; the African forest elephant of the Congo is relatively small.[1]
The concave slope of the African elephant's back and the slightly
more upright angle at which it carries its head lend the species a
kind of grandeur and stateliness that some may find lacking in the
Asian species. The African elephant's ears are huge and splendid
while the Asian elephant's are rather small. Many graphic designers
surely appreciate how the African elephant's forehead rises seam-
lessly from the line of its trunk. The Asian elephant's forehead, by
contrast, juts upward into a bumpy, domelike protrusion. Both species, of course, are beautiful and majestic in their own right, and
certainly many artists have found ways of conveying the magnifi-
cence of the Asian elephant. But visually comparing the two animals side by side, it's not difficult to discern why many modern

illustrators, designers, and iconographers have been drawn to the African species.

African elephants exist almost entirely in the wild, whereas a quarter to a third of Asian elephants are working animals, most with mahouts. Thus while Polo Ralph Lauren's logo shows a horse with a rider, Banana Republic's shows an African elephant, who like virtually all African elephants is riderless. The mahout would be a better-known figure to the world if Asia's long-standing cultures of elephant domestication and mahoutship were mirrored in Africa. Why aren't they?

Understanding the divergence in the two species' experiences with humans requires a look at human attempts at domesticating both African and Asian elephants over the past several thousand years. This story takes us far beyond Southeast Asia and India, to the Mediterranean world in classical times, including much of North Africa, Southwest Asia, and southern Europe. In turn, by looking at how efforts at domesticating African elephants succeeded briefly in this Mediterranean and African zone but did not endure, we can throw into sharper relief the complex and unique dynamic that emerged between humans and elephants in South and Southeast Asia, and that continues to shape the Asian species to this day.

THERE ARE ROUGHLY ten times as many African elephants on the planet today as there are Asian elephants.[2] But unlike in Asia, elephant domestication in Africa has never been widespread. Furthermore, while the history of elephant domestication in Asia has been continuous over the past three millennia, in Africa the practice has occurred only in fits and starts. It is possible to misconstrue the contrast as evidence that Asia's long-standing tradition of capturing wild elephants has caused that continent's elephant population collapse. But comparing the histories of Asian versus

African elephants over the past several millennia reveals a more complicated picture.

The earliest evidence of elephant domestication appears in the archaeological record of the ancient Indus Valley, or Harappan, civilization, whose excavated legacy has left us several stone seals showing an elephant with a cloth, or pannier, draped across its back. The imagery strongly indicates that the Indus Valley civilization was familiar with taming elephants.[3] Scholars disagree about whether to date elephant domestication in the Indus Valley to the second millennium B.C. or even earlier, a debate that won't be settled here. A more pertinent question, perhaps—though the archaeological record gives us no means to answer it—is just who *invented* elephant domestication. Did the inhabitants of the Indus Valley civilization invent it themselves, or did they learn it from a nearby culture that was perhaps more adept at befriending forest animals than at stone-carving?

Whatever the case, by the first millennium B.C., elephant domestication was widespread throughout the Indian subcontinent. Powerful kings and princes demanded elephants as beasts of combat for their armies. Elephants were also employed for nonviolent tasks, like logging, transport, marching in parades, and so on. But the use of elephants for military combat appears to have been especially important during this epoch. A kind of war elephant "arms race" among ancient Indian kings motivated many to institute royal forest preserves, where agricultural development was banned, so that a steady supply of elephants could be caught for the military. Some have proposed that these royal preserves even helped to conserve the species' numbers.[4] The idea is intriguing but somewhat unlikely: even when ancient kings fastidiously protected elephant forests, their ultimate aim was to capture elephants at a massive scale and march them toward death: either immediate death in bloody battle, or genetic death in the military's elephant corrals, where they were unlikely to mate. The forest-based economic activities in which the elephants were engaged—that is, in logging or in cross-forest transportation—would have placed domesticated elephants in a far better position to reproduce.

An African tradition of elephant domestication shows up in ancient records too. At Meroe, along the Nile River in present-day Sudan, a civilization that historians refer to as the Meroites (or sometimes the Kushites) appears to have had an elephant-domesticating culture as early as 400 B.C. A stone relief excavated from the Meroite temple site Musawwarat-es-Sofra shows a king riding an elephant, with an attendant kneeling for them and holding the elephant's trunk. The excavations here indicate that the complex had a large enclosure, possibly a corral for the domestic elephants.[5]

Little is known about the Meroites; and nothing about how their tradition of domesticating elephants came about. Meroe was a major metalworking center in the ancient North African world—one archaeologist has whimsically dubbed it the "Birmingham of Africa," after the metalworking city of the English Industrial Revolution.[6] As a center for metal crafts, Meroe had significant trade networks extending in all directions, including eastward to Yemen and the Arabian Sea. Since Indian trade also extended to Yemen, it's plausible that the Meroites learned of elephant domestication through contact with Indian merchants. Of course, Indians had been domesticating a different species—the *Elephas* genus, of which the Asian elephant is the only surviving member, split from the African elephant's *Loxodonta* genus millions of years ago—but there's no reason this modern, Linnaean sort of distinction would have prevented the Meroites from trying to do in their own backyard what their tradesmen informed them the Indians were doing in theirs.[7] That said, it's equally plausible that the Meroites innovated their own local domestication methods, independently of their trade contacts.

The Meroites' use of elephants seems to have been an isolated phenomenon in Africa for another century. Of course, we can't discount the possibility that a culture in southern Africa domesticated elephants during this period but never left a stone record of it. Training the sub-Saharan African elephant as a work animal would have been especially practical and useful. Other large herbivorous mammals in southern Africa (giraffes, zebras, gazelles, and so forth) are far more difficult to domesticate than African elephants. Nor could horses or cattle easily have been brought from northern to southern Africa. A biting insect called the tsetse fly is widespread in tropical southern Africa and carries a parasite called the nagana pest, which is especially toxic for most work animal species originating from Eurasia—but not to African elephants. In the historical record, though, it's only at Meroe in Sudan, and not in southern Africa, that we find hard evidence of elephant domestication in Africa during this time.

This isolation had changed dramatically by the third century B.C. What changed during the intervening years was the incredible influence, throughout the Mediterranean world (which included North Africa), of the Hellenic Macedonian king Alexander (popularly known as Alexander the Great), who conquered lands from the Balkan Peninsula to the Indus River Valley between 336 and 323 B.C. Alexander's experience at the easternmost reach of his empire proved decisive in launching Europe and North Africa's own brief but often spectacular "war elephant" era. In 326 B.C., on the upper reaches of the Indus, Alexander was impressed by the elephant cavalry of the enemy Indian king Porus (or Puru). Alexander had seen trained elephants before, in Persia, but they had been mostly transport elephants carrying supplies or hauling wagons along roads.[8] But Porus's terrifying elephant cavalry made an indelible impression on the Greek soldiers at the battle of the Hydaspes, in modern-day Punjab. This in turn shaped Alexander's subsequent military thinking, as well as that of his generals, especially his lead general Seleucus, whose infantry had borne the main brunt of the Indian elephants' attack.[9]

The tactical strength of Porus's war elephants lay partly in their ability to carry several soldiers at once, who could fire arrows in multiple directions. More importantly, though, the elephants were incredibly effective as a first line of attack, sweeping aside the Hellenes' defenses with their great tusks and powerful trunks, then stomping and kicking stunned infantrymen, while even the best-trained horses scattered in fright. Alexander's forces ultimately prevailed in the battle, but his and Seleucus's immediate thought was to gain elephants of their own as tribute, along with these elephants' Indian mahouts, who could teach the Hellenic soldiers the art of mahoutship.[10] The Alexandrian forces would send the elephants and mahouts westward, as a new weapon of war to wreak havoc upon enemy armies around the Mediterranean.

Alexander died only a few years after this battle, but many of the post-Alexandrian Hellenic successor states, inspired by Alexander's experience, built up armies with large elephant cavalries. The general Seleucus gained control of the largest of these successor states, the Seleucid Empire, in which elephants played a crucial role as pack animals, both in military and civilian life.[11] The Seleucids, as the rulers of this empire came to be called, had an ecological advantage over the other post-Alexandrian successor states in acquiring elephants, because during this time the natural habitat of the Asian elephant still extended across Persia into Mesopotamia—both fully within the Seleucid domain.[12]

Nonetheless, the Hellenic states cut off from a natural supply of Asian elephants could still trade for them or seize them (and their attendants) as war booty. Thus the Greek king Pyrrhus, who ruled the small Hellenic kingdom of Epirus, was able to build up a significant cavalry of Asian combat elephants, even though Epirus was located in northwestern Greece on the Ionian Sea, far from the Asian elephant's natural range. Vying for control of the central Mediterranean, Pyrrhus and his generals used their elephants to great effect, marching on southern Italy in 280 B.C. and wresting the island of Sicily from the Carthaginian Empire in 277 B.C.[13]

After their defeat, Carthaginian leaders built elephant cavalries of their own. They had some elephants shipped from the east, but the city also had its own local supply of elephants: African pachyderms in the foothills of the nearby Atlas Mountains, in modern-day Tunisia and Algeria, whose river valleys in classical times were wetter and greener than they are today. These elephants of North Africa looked somewhat different from the large savanna elephants to the south, though they were of the same species. The North African elephants were smaller—a bit smaller, even, than many Asian elephants. But they were still physically imposing and seemed promising as combat animals.

The Carthaginians hired the Numidians, a tribal group from the Atlases, to catch and tame the local elephants. Carthage's elephant cavalry became a mixture of Asian and African elephants.[14] The elephant tamers and mahouts were also a mixed lot, composed of both Indians and Numidians. Despite the tamers' mixed origins, though, Carthaginians referred to mahouts as "Indians"—a word that, in the context of elephant culture in the classical Mediterranean world, came to refer to a profession (mahoutship) rather than to a people from the landmass of India.[15]

Some Mediterranean geographers at this time conflated India and Africa, imagining them as connected at their extremities by a land bridge out beyond the Indian Ocean. The Indian Ocean was surely an inland sea, these geographers supposed—otherwise how could India and Africa both have elephants? Other classical geographers, who lent more credence to the tales of sailors, disputed the theory. But the proposed Indo-African "land bridge" would show up on some European world maps as late as the medieval era, over a thousand years after Carthage first mixed Indian with African mahouts, which had contributed to the original misperception. Only in the fifteenth century, when Vasco da Gama reached India from the Atlantic, were Western geographers satisfied, once and for all, that the hypothetical land bridge did not exist.[16]

Carthage was not the only North African power to train African elephants for war during the third century B.C. Egypt, which had become another Hellenic successor state, ruled by a royal line called the Ptolemies, clashed with the Seleucids over control of the Levant, the far eastern Mediterranean coast. Wishing to build an elephant cavalry of their own to compete with the sophisticated elephant divisions of the Seleucids, the Greek-speaking kings of Egypt established elephant-hunting ports along the so-called Troglodyte (or "cave-dweller") coast, today's Sudanese and Eritrean shore of the Red Sea. The largest of these hunting ports was Ptolemais Theron (Ptolemy of the Hunts).[17]

This area was outside the Ptolemies' sphere of direct influence, and handsome sums had to be paid to local elephant hunting tribes (referred to in records as "Troglodytes" and "Blemmyes") to capture elephants alive rather than kill them for ivory and meat. The captured African elephants were taken by specially designed ships up the Red Sea coast and then by canal across the desert to Memphis on the Nile, the Ptolemies' major city. (Eventually the canal route was deemed impractical, and the elephants were marched overland instead.)[18] Here they were trained for warfare. The Ptolemies' elephant specialists seem to have been a mix of Indians and Meroites. Possibly some of the Troglodyte elephant catchers came into Egypt as well, to become war mahouts. The Ptolemaic elephants' most famous deployment was at the Battle of Raphia in 217 B.C., at the modern site of the Gaza Strip. The Egyptian Ptolemies had 73 African elephants; the Persian Seleucids had 102 Asian elephants. This was, evidently, the only battle in history where African and Asian combat elephants were made to fight each other. Records of the battle assert that the Asian elephants, who were larger and better trained, thoroughly outperformed the African elephants. But much else was going on in the battle, and the Ptolemies won the day.[19]

By this point in the third century B.C., Mediterranean military strategists were beginning to realize that Alexander and his successors may have overestimated the effectiveness of elephants in combat, and that the subsequent arms race in elephants, which had mobilized thousands of elephants, both African and Asian, away from their natural habitats and toward the Mediterranean, had been irrational. Combat elephants were most effective against armies that had no prior experience with them. Porus had deployed his elephant cavalry against Alexander with notable success, just as Pyrrhus of Epirus and his elephants had taken the Romans and Carthaginians by surprise during his campaigns in southern Italy and Sicily.

But Roman generals adjusted their field tactics in anticipation of further elephant-based frontline attacks. They realized that war elephants, though very fast when charging, lacked a horse cavalry's ability to change direction quickly, to avoid oncoming spears and arrows. In the forests of India, this disadvantage might be offset by the paucity of large open spaces needed to fire a projectile at an elephant from a safe distance, but the Mediterranean was drier and more sparsely vegetated. The Roman generals divided their own defensive front lines into comblike formations so that charging elephants could be easily enveloped and speared from the side. The strategy proved effective.[20]

The ancient Mediterranean world's most famous episode involving war elephants was the ambitious campaign of the Carthaginian leader Hannibal Barca against Rome in 218 B.C. Hannibal's army marched with thirty-seven war elephants from Spain through

France, across the high, white-peaked European Alps (though it's unclear through exactly which pass they crossed), and into the Italian Peninsula. The elephants seem to have been a mix of Asian and African. Hannibal's personal elephant was named Surus, sometimes translated as "the Syrian," so was likely an Asian elephant.[21]

The march looms large in Western memory, the stuff of epic narrative and stirring paintings—and yet one senses in accounts of the failed campaign the limits of the Carthaginian military commanders' elephant knowledge. For instance, when passing through France (Gaul, as it was known then), Hannibal's elephants were unable to ford the Rhone River—a far gentler stream than the Sissiri during monsoon season. The soldiers had to build a small fleet of rafts to ferry them across. Why couldn't the elephants do it themselves? Likely because these elephants had spent most or all of their lives in arid parts of the Iberian Peninsula or North Africa and so had little experience swimming.[22]

Nor would the Carthaginian commanders have known that elephants, if raised and trained near a proper river, could develop incredible swimming and fording abilities—more useful, even, than their abilities during combat. The value of elephants for logistics, rather than for combat, does not appear to have dawned on any of the North African or European military strategists of this era—an oversight that surely stemmed from Alexander having ignored the transport elephants he encountered in Persia a century earlier.[23]

From the second century B.C. onward, the use of war elephants in the Mediterranean world declined, all but disappearing by the first century A.D. Part of the explanation for the decline appears to be geopolitical: the triumph of the Romans, ruling from their European seat of power, and the defeat of the other ambitious Mediterranean powers to the south and east, closer to the natural ranges of African and Asian elephants. The Romans did employ war elephants in a variety of military campaigns throughout the European continent, from Greece and Macedonia to Iberia and Gaul. But they never invested as heavily in the development of large-scale elephant cavalries as had Carthage and most of the Greek-speaking powers—rivals whom the Romans ultimately vanquished.[24]

An even more important reason for the decline of the Mediterranean combat elephant was that the natural ranges of both Asian and African elephants rapidly contracted during this period. In the late classical era, Asian elephants retreated eastward, and the African ones moved south. The animals disappeared not just from Southwest Asia and the North African coast, but also from places as far south as Meroe. Wild elephants adjacent to the Mediterranean sphere may have been overcaptured and overhunted by humans, but the more decisive factor in this spatial retreat was that North Africa and the Middle East both became hotter and drier over the course of the late classical period, as the Saharan and Arabian deserts encroached upon what had formerly been verdant grassland.[25]

The domesticated African elephant fades from historical view until modern times—or nearly so. In the region along the Red Sea coast where the Ptolemies had established their elephant ports, a kingdom arose during the first millennium called Axum, located in modern-day Ethiopia and Eritrea. Numerous records attest to the Axumites' use of domesticated elephants hundreds of years after the last elephant cavalry had been vanquished in the Mediterranean region, and the last Ptolemy was deposed from power in Egypt. In A.D. 533 the Byzantine emperor Justinian sent an envoy to Axum; the Axumite king greeted him on a chariot drawn by four elephants. Later in the century, Islamic accounts (which may be apocryphal) say that an Axumite king sent an army with an elephant cavalry to sack Mecca, but the elephants refused to approach the city.[26]

During this period, an Ethiopian hill tribe on the margins of Axum, the Beja people, are reported to have used a large number of trained elephants in a battle against Arab invaders.[27] A British colonial administrator in Sudan opined in the 1950s that these Bejas were the descendants of the Blemmyes, or Troglodytes, who had caught wild African elephants for the Ptolemies of Egypt eight centuries previously.[28] The Axum ruling class spoke and wrote Greek for many centuries, so it seems plausible that the Axumite elephant-domestication culture came directly from Ptolemaic Egypt. Alternatively, perhaps the Meroite elephant catchers and tamers migrated into the Axumite region, following the elephants in their retreat from an expanding Sahara. Or perhaps the Bejas and Axumites developed an elephant-domesticating tradition independently of Meroite Sudan and the Hellenic world. In any event, as late as the sixth century, a culture of elephant domestication appears to have persisted in the region of Axum.[29] It disappeared with subsequent Arab conquests. The Arabs, unlike the Axumites, were camel domesticators, which gave them an enormous advantage as the Sahara gradually expanded.[30]

Domesticated elephants retreated from the Western experience for over a millennium. As the centuries passed, dim Western memories of trained elephants manned by mahouts tended to be negative, a symbol or storytelling trope signaling outside military incursion against the sphere of the Abrahamic religions. This is likely why the story of Hannibal's elephant-mounted march against Rome, the eventual focal city of much of Christianity, looms large in Western memory; and why the biblical story of the Maccabee rebels' resistance against the Seleucids' war elephants looms large in the Jewish narrative tradition; and why Muslims refer to the failed Axumite campaign against Mecca as the Year of the Elephant. The trope shows up in modern storytelling too, in J.R.R. Tolkien's Battle of Pelennor Fields and in George Lucas's Battle of Hoth.

This negative narrative legacy contrasts with the impressions formed by British refugees fleeing Burma in 1942, for whom elephants meant salvation. In recent history, elephants have been used in war not to scatter and intimidate the enemy's front line but to avoid confrontation with the enemy altogether: to hide, avoid, and escape. This is a pattern which we'll see extended to Vietnam during the 1960s (Chapter 5) and to the Kachin Hills of northern Burma up to the present day (Chapter 8). But elephants rarely if ever play this role in storytelling conventions shaped, in part, by the ancient Western world's dramatic and ultimately abortive experiment with the elephant as a weapon of violent combat.

WHAT ABOUT African elephant domestication in lands farther south, beyond Axum? European explorers' records from the nineteenth century give us a few indirect hints of indigenous elephant domestication in central and southern Africa. These hints are obscure and unreliable but also tantalizingly suggestive. During the 1810s, the British missionary and explorer John Campbell traveled among the Tswana peoples of southern Africa. His guides told him of a group to their northeast—near Maputo Bay, in modern-day Mozambique—who "rode on elephants" and "used elephants as beasts of burden." The Tswana called this group the Mahalaseela people, which may translate as "people of the road" or "people of the cloth." According to Campbell's informants, this northeastern neighbor also taught other tribes in the region how to inoculate against smallpox. Campbell opined that the Mahalaseela had coastal trading links with the Portuguese (whose maritime empire extended to India). Little else is known about the group.[31] Whoever they were, and whatever their true relationship with elephants, their way of life was likely radically disrupted by the Mfecane or forced migration wars among the region's polities, which took place soon after Campbell's information-gathering expeditions of the 1810s.

A comparable secondhand mention of indigenous elephant domestication in southern Africa comes from the records of the

Scottish explorer David Livingstone. In 1869 Livingstone reported in a letter to a friend that he had found an indigenous people in the Maniema region of central Africa, just west of the African Great Lakes, who said their ancestors "tamed and rode elephants." Livingstone added that there was "a total absence of the idea south of this"—so we can deduce that he was unaware of Campbell's report from a half-century earlier, about the supposed Mahalaseela elephant riders.[32]

One reason Livingstone pressed his Maniema hosts for information about local traditions of elephant riding was his desire to suggest a historical link between the peoples of the African Great Lakes and the peoples of the classical Mediterranean world. Livingstone, like numerous other European explorers of the African interior, hoped to demonstrate that after the classical era, "Hamitic" peoples from northeastern Africa, with strong genealogical and cultural links to Egypt and to Hellenic antiquity, penetrated into the interior of the African continent, following the Great Rift Valley, and settled near the source of the Nile. The theory was based mainly on the fact that the Ptolemaic Egyptians had possessed some partial understanding of the Nile up to its source. The ancient Greek-Egyptian geographer Claudius Ptolemy had recorded that the river began at two lakes that drained the "Mountains of the Moon."[33] These could very well be lakes Victoria and Albert, which drain into the Nile, and the Rwenzori Mountains, which have snowy peaks and partially drain into Lake Albert. Livingstone and his contemporaries supposed that if quasi-Hellenic, "Hamitic" peoples living in the Lower Nile during the classical period had good geographical knowledge of the upper Nile, then perhaps during the eventual Arab invasions of northeastern Africa, these groups retreated southward, passing through Meroe and Axum, and settled in the continental interior—bringing their knowledge of elephant domestication with them. Bolstered by nineteenth-century

Western racial attitudes, these searches for lost "Mediterranean" peoples stimulated popular interest in and support for expeditions at the outermost frontiers of European empire.[34]

Subsequent ethnographers in the Maniema region do not seem to have found anything echoing Livingstone's report. Maybe Livingstone, overeager to find some artifact or oral memory that could link the African interior with the ancient Mediterranean world, had asked the indigenous people in Maniema a set of leading questions in order to get a desired result. Or perhaps some Maniema tribes really did have such a tradition, and Livingstone talked with the last individuals who still spoke of it. If they did have such a tradition, it would not necessarily follow that their elephant-domesticating knowledge came from the Mediterranean sphere.

Livingstone likely had elephant domestication on his mind for additional reasons, besides this wish to associate Great Lakes peoples with the classical Mediterranean. In 1868, a year before Livingstone's letter, the British had invaded Ethiopia (then called Abyssinia) and brought with them forty-four Asian elephants, with Indian mahouts, to assist in transportation and logistics. The idea of instituting elephant-based transportation in sub-Saharan Africa gained momentum among European explorers and colonists between the 1860s and 1890s. European colonists were aware of the severe limitations that the tsetse fly placed on horses and mules in the African tropics. African elephants seemed impervious to the fly, but nobody knew if they could be tamed effectively. If Asian transport elephants could be brought into Ethiopia, which is at a transitional latitude between northern and equatorial Africa, perhaps they could be brought into the tropical tsetse zone as well. And if such an experiment failed, then Europeans could try to devise a way to train African elephants, or perhaps find some half-lost indigenous tradition of doing so, such as the Maniema tradition referred to by Livingstone.[35]

The Belgian Empire's King Leopold financed the one major experiment in introducing domesticated Asian elephants into tropical Africa as a means of transportation. It took place in 1879. Leopold was especially eager to establish an elephant-based transport service for his vast domain in the Congo, where human porters, nearly all of whom were enslaved laborers, tended to flee at the first available opportunity. Leopold hired an Englishman who, along with a group of Indian mahouts, brought four Asian elephants from India to Tanganyika.

The elephants were marched across the arid grasslands toward Lake Tanganyika, the huge, long body of water that marks the beginning of the westward-flowing Congo basin. Many of the Indian mahouts, seeing the conditions of the landscape and the available vegetation, had misgivings about the expedition and turned back. The elephants got sick, either because many of their skilled attendants had left, or because the ground vegetation was inappropriate for them. The problem was not, apparently, the tsetse fly. At any rate, Leopold's experiment had failed.[36]

In the early twentieth century, Belgian colonists in the Congo turned their attention to the domestication of the native elephant species. Hiring mahouts from Ceylon and eventually employing indigenous labor from the Congolese Azande people, the Belgians created training centers for African elephants at several locations in the northeastern Congo. By the 1930s, the mahouts at the domestication camps were all Congolese, and they'd developed methods quite unlike those in South Asia. The African elephants mainly pulled large wagons. One English visitor was impressed by the African pachyderms' acumen in performing the job. Should the wagon brakes fail going down a hill, noted the visitor, the elephants would "seize hold of the wagon-pole in their trunks and throw back their full weight on the loaded wagon. . . . I have seen them doing this on their own initiative."[37] Though the training centers showed the promise of the domesticated African elephant, the need for elephants as a mode of transportation declined in sub-Saharan Africa as motor transport became more widespread.[38] Nonetheless, the precedent set by the Congolese camps eventually proved useful in the establishment of elephant safari parks elsewhere in southern Africa, such as in Botswana and South Africa.[39]

EVEN IF WE SUPPOSE that Campbell's and Livingstone's nineteenth-century informants provided them with good information, and that the Mahalaseela and Maniema peoples really were riders of African elephants—and even if we suppose that other sub-Saharan African peoples elsewhere domesticated elephants too but left even less trace of having done so—a question still lingers: why does Asia have a continuous history of elephant domestication, enduring for millennia, whereas in Africa it occurred so sporadically? The Luba kingdom in the eastern Congo, the powerful Songhai Empire in West Africa, the Great Zimbabwe kingdom in the south—they were all surrounded by large herds of elephants. Yet people in these areas either hunted them or simply left them alone. Being strong and intelligent and naturally resistant to the tsetse fly, the elephants were the best local candidate for animal domestication. So why weren't Africa's powerful kingdoms and empires domesticating elephants as the kingdoms of India and Southeast Asia were?

The likely explanation is perhaps counterintuitive and has to do with the intensity of historical processes of deforestation in Asia as opposed to Africa. In Asia, the growth of immense agricultural civilizations in the Indo-Gangetic Plain and the Great Plain of China erased vast forestlands. Over several thousand years, these societies built up dense human populations and expanded deep into the surrounding sylvan regions. Biological evidence shows that only a few millennia ago, Asian elephants, today so closely associated with hills and forests, once dwelled on these open plains—that they used to be grazers feasting on grasses, rather than forest browsers munching on bamboo leaves, creepers, and vines.[40] The large, agriculturally intensive societies of India and China, which together over many millennia have contained a significant percentage of the world's human population, pushed the elephants out of these plains.

As these agricultural civilizations expanded into elephant habitat, an individual elephant faced four possible trajectories. One, if the elephant maintained its original habitat in the plains, it faced great peril from the farmers tending new paddies and fields. Two, the elephant could flee into the forest, having learned that all humans are the enemy. This elephant would have a better shot at survival than the first one, but in the forest, it could easily meet people who hunted elephants for ivory or meat. Furthermore, the elephant would likely have no real sense of where the farmers would next breach the forest margin. This elephant could easily find itself trapped in a small, isolated pocket of forest—still alive but unable to mate with a large herd.

In a third scenario, the elephant might be captured by humans associated with an expanding agricultural kingdom. This elephant would march in royal parades and religious festivals, or it would become a combat elephant and fight armies in some distant battlefield. This elephant would likely spend much of its life in a stable with very limited mating opportunities, or perish in battle, either fate being a genetic death.

Needless to say, none of these first three possible trajectories was particularly good for contributing to species survival. But there was a fourth possible path. As agricultural societies were expanding, they were displacing not only large animals like elephants but human populations too, usually smaller farming cultures. Faced with the prospect of absorption into a much larger and more expansive agricultural empire, these groups chose, for one reason or another (fear of enslavement, determination to preserve language and spiritual practices, etc.), to migrate into the forested hills rather than stay put. Fleeing their old lands and arriving in new ones, these "fugitive" cultures would clear forestland and irrigate paddies to some extent; but mostly they had to adopt new crop-production techniques, especially swidden (shifting field) agriculture, more in keeping with the limits and possibilities of mountain ecology.[41] Some political geographers and anthropologists even use a special toponym for the uplands of South and Southeast Asia, "Zomia" (from *zomi*, which means "highlanders" in the patois of the Naga Hills). This region has been a kind of layered receptacle for different waves of people who fled powerful kingdoms in the adjacent lowlands and underwent self-reinvention up in the hills.[42]

Most of northeastern India and Southeast Asia's elephant-domesticating hill tribes underwent this experience of group exodus and self-reinvention. The Kachins were pushed out of Yunnan after a series of Mongol and Han invasions there.[43] Moving into the upper Irrawaddy Valley and the Hukawng Valley, they then displaced many of the Hkamti Shans of that region, many of whom in turn fled across the Patkai Mountains to the Lohit and Dihing valleys.[44] The Was, a swidden-practicing, elephant-domesticating people in the northern Shan Hills, were displaced into that region's mountain forests by expansions of Tai-speaking kingdoms in nearby valleys.[45] The Khas, who have had a mahoutship culture in the forests of Laos, fled from the Vietnamese coastal plain in 100 B.C., pushed out by Lao peoples who were fleeing an invasion from China.[46] The Karens, along the hilly border country between Burma and Thailand, appear to be an admixture of different groups that migrated from expanding agricultural kingdoms in different lowland areas: from the lower Irrawaddy (in Lower Burma), from the lower Chao-Praya (in central Thailand), and from the Zimme

Plain (in northern Thailand). Hence the various Karen languages mix elements of Tibeto-Burman, Austro-Asiatic, and Tai.[47]

Such groups all sought to keep at arm's length the large agricultural societies that had just displaced them.[48] This meant they had to adjust to forest life. But unlike the already established human inhabitants of the forest, they could not base their new lives entirely on hunting and gathering. If they infringed upon the preexisting groups' hunting grounds, they risked starting a war. So these forest newcomers turned to activities like logging, mining, and portering.

Now, imagine an elephant like Pagli—the "crazy" female elephant at the Mithong logging area that we learned about in Chapter 2. Imagine that a Pagli-like elephant met such a displaced band of humans in the forest and, rather than avoiding them, followed them, hoping for attention and food treats. Imagine she refused to follow a wild herd. After a period of puzzlement at the elephant's behavior, the group might choose to befriend her. They might attempt to train her for work—or better yet, they'd try to train one of her offspring, who'd be a better candidate for domestication, being familiar with the humans from birth.

The forest location of the work would give the Pagli-like elephant and her offspring free foraging time, which would also mean ample mating opportunities. What's more, if the displaced human group became sufficiently wealthy and powerful, based on its cultivation of forest resources, it might be able to pressure the hunter tribes deeper in the hills, and the farmers farther down the valley, to spare its elephants should they happen to wander into these other groups' areas. The displaced group might even have the ability to politically counteract further agricultural incursions into the forest.

In this scheme, then, such Pagli-like elephants, cooperating with displaced or "fugitive" human cultures, would have reasonably good odds of genetic survival—and of producing especially high-performing work elephants, like Air Singh, as progeny. The forest elephants who avoided humans would have decent but lower chances of genetic survival. And the elephants who refused to flee into the forest at all, or who wound up in royal stables or as combat elephants, would have very poor chances of genetic survival.

Thus, over time, the elephant species as a whole would gradually become more likely to possess traits conducive to the needs of the fugitive cultures. With each passing generation, the elephants would become more cooperative with these humans and more attuned to their practical needs. They would become more dexterous at handling logs, and more agile and ingenious at crossing seemingly uncrossable monsoon rivers with human passengers on their backs—more useful, then, in helping these communities keep the expanding agricultural kingdoms at arm's, or trunk's, length.

And unlike the domestication of cattle or other livestock, all this would take place without the humans ever implementing a plan for selective breeding. Humans would simply catch elephants in the forest, then train them for types of work that created wealth for the community and gave the elephants freedom to wander the forest at night. Other elephant lineages would peter out due to the activities of other human groups. Thus, even without human-imposed selective breeding, a process known to environmental historians as anthropogenic evolution—the evolutionary alteration of a nonhuman species through human activity—would occur.[49]

To follow the scheme further: eventually, a powerful agricultural kingdom might see in the nearby hills an abundance of highly trainable elephants and high-quality mahouts. The medieval Burmese kingdoms tended to bring Hkamti mahouts from the northern hills into the royal capital cities to train the valley Burmese in the art of mahoutship. The Burmese royal elephant minister's main assistants were traditionally Hkamti, and numerous words in the Burmese elephant command system are Hkamti.[50] Some kings, especially in India, came to value elephants to such an extent that they began to set up forest preserves for the elephants—thus reinforcing the hill tribe mahouts' ability to discourage hunters and farmers from killing elephants. Such measures were also put into place, to a lesser degree, in many Southeast Asian kingdoms.[51] By contrast, such measures were never adopted in China, where the elephant has almost entirely disappeared over the past two millennia.[52]

Adding an extra layer to the dynamic, many kings in South and Southeast Asia likely found their elephants most useful not when these kings were actually in power and keeping their elephants in royal stables, as trophies of prestige or weapons of combat, but rather when the kings were overthrown and fleeing with their elephants into some forested refuge, to become bandit chiefs there—to become "Zomian." Medieval Asian chronicles and European sources often speak of such kingly escapes: leaders' absconding from lost battles or palace coups on elephant-back into the monsoon forest. Here too the elephants who bore the kings into the wilderness went from a poor situation for elephant reproduction to a good one.[53]

The African elephant faced an entirely different situation. By the first millennium, elephants had been pushed out of North Africa once and for all, primarily because the North African grasslands had turned to desert. Some North African elephants likely migrated south and interbred with the herds there.

In the sub-Saharan zone, humans were not destroying elephant habitat to anywhere near the same extent as in Asia. This meant that the non-Paglis of the African elephant species had at least as good a chance at survival as the Paglis. The complex dynamic in Asia—where dense agricultural kingdoms were rapidly erasing forestland, thus engendering a kind of unique socio-evolutionary "alliance" between elephants and human groups wishing to flee these expanding kingdoms—simply does not have an analog in Africa.

The African elephant thus didn't have to coevolve in tandem

with a set of human needs. This doesn't mean that African elephants wound up less intelligent than Asian elephants or less easy to train. The experiences of the combat elephant culture in North Africa in classical times suggest otherwise, as do the Belgian domestication experiments in the Congo during the colonial period (as do the experiences of modern elephant safari parks in Africa, and of circuses that became adept at training both elephant species for shows). It means, rather, that unlike the Asian elephant, the African elephant's physical and cognitive abilities never became organized around sustaining codependent work relationships with groups of human beings connected to the resources of the forest. And so rather than sustaining themselves over the millennia, cultures of elephant domestication in Africa occurred far more spasmodically than they did in Asia.

Chapter 5

BREAKABLE
CHAINS

THE EPOCH OF THE "COMBAT ELEPHANT" ENDED TWO millennia ago around the Mediterranean and in Southwest Asia. In India and Southeast Asia, the use of combat elephants lasted much longer, up until just a few centuries ago. But the introduction of increasingly powerful guns and cannons to Indian and Southeast Asian warfare brought the era of the combat elephant to an end here as well.

Yet the story of domesticated elephants was not subsequently disentangled from stories of warfare among human beings. We've already seen how important elephants were to people fleeing Burma during World War II. And just as elephants can be instrumental in such escapes and rescues, or in furtive forest work, they also can be useful for rebel soldiers seeking to avoid stronger armies. This use of elephants—for the logistical needs of rebel armies—extends into surprisingly recent decades. Indeed, since World War II, such rebel forces as the Kachin Independence Army in northern Burma, the Karen National Liberation Army in eastern Burma, and the Vietcong in Vietnam have employed elephants for logistics—transporting supplies through the forest, hidden from the watchful eyes of aircraft flying overhead.[1]

As we saw in the case of Maggie—the elephant who ferried refugees across the Namyung River during World War II, then disappeared into the wild—"war elephants" who assist in emergency escapes or evasive maneuvering (as opposed to combat) can actually improve their ability to commingle and mate with wild forest herds. But this can bring about a conflict between the elephant's awakened desire to mate with a new herd and the urgency of the surrounding human situation. A complex negotiation between elephant and mahout can ensue. Several accounts—both historical and based on interviews I conducted with Trans-Patkai mahouts in 2015 and 2016—indicate that the fettering chain is a focus of this negotiation, in particular its capacity to be broken. The fettering chain, we'll remember, binds the elephant's two forelegs when he or she is roaming at night. The chain is slack enough that the elephant can walk through the forest at an unhurried pace, and tight enough to prevent the elephant from running.

Yet these chains often break. We saw this occur with Maggie in the forest country beyond the Namyung. Holt Hallett, a British civil engineer traveling with mahouts and their elephants through the Shan States in the nineteenth century, complained of the frequency with which the nighttime fetters failed. The travel party often became delayed as the mahouts wandered through the forest to locate their elephants.[2] Tenam, the long-haired Hkamti mahout at the Mithong logging area, told me that Air Singh sometimes breaks his chains. In the same region, an Adivasi mahout named Gudu reported the same thing with his elephant. And a former commander of an elephant brigade for the Kachin Independence Army remarked to me that his elephants would sometimes break their fettering chains, thus delaying the convoy.[3]

Why not use stronger chains? I asked.

Nobody had a clear answer. I began to suspect that the breakability of the fettering chain acts as a kind of safety valve. At times, an elephant's urge to follow a wild herd becomes so great that the

giant might injure himself or herself itself while attempting to shuf-
fle after them. Or due to pent-up spatial and psychological frustra-
tion, an elephant might pose a behavioral danger to the mahout
the following morning. When the urge is very strong, the elephant
exerts an extra amount of force against the fettering chain and—
snap!—it breaks. This is inconvenient for the mahout the following
morning, and it might be very inconvenient to the larger human
operation the mahout is part of. But it helps to sustain the always-
tricky balance between the humans' and the work elephants' needs.

That said, in emergency situations, the stakes for the humans
might be so great that this inconvenience becomes intolerable to the
humans. In such moments, the give-and-take between elephant and
mahout can become far more complex. A story from the Vietcong
side of the Vietnam War provides a rare window into this sort of
negotiation. The story is about a Vietnamese mahout, Xuan Thieu,
and his elephant, Pak Chan (which seems to mean, simply, "Pack
Elephant").[4]

Xuan was from a forested area of former French Indochina—his
account does not say exactly where, but it seems to be someplace
near the Truong Son Mountains. During the war, he was assigned
to work on the Ho Chi Minh Trail, the Vietcong's long logistical
lifeline. The path wound for hundreds of miles through the rainforest, hidden beneath the cover of leaves, from North to South
Vietnam. When Xuan first reported to the trail, he was recruited
by an elephant convoy commander, Kien. Xuan was to become
a mahout.[5]

Xuan was not from a village with elephants or mahouts, and
at first the assignment worried him. "I found all sorts of reasons
not to accept the new job," Xuan would later write. "Recalling
all this I am still now ashamed of my first reaction." He regarded
the mahouts of the Truong Son as something of an alien group.
Everyone bowed to them in respect, but nonetheless their life was

secretive. He was under the impression that mahouts were banned from marriage. When pressed to join the brigade, Xuan blushed and insisted he was already married, so he couldn't possibly take the assignment.

The superior officer of the elephant brigade, Kien, would have none of it. "I am married too," Kien replied. "Have you ever seen the sea? You haven't? I come from the sea. All year round I worked in the salt marshes. I was used to the sun, sea air and wind, not to the forest like you." Kien, a maritimer, wanted Xuan for his forest skills.

And with that, Kien presented Xuan with Pak Chan the elephant. He demonstrated the command terms, mostly Tai-derived, and Xuan was astonished to see that the elephant understood Kien's intentions—as if they were using a special language of their own. Pak Chan eyed the new recruit and waved his big ears.[6]

Despite his initial misgivings, Xuan became very close with Pak Chan. The elephant was mischievous but also strong and intelligent: a potential lead elephant of the convoy, if not for his streak of disobedience and troublemaking. Xuan recalled an episode on the southern front where Kien took his own elephant, Pak Ve, across the Mekong on a ferry.

When my turn came Pak Chan seemed reluctant to get onto the ferry. I urged him on. He leisurely put his trunk on the plank to test his strength. I said to myself: "What strange behavior! Pak Ve has already crossed the ferry, you must follow suit." I let him carry on. *Crack!* Unfortunately, he broke the plank in two.

Pak Chan seemed to have done this intentionally, placing his weight right where the plank was weakest. Annoyed, the ferrymen went ashore to look for another plank. Pak Chan stood by, carelessly watching the boats go by along the river. The ferrymen fastened a new plank in place. *Crack!* The elephant broke this one too. Pak Chan and Xuan wound up swimming across.[7]

Xuan recalls another story, one that illustrates the complex relationship between elephant and soldier-mahout along the trail. It was later in the war. Kien's elephant Pak Ve had died of pneumonia, and Pak Chan had replaced Pak Ve as the lead elephant of the convoy. Though he was the best elephant on the team, he still possessed a certain flair for mischief. One day he walked through the cassava fields of a tribal minority people in the village of Ta Noi. Xuan decided to punish Pak Chan by chaining him to a barkless ironwood tree. The villagers informed the brigade mahouts that a herd of wild elephants was nearby, so the mahouts decided to chain the other convoy elephants too for the night, to avoid trouble with the wild herd.

But Pak Chan broke loose! He found a weakness in one of those faulty fettering chains that so often figure in forest mahouts' tales. The next morning Xuan and several other mahouts looked for Pak Chan. They knew it would be easy to find him if he'd simply wandered off in search of food, and much harder if he'd joined a wild herd. Pak Chan was a male in his prime. But domestic males, unlike domestic females, tended not to join wild herds. More typically they mated with a female and then returned to their mahouts. So even in this scenario, there was hope of retrieving Pak Chan. Looking at their missing elephant's footprints, Xuan and the other mahouts knew that he was after a mate.

At last they came upon the elephant, deep in the forest—and sure enough, he was there with a wild female: "Playfully, he was twisting his trunk with that of his mate." The mahouts hid behind some trees. One of them made a birdcall to get the elephant pair's attention, and the sound echoed across the ravine. "Pak Chan let loose of his mate, raised his head to listen. He looked perplexed."

Xuan cupped his hands and yelled, "Pak . . . Chan! Pak . . . Chan!"

The gray giant looked "stunned, like a criminal caught red handed, his trunk and ears hanging down."

The female, alarmed, darted into the woods. Pak Chan hesitated, and then followed after her. The two animals crashed through the woods away from the humans. This initial attempt to retrieve the lead elephant seemed to have backfired.

The mahouts stopped to discuss what to do. One of them proposed killing the female, the obvious source of Pak Chan's recalcitrance. The rest of the circle rejected the idea: "He would probably go wild or grow listless from missing her." Pak Chan's feelings and desires had to be taken into consideration. Discussing the matter further, the mahouts determined that they needed to frighten the wild female into the forest without hurting her, but also somehow warn Pak Chan of their resolve not to let him follow her again.

The next day at around noon they caught up with the pair, who were romancing each other ("romping," Xuan writes) by a brook. The mahouts waited quietly. Pak Chan and the female finished the activity, and Pak Chan wandered off in search of leaves. This was Xuan's chance. He approached his elephant again and murmured, "Pak . . . Chan . . ."

Pak Chan stopped eating and peered at Xuan. At this moment the other mahouts fired their guns into the air, and the female raced off into the forest. Pak Chan stood still, once again uncertain what to do.

Xuan walked straight up to him. The elephant "looked straight at me," Xuan remembered. "His eyes were fierce and tense under the glittering sun." The other mahouts pointed their rifles, expecting the worst. But Xuan, trusting his elephant, waved them off and stepped closer. "Would Pak Chan be so reckless as to snatch me and throw me down? Frankly speaking, I had never imagined such a situation. On seeing him, I had the feeling he was something of a prodigal son and my anger was overwhelmed by my affection for him. As for him, I was confident that he wouldn't forget so quickly our times together."

Pak Chan looked bashful and tried to avoid Xuan's eyes. "As I caressed his rough trunk I felt his skin twitch with emotion and heavy tears fall on my cheek and shoulder. He looked sad and depressed." The elephant let the group of mahouts climb onto his back, Xuan onto his neck.

"Pei!" said Xuan, meaning "Go." The mahouts began to relax and laugh together, and hearing this, Pak Chan's mood improved. The great animal "jerked up his trunk, looking far ahead, and took big strides forward."[8]

This affecting story exemplifies the complexities of the mahout-elephant bond in wartime. Xuan perhaps intuited that the chance to mate with this amorous wild female was one of the few benefits Pak Chan could expect out of his service in the terrible conditions of the war. To kill the female, who was possibly already carrying the kernel of Pak Chan's future offspring, was therefore out of the question. Nonetheless, from the human perspective, the two elephants' "honeymoon" period had to come to an end, for Pak Chan was needed to bring supplies through the forest to soldiers at the front.

And what of Pak Chan's side of the negotiation—why didn't he ultimately follow the female? Several deliberations were perhaps at play. One, he likely anticipated that the wild herd wouldn't easily accept him, since he was a male in his prime. Two, Xuan possibly managed to confront him at a brief moment of postcoital disinterest in the wild female. Three, perhaps at some level, Pak Chan grasped that though his odds of surviving this war were bleak, they were somewhat better with Xuan at his side—and that anyway, marching up and down the Ho Chi Minh Trail gave him opportunity to mate with females in different wild herds. If these mates then headed away from the fighting, toward the west, the odds of his offspring surviving would go up.

As the war progressed, Pak Chan became one of the most capable transport elephants along the Ho Chi Minh Trail. His skill wasn't just in moving the war matériel—the food, clothes, medicine, ammunition, fuel barrels, tires, and so on—but in helping the platoon detect danger ahead and stay clear of it. With his huge, sensitive ears, he could hear all kinds of noises from afar. He knew that the sound of propellers in the wind meant he should dash under the forest canopy, for this was the sound of a reconnaissance plane. The sound of a jet engine meant he had to get to a ravine for cover as quickly as possible, for a jet meant bombs or napalm. He also knew that the sound of a truck engine meant that no sudden evasive action was needed at all, for this was almost certainly the motor vehicle of a friendly battalion. The other elephants would imitate Pak Chan, and the elephant corps remained relatively safe.[9]

ANOTHER STORY comes to us from the Ho Chi Minh Trail. A Vietcong platoon was crossing through the rainforest along the base of the Truong Son Mountains. Like many platoons along this route, they had with them a few elephants to carry heavy baggage. But no sooner had they left the camp than one of their elephants became trapped in quicksand.

The soldiers tried for two hours to save the unhappy creature. It was suggested that the elephant should be shot, so the platoon could take its tusks and distribute the meat to the surrounding villages. "But," one soldier recalled later, "we felt we couldn't do that: these elephants had done a lot for the regiment."

Seeing the huge animal sink, sorrowfully, deeper and deeper into the mire, the soldiers lost hope of saving it. But the commander of the unit, a man named Thuan, refused to leave the elephant to die. He ordered his men to cut trees down and drag them into the swamp. Watching them, "the elephant quickly understood: it grabbed hold of the logs with its forelegs and trunk and gradually pulled itself from the mud and out of danger." The soldiers were overjoyed and set off immediately. Later in their journey, the platoon crossed through an open area, and this same commander, attuned to the value of the elephants for making hidden movements across the dangerous landscape, told the soldiers to "hide behind the large ears of their elephants."[10]

Stories like this one, as well as the story of Pak Chan and Xuan, give us a sense of the strong culture of forest mahoutship that existed in the Vietnamese highlands up through the war—a culture that is, sadly, all but extinct in that region today. The elephant-domesticating hill peoples in the vicinity of the Truong Son are in some ways analogous to mahouts we've met in the Trans-Patkai region, or to the Karens along the Thai-Burmese border. The Truong Son mahouts mostly hailed from a diffuse group loosely referred to as the Kha people, a kind of ethnonymic blanket term. In effect a set of "fugitive" groups, the Khas of the Truong Son had been driven from the Annam and Mekong coastal plains by warfare around 100 B.C. Retreating into the mountains, they ultimately learned to practice swidden agriculture and to catch and ride elephants. Kha elephant skills persisted across the generations. Even today, a Kha group in Laos called the Khamus domesticates elephants.[11]

An unusual piece of writing from Vietnam during the 1970s, *The Story of a Mahout and His War Elephant*, describes Kha resistance on elephant-back during the First Indochinese War, against the French, following the conclusion of World War II. The book is peculiar in that it is semifictional, yet it was clearly written by someone with extensive knowledge of Kha elephant domesticating cultures in the Truong Son Mountains. It's unclear how the book's author, Vu Hung, came by this knowledge. The level of detail is striking. Kha elephant command terms (most with Tai etymology) are quoted throughout the text. Hung also describes the Kha training and initiation rituals, for both elephants and mahouts. In an early scene in the book, the old mahouts of an elephant village test the boy Dik, a teenage mahout-in-training and the book's main protagonist, in his knowledge of elephants' diseases. Dik is brought a sickly elephant and asked to diagnose what's wrong. After studying the animal, Dik determines that the elephant has swallowed several jungle leeches. He mixes some medicinal wild herbs with fruit and pours a jar of the remedy down the elephant's throat. The elephant is cured![12] Elsewhere in the book, Dik must desensitize his elephant, Lumluong, to gunfire so that the tusker can tolerate passing by battlefields. This account too appears to be based on actual wartime elephant training.[13]

The book is also noteworthy for the Exodus-like narrative themes and imagery that appear throughout—curiously similar to S. Farrant Russell's *Muddy Exodus*, where Russell tells his own story of escaping from Burma during World War II, riding Maggie the elephant. When war with the French breaks out, the elders of Dik's village decide it will be best to flee into the hills. The villagers evacuate, their possessions carried by elephants ridden by "grim and silent" mahouts. Hung continues: "Neither did the elephants show any unwillingness to take the unusually heavy loads. They seemed to know something was amiss. . . . The exodus began."[14]

The fleeing villagers become lost, cut off and disoriented by new water channels opened up by monsoon storms. Their elephants crash a path through the unexpected barriers. In the animals' wake, "the refugees trudged on," a crossing recalling the ancient Hebrews' passage across the Red Sea. As a "promised land" takes form in the Kha refugees' minds, they stumble through the territories of hostile hunter-gatherer tribes deep in the hills, a kind of Wilderness of Zin.[15]

Here the thematic parallels with the Book of Exodus break off. Dik decides to stop fleeing, and he and his elephant Lumluong return to the lowlands, to join a liberation army fighting the French. Lumluong becomes a transport elephant, much like Pak Chan. The rest of Dik's village proceeds with their elephants "for where the sun was setting"—likely to the westernmost forests of former French Indochina, in Sayaboury province of modern-day Laos. Today Sayaboury contains Laos's largest concentration of domesticated elephants. Though semifictional, Vu Hung's tale gives us a sense of two different migrations of Vietnamese domesticated elephants during the period of anticolonial struggle: either eastward to the coast, to supply the liberation soldiers, or westward to jungle refuges, in flight from the war.

Very recently, in 2018, an incident took place that echoes this narrative. The incident occurred not in Vietnam but in northern Burma. Here, fighting between the Kachin rebel army and the Burmese central military, or Tatmadaw, reached the small forest village of Awng Lawt, which is nestled deep in the Hukawng Valley. In May, hundreds of villagers fled the violence, seeking a displaced persons camp in Tanai. They took their elephants with them, about ten giants overall. The large refugee party marched through the jungle and came upon a river called the Mau Hka. Some had smartphones with them, and their astonishing photographs and video footage show the elephants carrying the elderly, the young, and many people's possessions across the river and through the surrounding forest.[16] Like Vu Hung's story, and like the stories of the elephant-mounted rescues during World War II, this episode conveys the significance elephants can hold for people in flight.

NEAR THE END of the conflict with America, Xuan Thieu the Vietcong mahout was still working along the Ho Chi Minh Trail. One day he thought of his old commander and mentor, Kien, the maritimer who had first recruited him to the elephant brigade. He remembered how Kien had brushed aside Xuan's initial fears of becoming a mahout. Over the ensuing years, Pak Chan the elephant had proven Kien right. Now, if Xuan were asked to be transferred to a mechanized transport unit or a boat transport unit, he knew he would refuse, so profound had his bond with the brigade elephants grown.

Xuan wrote a letter to his old commander, who had long since left for the coast. He wrote of his many adventures with Pak Chan along the Trail. "Each animal is special and has his own character," the mahout reflected.

"Dear Brother Kien," Xuan continued, "this is the sad news I had to tell you": Pak Chan was dead. Nobody knew the cause for sure—maybe an old battle wound, or maybe something else. "For me, nothing can replace my life as a mahout with our elephants, and I hope I shall never have to part with them," wrote Xuan. "We transport goods to the front by whatever means available, primitive or modern, but ours has a life and feeling of its own."[17]

The American war in Vietnam was calamitous for the elephant population there, doing vastly more damage than World War II had done to the elephants of Burma and northeastern India. During World War II, it had not occurred to either the Allied or the Japanese side to declare war on the forest itself, whereas the American strategy in Vietnam hinged upon the use of napalm and defoliating agents like Agent Orange to eradicate forest cover. The ecological damage was not a side effect but the very goal.

At least during certain stages of the war, the U.S. air command (like the British Royal Air Force during World War II) appears to have had a policy of specifically targeting elephants, with gunfire or rockets. Fred Locke, a former helicopter pilot, recalled being under order to fire on elephants, on the grounds that they might be with the Vietcong. But the South Vietnamese army had elephants of its own, and during one briefing a commanding officer "casually admonished the chopper pilots to be sure not to ask for air strikes against friendly elephants." Locke, a flight leader, inquired how they were supposed to tell the "friendly elephants from the enemy ones." The briefer explained: "the 'enemy' elephants would have their bellies tinged red from the clay mud of The Trail," that is, the Ho Chi Minh Trail. As Locke recalled, in subsequent flights, "I'll be doggone if we didn't see a whole bunch of elephants and, they did. . . . The 'pink elephants': there they were, right in front of me!"[18]

Robert Mason, another American helicopter pilot, recalled overhearing a radio conversation where a U.S. gunship ordered a vehicle code-named Raven Six (likely an armed helicopter) to shoot elephants. The bullets weren't effective, so the gunship ordered Raven Six to use rockets instead. Mason and his copilot listened to this radio exchange dumbfounded. "Elephants?" Mason wondered. "We're killing fucking elephants?" Then they heard Raven Six say someone should "go down and get the tusks." "I'm sick," Mason's copilot said, listening to this exchange. "Killing elephants is like blasting your grandmother."

Like the British Royal Air Force pilots who protested orders to target elephants in the Burma theater, many American soldiers considered such directives beyond the pale. Back at the company's camp, Mason recalled, there was "general outrage" that the ivory had indeed been recovered from the jungle and delivered to the division headquarters.[19]

The total number of elephants purposefully killed in air strikes is not clear. The elephant conservationist Richard Lair has noted that in one town, Nhan Hoa of Gia Lai province, more than twenty-eight local work elephants were killed from the air. In another village, Dak Lak, many owners fled with their elephants to Cambodia to avoid being strafed and bombed.

The use of forest-destroying weaponry, the scattering of land mines, and the U.S. air command's policy of purposefully targeting elephants—all this combined to effectively eradicate Vietnam's elephant population. Elephants in the country before the war seem to have numbered in the thousands. Afterward, the number had plummeted to just a few hundred. Today the number seems to be lower still, due to deforestation caused by postwar economic development.[20]

And yet there might be another way to look at the loss of elephants in Vietnam. Just as the collapse in the number of registered logging elephants in Burma during World War II likely reflected a partial exodus of domestic elephants into the wild, it is also possible that a significant number of elephants escaped Vietnam and went into the highlands of Laos—following the path of those displaced Kha mahouts in Vu Hung's tale. Some aspects of the present-day geography of elephants in former French Indochina lend credibility to this theory. The elephant population of Laos is estimated at somewhere between 1,000 and 1,500, some two-thirds of which are domesticated. Much of the domesticated population is concentrated in the far west of the country, in Sayaboury, likely as the result of two distinct recent mass movements of wild and domestic elephants: out of northern Thailand, as agricultural development there has erased forestland, and from Vietnam, fleeing fighting and deforestation.[21] So perhaps somewhere in Sayaboury, Pak Chan's children roam the forest.

It is geographically unfortunate that no further forest corridor links Laos's Sayaboury Province, with its significant elephant population, with the Kachin Hills and the Trans-Patkai region, where there are even more elephants. Such a link would enable a much-needed genetic transfer and diversification within the species. Blocking the way is the Shan Plateau. In Sayaboury and the Trans-Patkai, the coalition of human groups dependent on the forest has thus far counteracted the deforestation pressures associated with agricultural development. But the forests in the Shan area aren't as abundant in valuable timbers, and there's less bamboo. The diminished severity of monsoon flooding here also tends to make it attractive for irrigation-based farming, which entails permanent clearance of forestland.[22] All this swings power away from forest-based economies and toward paddy farming and regularized agriculture. Though the geographic distinction between the regions is subtle, and the Shan Plateau still has plenty of remaining forest cover, during the past half-century the balance here has "tipped" in the direction of local farming interests, rather than local forest interests. By contrast, the Trans-Patkai and Sayaboury remain, for now, forest-centric economies with large numbers of elephants.

Chapter 6

STRANGE BEHAVIORS

THE DUAL WORLD IN WHICH ASIAN WORK ELEPHANTS live—as members of a human community by day and of a wild ecosystem by night—can lead to some strange elephant behaviors. Some elephants can become difficult.

I met the mahout Mong Cho, and his tusker Neh Ong, at a tiny logging camp nestled in a glen in the southwestern hills of Kachin State. Far below lay Hpakant, the jade-mining area, and next to it was a huge placid blue lake, Indawgyi, the largest in Burma. The bumpy ascent by motorcycle to Mong Cho's hill camp had taken half an hour, the vehicle scurrying goatlike up the rockface along a route that could barely be called a footpath but that the motorcyclist had somehow mastered. I clung to his back. The driver was a Hkamti, like Mong Cho. In the motorcycle following us was J., a Kachin American spending her year after college graduation teaching English in Myitkyina. J. had helped arrange to get me to this spot.

We arrived at the camp, one of the smaller ones I saw during my travels. It contained a small group of six elephants: a large adult tusker, two adult females, two juveniles who were already taller at the shoulder than their mahouts, and one baby just a few years old. The youngest followed his mother around all day, observing her as she did light tasks. Usually the other adult female would attend to the calf as well, acting as an "auntie"—an arrangement borrowed from the family structure of wild elephants, where an infant is often raised and protected by two adult females. The older juveniles at the camp, around ten years in age, were able to do modest tasks like hauling smaller logs or piles of bamboo. Work elephants hit their prime at around twenty to twenty-five years of age and remain robust workers for about two decades.[1]

Mong Cho was the head mahout and owner of all the elephants here. There were three other mahouts to assist him: another Hkamti and two ethnic Burmese. The elephants were lounging under a grove of trees, munching on leaves. The three adults were tethered, while the young elephants were free to roam. The mahouts weren't paying close attention and trusted that the younger generation wouldn't wander too far from the adults. Next to the elephants was a small shelter for the mahouts, a green canvas roof suspended by several well-placed bamboo poles. A radio played traditional Burmese country music. The tinkling of the wooden bells worn by the adult elephants also filled the air. The camp would have been entirely secluded in the tree shade, but a small landslide from the rains had recently denuded a side of the glen, letting in streams of sunlight. A brook wound its way alongside the canvas tent, and the mahouts had built a kind of aqueduct for themselves, made of rubber and bamboo, transferring some of the running water into a basin. Next to the basin were also several smaller shelters protecting pots and pans from the rain and sunlight. The grounds looked comfortably lived in.

"He's looking at us so skeptically," J. remarked of the big male elephant. She called across the camp to Mong Cho, and then said to me, "The big one is Neh Ong. And that one there is his mate, Pwa Oo. They're both about thirty-seven years old."

Up until now Mong Cho had been on the other side of the camp with one of the juveniles, reciting command terms in a gentle voice and rewarding the elephant with cooked rice when it performed the right action. Now he approached us to talk. One of the other mahouts was readying equipment for the workday, which had been delayed to make time for my visit. The others were smoking and eating in the main tent.

"Mostly we do logging work here," Mong Cho explained. He had a boyish voice, though he was in his mid-forties. He spoke in a pleasantly relaxed cadence. "Later in the rainy season, the roads in these hills get bad, so at that time of year we also use the elephants to transport people's things. It used to be that we'd transport a lot of jade from the mining area down below." He gestured to a large wooden basket resting by a tree that they'd use for moving the gems. "Or we'd transport gold"—likely mined from the Uyu Valley.

"That was lucrative. But then about a decade ago, the roads to Hpakant were improved. Even so, in July or August, the roads there still flood. I'll go with Neh Ong to help pull jade trucks trapped in the mud. A lot of the time, we'll just follow along behind a truck, which will get stuck every few hundred meters. The trucks can't go very fast on those roads when the conditions are like that, so it's not hard to keep up. It was more lucrative for us when we carried the jade ourselves, though."

Next to us the smallest elephant, the baby, was rolling around playfully in the dirt. The infant would stay extremely still, almost like a cadaver, then twist suddenly and happily into a new position, batting at pebbles with its tiny trunk. The two adult females looked on and ate leaves. The big tusker, Neh Ong, was off to the side facing away from the group, toward the wooded mountain pass up beyond the glen.

"Recently the logging work here has also been not so good," Mong Cho continued. "The valuable wood here is teak, but we logged most of the mature timber. A lot of mahouts in the area recently went with their elephants to Shan State, where there's some logging to do, while we wait for our trees here to grow back."

"Who are the other mahouts in the area?" I asked, attempting the question in Burmese. J. had to intervene and rephrase.

"Owners like me are all Hkamtis or Kachins. The helper mahouts, who don't own the elephants themselves, are mostly Hkamtis or Kachins too, but there are some ethnic Burmese helper mahouts. There is also a government-run elephant logging village beyond the lake. They have many more elephants than any single owner does here in the hills. But really, a lot of the elephants here are now in the mature logging area in Shan State."

Mong Cho described the route by elephant from here to Shan State. First the mahouts would trek with their elephants through the Japi Bum Pass. (I could not locate it on any map.) From there, they'd cross the large Kaukkwe forest, which has hardly any villages or human settlements of any kind. At this point they wouldn't be far from Katha, the town where George Orwell worked as a police official during the 1920s. Past the Kaukkwe forest, they'd get to the broad Irrawaddy River, which the elephants would swim across, with mahouts and supplies on their backs. Finally they would enter Shan State, which contains the provincial city of Lashio, an important hand-off point on the Burma Road during World War II.

I hoped to ask more about the routes the mahouts like to take to get to the surrounding regions in search of work—I'd heard about other logging areas in the Hukawng Valley, as well as large amber mines—but just then Mong Cho leaped up, shouting at Neh Ong. The tusker had quietly moved toward the main tent and was about to grab its canvas roof with his trunk. The other mahouts began shouting at the elephant as well. He squinted, then retreated back to eating his leaves.

"He is a difficult tusker," Mong Cho confessed as he returned to J. and me. "Very difficult. No one can ride him except for me." Our attention was now on this huge gray mass of flesh. The tusks on the large male elephant had been trimmed down to roughly a foot, the length preferred by logging mahouts so that the elephant can "scoop" the tusks under a log and hoist it upward, a bit like a fork-lift.[2] The trimmed tusks also provided some supplemental income. Most elephants permitted the trimming to occur, provided their mahouts were seated overhead, muttering words of encouragement into their ears. The important thing was not to cut through the interior nerve, near the base of the tusk.[3] Elsewhere I heard stories about forest mahouts who, greedy for an extra few inches of ivory to sell, trimmed the tusk right down to the nerve, which then became infected. Mong Cho had trimmed these tusks expertly. They were growing back at the rate of roughly an inch per year, and a new trimming was still several years away.[4]

J. was right that Neh Ong appeared to be looking at us "skeptically"—though this might have been an effect of the tusker's peculiar eyes, which were very small, nearly lashless, and orange. These eyes, combined with the pyramid-like shape of his forehead, gave the elephant an imposing, beastly appearance. He was not a "beautiful" elephant like the female Pwa Oo, who had larger, darker eyes, long lashes, a pleasantly plump trunk, and a mouth that curled upward in the shape of a gentle smile. Some of these features, of course, signified nothing about the elephants' actual personalities—they merely had shapes, colors, and proportions onto which an observer might project human qualities. Yet other features, the eyes in particular, seemed to reveal something real in an elephant's personality.

"He's a very good work elephant when I ride him," Mong Cho explained. "He can carry heavy loads, and he's very good at handling the timber. He's also very smart and agile when we're on these slopes"—Mong Cho gestured to the landslide next to us—"getting out of the way of falling logs, boulders, things like that.

"But he is a killer elephant. Last year we hoped to mate him with a new female, but when she wandered over this way during the night, he became territorial and killed her." For a male to attack another elephant during the nighttime roaming period wasn't entirely unusual, but Neh Ong's hyperprotectiveness of the other elephants in his camp was a bit strange. "They're his family," Mong Cho continued with a trace of exasperation, "so when strange elephants approach them, he becomes very aggressive, even when the strange elephant obviously means no harm or simply wants to mate."

By now we were back in the tent. The mahouts, who had never had a foreign guest at their camp before, were enjoying their role as hosts. They showed me the various tools they used for disciplining the elephants. There was a metal-tipped hammer-like tool—an *ankus*—that could be struck into an elephant's ear. There was also a smaller metal pointer used on an elephant's back. I'd seen tools like these, in the Moran area of the Dihing Valley, with elegantly carved, decorated handles, but here the instruments were less adorned. A mahout fetched tea for us, as well as a strong alcoholic drink they'd been brewing, a rice wine mixed with wild sun-dried tubers.

Mong Cho continued to talk about Neh Ong. "It's more normal for someone like me, the owner of the camp's elephants, to be able to spend more time down in the valley, in the village with family," he said, pouring his tea. "So, for a while my nephew was Neh Ong's mahout instead. But he killed my nephew. That was about a year ago."

The revelation was startling, both to J., who had been translating, and to myself. In other conversations with mahouts, I'd heard about the dangers of the trade: about falling off an elephant, or encounters with enraged wild elephants during the capturing process, mela shekar. Sometimes a mahout or fandi would vaguely allude to incidents where an elephant had killed his rider, but he would say very little about it. This was my only field interview where a mahout openly discussed one of his own elephants killing a person. Moreover, the person had been a close relative, and the elephant in question was standing just fifteen feet away. The Hkamti mahout went on: "So now I always ride him, and he has no problem with me. He always obeys me and cooperates with me. But it keeps me up here in the camp a lot of the time. I'm here even more than my helper mahouts. And since I'm the owner, that's a bit unusual."

The dark cloud hanging over the elephant Neh Ong indicated the psychological toll that captive life could take on these elephants, even when they had competent, caring mahouts like Mong Cho. The mahout-elephant relationship, in these work environments in the forest, was not morally or emotionally simple, for either human or animal. I recalled the words of a song that the Moran fandis, like Miloswar, sing to elephants they've caught out of the wild:

O *wild elephant:*
Earlier you were in the mountains eating green grasses,
But then we fandis caught you to take you farther down into
   the plains.
Do not mind when I tie these ropes around your
   neck and feet,
They are like necklaces and bracelets in your honor.
Though sometimes we'll have a hard time, I will give you the
   best food,
And life will be better than before.
You will change your heart.
Though once you were in the jungle,
Now you will adopt the heart of a human.[5]

Miloswar sang these words for me in a melancholic, minor key that almost resembled Appalachian bluegrass. He said the song was "something between a lullaby and a love song."

Many elephants clearly do wind up "adopting the heart of a human." But an elephant's instincts and loyalties then become caught between two worlds. A fandi in the Trans-Patkai told me about an elephant who had been caught only recently and was still "rogue," in the sense of being very difficult to control. He was a tusker, and as with Neh Ong, mahouts had died while working with him. The job of handling him was eventually divided among several mahouts, all brothers. One day this rogue elephant angrily shook and jerked his head to free himself of the mahout on top. The mahout fell. He wheezed in pain, and the other brothers gathered around to help him. The rogue elephant, seeing the rest of the group's concern, immediately perched himself over the fallen boy to shade him from the sun. Then the tusker picked a broad leaf with his trunk and began fanning the young mahout, who was catching his breath.

And yet this elephant had already killed several people. "The elephants are amazing creatures," the fandi said to me. "Even when they are rogue or raw, they still have kind hearts."[6]

This story spoke to a core confusion at the heart of that elephant's life. In some ways the lives of domesticated elephants could be grim. Getting caught could itself be traumatic for the elephants. "Mela shekar is like war," another fandi once remarked to me.[7] Usually mela shekar marks the last day an elephant ever sees its parents, offspring, or anyone else in its original herd. The targeted elephant finds itself surrounded by imposing khoonkies and tangled by rope. Then a sometimes-brutal training process begins. Training can last for many months, and during part of the time, all four of the animal's legs are fastened with ropes to nearby trees.[8]

The government-run logging camps in Burma tend to have gentler training methods, built more on positive reinforcement—food treats and the like—though this approach takes longer.[9] The Trans-Patkai fandis more often mix positive with negative reinforcement. Thwacking the elephant over the forehead with the blunt edge of a machete seems to be a common disciplinary device. The higher-quality fandis and mahouts do this gently, so as not to injure the elephant or leave a mark. But in the Trans-Patkai, I saw a number of elephants with several parallel machete scars on their foreheads. To relax or reinvigorate their elephants, the Trans-Patkai mahouts sometimes give them marijuana, rice beer, or opium. Again, the more skilled elephant drivers know how to do this in moderation. But sometimes the elephants become addicted to the opium, which has long-term consequences for their physical and psychological well-being.

Add to this the pressures of the work itself, and the physical frustrations caused by the nocturnal fetters. And add the slow march of modernity that everywhere fills the elephants' lives with the roar of engines and deprives them of their forestlands. All this can result in a number of macabre behaviors. An elephant at a government camp in central Burma had a reputation for charging off to the nearby human graveyard during his period of musth. He would maniacally dig up graves and chew on the remains of human bodies. He preferred the more recent graves. Families in that village had learned that if they held a funeral immediately before the onset of this male's musth season, he had to be watched, even chained if necessary. Nonetheless, during most of the year, the elephant was a fine work animal, with a close relationship with his mahout.[10]

I heard an awful story of another elephant, a mother, found dead one morning. She was still standing, her forefeet crushing her own trunk. Evidently she had committed suicide. I didn't understand how this was possible. Surely, as she lost consciousness from lack of oxygen, she would involuntarily breathe through her mouth, or the trunk would jerk free. Maybe this was just a story the mahouts tell to convey, both to the listener and to themselves, their mixed feelings about the work they do.[11]

James Howard Williams tells a story from the Shenam Pass evacuation during World War II. He was walking along the path toward Imphal with the elephant convoy, when he suddenly saw a "rider-less elephant, with its pack gone, coming up the slope towards me at a fast stride. Her ears were forward, and she had an expression on her face that, I thought, meant that she was off back to Burma." Mahouts scrambled behind her to grab her chain. To dodge them, she took a running start and jumped over a ravine—"an action I had never seen an elephant make"—injuring her legs in the landing. Investigating the affair, Williams discovered that her mahout had tried to get her to cross an especially rickety bridge. The elephant had snapped, kicking the bridge down in anger, and this motion had thrown the mahout and saddle from the elephant. Then she fled: "Like a convict making a bold bid for liberty, she had stam-peded up the hill, hoping to the return from the barren hills to a land of bamboos." But having injured her legs in the jump, she was easily caught. "She stood quietly to be saddled"—but after that point, she walked with a limp.[12]

Though forest-based work puts elephants in a better position to mate than elephants in tourist camps or in zoos, sometimes the stress and situation of the work can undermine healthy mating pat-terns. I encountered a tusker elephant in the Trans-Patkai, who, I was told, had mated with his own daughters. This was an area where there were few wild elephants left.[13] I met the offspring. To my nonveterinarian's eye, they seemed healthy enough, but such cases of inbreeding are obviously not what mahouts hope for, and a male elephant in a psychologically and environmentally healthy situation would be unlikely to engage in such behavior.

Thinking through such stories and scenes, it's hard not to won-der whether the practice of keeping elephants as work animals is defensible. Animal rights proponents concerned for the elephants' welfare may argue that these elephants really ought to be released, to join or form wild herds. To be sure, this idea holds a strong moral appeal. But such an idea also misses the real danger facing the elephants, which is not the stresses of working life but rather eradication of forest cover.

Advocacy of expanding forest preserves, and improving legal protections, is another morally intuitive rallying cry for outsiders hoping to see the elephants (as well as other animal and plant life) here flourish. But effective protection of forest ranges requires economic resources, and the more developed countries inside the Asian elephant's natural range—Thailand, Vietnam, and Malaysia—have all developed to a point where forest cover is scarce. Indeed, this is a large part of *how* such countries became more economically developed: by stimulating agricultural output through expansion of farms into former forest. Less developed countries—Burma, Laos, much of India—have more forest area but fewer financial resources to establish and sustain wildlife preserves.

The situation of elephants in South India provides a counterpoint to that of the work elephants in Burma and northeastern India. In South India, elephants are almost entirely wild, and they are relatively numerous: roughly a quarter of the world's Asian elephants live in South India. (Together, Burma and northeastern India have about a third.) They live primarily in forest preserves that are reasonably well protected. And there are official "elephant corridors" that, at least in theory, allow elephants to migrate from forest to forest. In reality, these forests are isolated from each other, enveloped by areas of incredible human density.[14] Indeed, no other region on earth has significant numbers of Asian elephants and human density levels even approaching those of South India. South India's system of wildlife preserves exists only with support from tax revenue generated through intensive human settlement and development in surrounding areas: that, in turn, constrains the size of the parks and fills the intervening elephant corridors with towns, villages, roads, and farms.

The Trans-Patkai forest is far less fragmented than the remaining forestlands in South India, and it is well positioned along major surviving elephant migration routes. There appear to be several major "trunks" in this system of natural migratory corridors: one is a north-south route following the Patkais, from the Rakhine and Chin hills in the south to the Kachin Hills around Putao. Another begins around the Kaukkwe forests near Katha. From here, the wild herds proceed along the Kumon Range past the Hukawng Valley, then into the Patkais in the Chaukan area. Two major routes branch westward from Chaukan: one along the foothills of the eastern Himalayas toward Bhutan; another straight along the Lohit River toward the Brahmaputra River. Some wild elephants migrate all the way to Kaziranga National Park, hundreds of miles away in central Assam, either directly along the Brahmaputra's floodplain or by a southern route across the Naga Hills and then the Karbi Hills. During the wet season, the elephants tend to stay in high areas, drawn to salt springs there. During the dry season, as the hills run out of water, the elephants come into the river valleys, where there are fresh bamboo shoots. This alternation between highlands and lowlands happens annually. Mahouts in both Burma and India told me the wild herds sometimes cross the international border, but nobody was sure how often.[15]

Some of these migration routes are becoming disjointed. I learned of a herd of wild elephants in the Patkais whose males were "all *mokona*"—that is, all born tuskless. This indicates that the herd had become isolated and was deprived of the tusker gene over time (likely due to poaching, but perhaps also due to loggers' heavy demand for tuskers to hoist beams of wood).[16]

Yet overall the wider Trans-Patkai area, encompassing much of Upper Burma and northeastern India, is the last place on earth where Asian elephants can at least approximate the mobility they had before humans conquered and cleared much of the Asian forest. For the most part, these forests have not been preserved by governments (though small sections of the wider system of migratory routes, like Kaziranga National Park in Assam, are indeed protected parklands). They remain intact because the forests in the Trans-Patkai generate value: profit from trading forest commodities like timber and minerals; refuge for local militias or other political fugitives; and support for "off-grid" ways of living based on forest ecology.

The work elephants of Burma and northeastern India are thus in a peculiar situation. On the one hand, they have been conscripted by forest-oriented humans; on the other, they "buffer" their wild counterparts deeper in the forest, helping the humans hold off potent economic, demographic, and political forces that have destroyed enormous swaths of forestland elsewhere. This vexed situation places the work elephants under varying degrees of psychological duress. Hence the elephants who are "difficult," and hence the mahouts who deal with this dilemma, which is in part a moral one, as best they can.

"**ARE YOU EVER** afraid of the big one?" I asked Mong Cho, referring to Neh Ong.

"I try to be careful. But really, it wouldn't make sense to be afraid."

"Do you think of him as your friend?"

At this, the other mahouts laughed. "No!" cried one. "You're not supposed to think of them as friends."

Mong Cho smiled, ignoring the others. He looked thoughtfully at some tools in the tent and reached over to sharpen one. "Well, I've been with him for a long time—since he was very little. It's been nearly thirty years now. He is more like a son than a friend."

I thought of what the Vietcong mahout Xuan had said about Pak Chan: *"I had the feeling he was something of a prodigal son."*

"Would you miss Neh Ong?" I asked.

"Of course!" the other mahouts exclaimed, laughing more.

"Of course," Mong Cho said too, while sharpening the ankus in his hand and smiling sentimentally.

At night, I learned, the other mahouts usually went home to their families in the village below, but Mong Cho more often slept up here in the hill camp. At first, this seemed odd to me. Mahouts usually exit the camp at the end of each workday because the elephants have been released into the forest for the night. Even if Neh Ong got into trouble in the forest—which from everything I'd heard about him seemed likely—it would probably happen far from the tent itself, deep in the woods; having a mahout at the camp area wouldn't achieve much. I considered the possibility that Neh Ong was actually kept chained up at night, and Mong Cho slept nearby as a kind of warden. But if this were so, then someone would have to gather hundreds of pounds of fodder for the giant elephant every day. Neh Ong was well fed, and none of these mahouts were preparing to gather six hundred pounds of bamboo leaves that afternoon. Clearly Neh Ong was free to forage at night.

Then it occurred to me: perhaps Neh Ong wanted Mong Cho nearby. Mong Cho was one of the few creatures Neh Ong had in his life who put the huge tusker at ease. Perhaps he preferred to forage at night knowing that Mong Cho was nearby, in the tent. In that case, Mong Cho was sleeping up in the hills to soothe and comfort his powerful but troubled lead tusker, to whom he felt such paternal affection.

Mong Cho also had a young human son, back in the valley. Despite the recent doldrums in elephant work in his area, Mong Cho hoped his son would grow up to become a mahout like him.

Chapter 7

CAMPS
AND VILLAGES

ARE WOMEN EVER MAHOUTS?

I'd been asking this question for months, in both the Trans-Patkai area and in central Burma, always receiving a firm no. Some told me it went against custom for women to be mahouts. Others claimed it was against religion and spiritual instruction.[1] Still others said that the elephants themselves will not accept a female mahout—that a male elephant in particular will never permit it.[2]

Such responses never satisfied me. In James Howard Williams's World War II memoir *Elephant Bill*, women demonstrate excellent elephant handling skills. Williams, a British teak wallah in Burma, was doing construction and transport work with the mahouts and elephants of the upper Chindwin Valley. One day Williams found himself with more elephants than mahouts. Many of the Burmese mahouts had gone missing that morning, apparently absorbed into a Japanese work camp beyond the front lines. With no one to drive the elephants, Williams considered releasing the giants into the forest. But the mahouts' wives (or their "women," as Williams puts it, which could mean sisters, daughters, and so forth) were residing in a nearby village and heard of Williams's predicament. Anticipating the eventual return of the missing mahouts to the British side, they volunteered to "ride the riderless elephants" back into a section of the forest under British control. The women did so successfully, under tense circumstances. This surprised Williams, who like me had been told that the women could not be mahouts.[3]

I knew of a few contemporary cases where highly educated women in the elephant conservationist community had learned mahout skills.[4] But did village women ever become mahouts? I learned of several. In central Burma, in the woods beyond a government elephant logging village, I visited a charcoal camp, comprising a few makeshift bamboo shelters amid several smoking heaps of ironwood that would later become saleable charcoal. Some mahouts lounged on matted floors inside the main shelter. Several elephants passed by, carrying ironwood logs upon their tusks and crossing the stream that snaked past the camp. The hike here from the road had taken some thirty minutes.

A woman named Nyo was at the camp with her husband, Win, who was repairing a bamboo pipe for the main cistern while Nyo stirred rice over a campfire. At first I directed all my questions to Win, as I'd been advised, but gradually I directed more to Nyo. Smiling at my inquiries, she pointed out that even though everyone says women don't drive elephants, she used to do it all the time.

We were sitting in a group, some eight men and three women in all, and everyone was laughing. The topic was apparently a source of great amusement. Nyo had grown up in a farming area and learned how to ride and give commands to elephants when she first married Win. She had a few favorite elephants in her life, but in the government-run timber industry, elephants can change hands abruptly or be sent off to different logging areas, and that was what happened with the elephants she remembered best. She never did logging work, only the transport work, like moving bags of charcoal, or supplies for village life. Then Win became a head mahout, and she became pregnant, and she never worked as a mahout after that. That was twenty-five or thirty years ago.[5]

I asked whether, during that earlier period, she had been an official salaried mahout, receiving a wage from the government as the male mahouts did. She said no, the government paid wages only for the logging work, not for the transport work that she was doing. The government's timber enterprise has never shown much interest in using elephants for transporting anything other than its primary commodity, the teak logs. Anything else is "not its department" and winds up on the margins of the village's economic life.

Looking around this tiny charcoal-making camp, I realized why I had never seen women like Nyo—that is, women with mahoutship experience—in the tribal logging camps. At this camp, as in the elephant logging village to which it was a satellite, wives and daughters and other family members worked alongside male mahouts. Most human family members here, male or female, spent their days near the elephants. Some of the women, I was told, would sleep here overnight, while others would return to the main village a short hike away.

By contrast, in the Trans-Patkai region, the tribal logging camps like Mithong (Air Singh's camp) in the Lohit Valley, or like Mong Cho's camp in the hills of southwestern Kachin State, were almost entirely male environments. A Kachin mahout in the Trans-Patkai's Dihing Valley told me that wives occasionally came along to the logging areas to help load elephants or to give commands. But mostly the women attended to things in the village. Indeed, in the Trans-Patkai, the mahouts hail from villages far removed from the world of elephants. These villages have main streets with motor traffic and shops; farms growing rice and potatoes; and pigs, cows, goats and chickens roaming about. They look "normal"—one could pass through them and never know that many of the families here are mahouts' families. Go up a dirt side road, and on the outskirts of the village, one might occasionally see an elephant brought from the forest to a mahout's village house. Perhaps the mahout is loading the elephant. Likely, he is bringing food up to his comrades at the logging camps. His wife might be there to help, packing bags or giving a command or two to control the elephant.

But most of the elephants aren't here, they're at the logging camp, many miles up the road and deep in the forest. At Mithong, this road ends at a sawmill. No women work there. The rest of the way to the actual logging area follows difficult forest and mountain paths. The array of camps, like the sawmills, are entirely full of men. A geographer or sociologist might say that when visiting elephant camps in the Trans-Patkai, one passes through a series of processional "stages," from village center to village edge to timber mill to elephant camp. Women are more present at the earlier stages; elephants are more present at the later ones; men are present throughout.

By contrast, the government elephant logging village in central Burma collapsed these different processional "stages" into one. The village had a main street and shops and several hundred huts full of families, but it *also* had elephants, some five dozen of them. All family members, of both species, were in one place. The village was the "hub" from which elephants and mahouts could reach many kinds of outposts connected to village life. Paths to the teak-logging areas passed by satellite camps for charcoal, or sites where villagers were gathering bamboo and cane to reinforce their homes in preparation for the coming monsoon storms.

There was an endless march of elephant traffic through the village to and from these sites, going up and down the main road and its many side paths. Elephants dragged huge, heavy heaps of bamboo piled on wooden sleds; elephants went off to the teak-logging areas for the day; elephants carried nine or ten large bags of charcoal at a time to some hut or depot; elephants headed to a stream for their daily bath; elephants delivered sacks of rice to the huts of mahouts. There was even a kind of "rush hour" effect in the morning, when the mahouts had all fetched their elephants and were coming out of the forest seated on the giants' necks.

Everywhere the lives of the mahouts' family members were visibly intertwined with the elephants and the elephants' work. Family members helped unload the elephants or tied up the elephants' dragging ropes. The mahouts' wives handed tools up to the mahouts on the elephants' necks or backs. One woman ordered an elephant to kneel by a section of her bamboo hut that was elevated so she could haul the cargo directly from the elephant's back onto the hut's main landing. I occasionally saw children playing with calves. There was a special satellite outpost for "retired" elephants, who were too old for logging work. These elephants, in their fifties or sixties, were attended to by gray-haired mahouts, who had some family members with them as well.

I was at a campfire one night with the mahouts of this complex logging village. While drinking rum and eating rice, several of the mahouts recalled female mahouts in the area besides Nyo. A Karen woman, Naw Ko, had lived in the village some years ago. She was unusual. Not only had she had done the logging work, she had received regular government wages for it. Unfortunately she had died young. Another mahout recalled a woman who was a kind of "tomboy." She would do everything the men did. She worked with the elephants, dragged the teak, and slept in the group tent in the forest during the peak work season in August. This woman would even work with the large male tusker elephants, something the other female mahouts I learned about never did.[6]

Such examples of female mahoutship seem to stem from the spatial organization of the Burmese government's elephant logging system. In other words, in these villages where the elephants, the mahouts, and the mahouts' family members all share space, more opportunities open up for women to become mahouts. Yet other factors could direct the flow of mahoutship skills to women as well as to men. I met an elderly woman, Timeh, who lived with her husband, Imow, many miles down the road, at the former site of the logging village, which had since migrated to follow the mature teak. This elderly couple had moved to central Burma during the 1990s, from the town of Homalin on the upper Chindwin River, between the Chin Hills and the Kachin Hills. We sat outside their hut on a sunny afternoon, a cat circling us throughout the conversation and meowing.

Timeh and Imow were both born in Homalin. Imow had a Hkamti mother and a Kachin father and learned his elephant skills from both sides but especially the Hkamti side. My guide P., who was half Shan, was able to converse in Shan with Imow for a portion of the conversation. Imow knew as little Kachin as I did, having not used it in many decades. Timeh, his wife, smoked a cigar throughout the conversation. She was an ethnic Burmese and was locally nicknamed "the Shan lady" (after her Hkamti-Shan husband) or "the Chin lady." This latter nickname seemed to be based on a local misperception that she was Chin rather than ethnic Burmese, or perhaps it simply referred to her origin in Homalin, which is near the Chin Hills. Like Nyo, whom I'd met at the charcoal camps, Timeh learned her mahoutship skills from her husband, when they were first married.

"Homalin had a lot of female mahouts in those days," Imow explained. "There was a lot of gold panning work to be done on the Uyu River"—which joins the Chindwin around this spot—"and men who were mahouts would go off up the river to do this work." Gold panning is mostly barge work, not elephant work. Sometimes while approaching a forest river in the Kachin Hills, one happens upon a little floating village of bamboo rafts carrying heavy dredging machinery and conveyor belts, with workers sorting through the machine parts, sifting through piles of rocks encased in mud, or lounging inside the rafts' canvas shelters. While the male mahouts of the Homalin area were on these excursions up the Uyu, in search of a commodity more valuable than teak, someone had to carry on with the elephant work, and this responsibility often went to the women. Women also sometimes owned elephants in this area. Timeh and Imow remembered a woman who owned a dozen elephants, having inherited them from her father. Her hired mahouts, though, were mostly male.[7]

Homalin is in the same general area along the upper Chindwin where James Howard Williams had been so surprised to see the women take control of the elephants. Perhaps this area has an unusually strong tradition of women mahouts, which might be connected to the boom and bust cycles of the nearby gold-panning industry that periodically draws many of the men.

At one point earlier in their lives, Timeh and Imow wound up working for one of the Burmese government's timber enterprises on the upper Chindwin. In 1995 government logging officials announced that a number of elephants, including two of Timeh and Imow's, were to be transferred to the teak forests of central Burma. The married mahouts decided to follow their elephants from Homalin to the central Burmese forest, leaving two of their four children behind. The journey took several weeks. Seven elephants in all made the trip. By chance, I had already met two of these seven. Gunjai, the elephant I'd seen being fetched the previous morning by the mahout Otou—the elephant who disliked me because I was wearing pants—was one of the Homalin elephants. Another, Latai, had carried me down a large hill to a forest outpost earlier in that day.

At mention of Latai, Timeh's face brightened. "That was my favorite elephant," she said. "Though I couldn't ride him, since he was a male and a tusker. But I'd always bring Latai food treats."

I asked Timeh what kind of work she normally did with the elephants. "Always transportation," she replied. "Food, canteens of water, charcoal, stones, bamboo and timber, things like that. I wouldn't do the logging work; that was Imow's job."

The two had retired from elephant work some years ago, which was why they didn't follow the logging village when it moved nine or ten miles up the road. The two children who moved with them to central Burma were still in the area, but neither had become mahouts. Timeh and Imow hadn't seen their other two children in many years.

The Burmese government's teak-logging system is in many ways an updating of managerial organization put into place by the British colonial teak wallahs, who themselves mostly formalized methods of elephant-based logging they observed among the Karen and Mon mahouts in the hills around Moulmein in the nineteenth century. Present-day logging and forestry bureaucrats have inherited from this earlier period a strong preference for "roadless" logging, seeing trucking roads as prohibitively expensive, ecologically destructive, and damaging to the quality of the teak.[8]

Currently, there are about three dozen government-run elephant logging villages in Burma, scattered among the best Burmese teak forests in the Rakhine Hills, the Bago Hills, and the upper valleys of the Irrawaddy and the Chindwin.[9] Once or twice per decade, these elephant logging villages change location, following the teak harvest. The dwelling structures in these villages are usually built of biodegradable forest materials—bamboo, cane, and timber transported by elephant from the surrounding woodlands—in anticipation of these periodic moves. Visiting these teak-harvesting villages, one cannot help but be impressed by their unique organizational genius.[10]

The Burmese government's elephant logging system is also rife with problems, and its future looks uncertain. From one point of view, the villages are just large work sites—factories for roadless logging. But these are also places where people are raising families and building lives. With the economic liberalization of Burma in recent years, these families now have access to a wider array of consumer items and are investing more in their homes, turning them into permanent structures.

I visited a particular central Burmese logging village once in 2013 and again in 2016. During the first visit, the villagers were busy gathering bamboo from the surrounding forest to reinforce their homes in preparation for the coming monsoon storms. The homes were built of materials that anticipated eventual abandonment: thatched roofs, skeletal structures and divisions made entirely of bamboo, beams held in place by pegs and rope rather than with screws and nails, and so on. In 2016, by contrast, many of the homes had noticeably changed. There were more metal roofs now, made of corrugated iron sheets. The bamboo stilts were sometimes reinforced with metal rods or concrete. People's gardens looked more elaborate, with more fruits and vegetables growing and with decorative flowers.

The logging officials, in the meantime, who live in far-off cities, had declared the area overlogged in 2015 and had already built a brand-new logging village many miles away, in an area with plenty of mature teak. Exploring the forestlands around the currently occupied village, I could see why officials announced it should be abandoned. There were trees everywhere, including some teak, but the streams and springs in the area were drying up, a consequence of diminished tree density. When I followed the mahout Otou to watch him fetch his elephant Gunjai, the only usable watering hole in which Gunjai could take his morning bath (an important part of the morning ritual for both elephant and mahout) was barely a foot deep. Soon it too would run dry.

The new village the government had built was on a wide river with a good current: a fine location from the perspective of an elephant. Already a few mahouts had moved here, having been offered a premium in their wages. I spent an afternoon with some of them.

Pointing to various corners of their new homes, they observed that the government had done a poor job building the new dwelling structures. Rather than weaving the bamboo slats together in a full latticework, to create firm flooring and insect-resistant walls, the builders of the new village had used a faster but less effective construction method, where only a few perpendicular slats held all the parallel slats together.

There were huge gaps in the flooring and in the walls. The government had also cut corners when finishing and treating the bamboo, which in places was attracting termites. Joints had been fastened with nails, which were rusting, rather than with bamboo rope. The new village was also many miles up the river, far from the nearest road. For the most part, neither the mahouts nor their family members wanted to move here, even if the wages were better. [11] Comparing this new work site with the older village, with its main street and its shops and its well-built homes and pleasant gardens, I thought no one in their right mind would move their family from the old setting to the new one. And yet the forestlands around the old village were drying up, and the new village site sat adjacent to tracts of mature teak.

By contrast, the tribal logging areas in the Trans-Patkai region do not have this conflict. Loggers follow the harvest from tract to tract, and their families settle in a single village around which they build their lives. The Trans-Patkai mahouts are also more autonomous, making decisions about when to move a camp from one glen to another among themselves. Given their location deep in the forest, in places only they (riding their elephants) can access, no outside bureaucratic authority could possibly control the harvest schedule. But this system has its social disadvantages too: the tribal loggers must spend long periods of time away from their families.

From the perspective of government logging officials in Burma, the camp system would also have the disadvantage of being extremely difficult to administer from a central bureaucratic office. The government-run timber industry's village system gives outside administrators a kind of lever over the logging mahouts' lives. The villages usually have at least one main road and so are accessible to administrators or to veterinarians making surprise visits.[12] The villages are also where educational and medical services are provided and where wages are disbursed. The mahouts are still able to gather resources from sections of the forest beyond the administrators' view—the charcoal camps, for instance, are not condoned by the industry officials—but overall, the village system keeps the mahouts connected to a formal bureaucracy in ways that the camp system in the Trans-Patkai tribal areas does not.

Mounting tensions between administrators and mahouts over village location has strained the Burmese government's teak-logging system. The system has also encountered a new, more challenging issue in recent years. The economic design of the government's timber industry assumes that the best and most valuable teak will come from forests with very few roads scarring the soil. From this assumption flow two further premises: that logging done with elephants can be just as profitable as logging done by motorized machinery, and that a portion of these profits can then be directed toward the elephants' welfare. Yet in recent years, the foundational assumption—that teak grown in "roadless" forests is more valuable—seems to have held true only when Burma's economy was closed and protected. Of late, the Burmese teak industry has had to compete with its counterparts abroad, especially in Central America. This new market pressure, and the increased availability of machinery, has led to the motorization of larger and larger swaths of the Burmese teak industry.[13]

This in turn has contributed to overlogging. The situation is nowhere near as severe as in Thailand, which once had a thriving teak-logging industry but so deforested its hills that erosion and calamitous downriver flooding ensued, leading to a sweeping logging ban in the early 1990s.[14] But the Burmese situation is still serious enough that Burmese forestry officials have recently instituted temporary limits on logging, allowing mahouts to harvest only about a quarter of the timber tonnage they were harvesting before—a cutback that should, the forestry officials hope, give the forest time to recover.[15]

The cost is borne, in large part, by the mahouts themselves, whose wages are paid per ton. The timber enterprise has no plan to compensate the mahouts for their lost income. A number of mahouts have responded by gathering ironwood trees from the forest, to make charcoal. Charcoal is nowhere near as valuable as teak, of course, but it gives the mahouts a commodity to sell, to make up for their lost earnings, which are significant (and entirely avoidable, if the government would simply pay them more during the tonnage limitation period).[16]

The mahouts' charcoal-making camps, though surely not an optimal use of forest resources, can be fascinating in action. The scene is full of smoke and steam and elephants carrying great ironwood logs upon their tusks. Sometimes the logs are simply burned in piles. But in another method, large cavelike rooms are hollowed out from nearby bluffs, and a chimney is dug upward until it reaches the hillcrest above. Logs are loaded into the cavern through a hillside door, then lit, and the door is filled in with clay, except for a few small holes that allow oxygen to flow into the subterranean chamber. I saw several of these structures in a row along a steep incline by a forest stream. Elephants were unloading logs at open doorways. Other chambers had already been sealed, and smoke was puffing out through the chimney openings above. The sight was lovely and strange: cozy and funereal at the same time.

THE MAHOUTS of the main government-run logging village I visited in central Burma were mostly ethnic Burmans. The village was characterized by this relative homogeneity in spite of a large nearby population of ethnic Karen mahouts. The Karen mahouts worked on private logging tracts. I would see their trucks pass by the government area frequently. The trucks were easy to pick out because they had a crucifix hanging behind the windshield. The government logging village had no church and was intended to be a Buddhist-only community: it had a Buddhist religious building near the main road and several shrines for the worship of forest spirits, or *nats*.

By contrast, the elephant logging camps in the Trans-Patkai allow people from multiple religious and ethnic backgrounds to work side by side during the day and to return to their respective villages at night. Thus, in the southwestern hills of Kachin State, Hkamti, Kachin, and ethnic Burmese mahouts worked in relative harmony together, even though the Burmese and Hkamtis return every night to villages whose main religious structure is a Buddhist stupa or monastery, while the Kachins return to a village with a large church.

Tenam, the long-haired mahout who brought me into the Mithong logging forest to meet Air Singh, was Hkamti, but he preferred to wear a traditional Kachin hat. I asked him about it over lunch. He laughed and answered that a Hkamti hat is too ornate and impractical for logging work; the Kachin hat was simpler and more comfortable. The choice was pragmatic but also signaled the sort of social intermixing that occurred in this work milieu. Tenam had many Singpho-Kachin mahouts working under him and in some cases alongside him.[17] Air Singh's mahout was a

Kachin teenager, Gam, whose fellow mahouts hailed from a wide array of groups: Hkamtis, Singpho-Kachins, Nepalis, Assamese, and Adivasis. The lead mahouts and tract owners were all Hkamtis and Singpho-Kachins, who'd divided the forest between themselves using a streambed as a border.[18] But the workers under them were a mix of all five groups, if not more. The lingua franca among the mahouts was Assamese.

Of these groups, the Hkamtis have played the most important historical role in diffusing forest mahout skills throughout this part of the world. Even the proudest Kachin mahouts I spoke with conceded, with a grudging smile, that the Hkamtis were in effect the core group, with the longest-lasting traditions, within the Trans-Patkai's mahout culture. The elephant skills seem to have originally come from the west—from Bengal and Assam. Nobody is sure when this was exactly. Apparently it was well over a thousand years ago, before today's ethnonyms (Hkamti, Kachin, etc.) show up in any historical record. Up until the nineteenth century, the Hkamtis had their own tiny kingdoms in the Hukawng Valley and the Putao Plain, political nodes that aided the spread of elephant skills eastward and southward. The Kachins, who originally migrated from Yunnan, became associated with elephant work much more recently, in the nineteenth century, learning the art of mahoutship from the Hkamtis.[19] The Morans seem to have been engaged in elephant work for as long as the Hkamtis but did not play as prominent a role in diffusing the culture.[20]

These groups have a history of struggling over territory, yet they share in common the experience of having fled powerful, expanding kingdoms and empires. The Morans were pushed into the Trans-Patkai when the Ahom kingdoms expanded up the Brahmaputra River. The Kachins fled Mongol and Han invasions in Yunnan. The Hkamtis migrated from larger Tai polities to the southeast. Once they reached the mountainous refuge of the Trans-Patkai, these groups became intermixed, though in ways that preserved certain distinct languages and cultural traditions.[21]

Imow, we should remember, was half Kachin and half Hkamti. Miloswar, the elderly Moran fandi who told me the story of the khoonkie elephant Sokona, had a Hkamti daughter-in-law. Intermarriage between Morans and Kachins in the Lohit and Dihing valleys seems to be rarer, perhaps due to the groups' topographic ordering: the Kachins are associated with a relatively high contour line up in the hills, the Hkamtis with a transitional area between hills and plains, and the Morans are mostly in the lower Dihing Valley. The scheme has lots of exceptions, but it generally helps an outside visitor make some sense of the dizzying network of interfamilial and intertribal ties. Nevertheless, some social scientists have reported a kind of ethnic "shape-shifting," in which individuals or clans shift from "Hkamti" to "Kachin" under certain political circumstances, or vice versa.[22]

Such an interpretation is disputed, but tribal fluidity and heterogeneity would perform a useful law-evading function as well. Forestry officials might hear that an illegal activity is taking place in a certain sector of the forest (illegal elephant capture, illegal logging, smuggling of goods, etc.). If the investigators know that the mahout they're seeking is, say, a Hkamti, then they go directly to the nearby Hkamti village and begin their interrogations there. But if the sector of the forest is associated with mahouts hailing from many different groups and villages, the investigation has no obvious next step. People at the Hkamti village will say that a Moran mahout must have done it; people at the Moran village will say that a Kachin mahout must have done it; and so on.[23]

In the Lohit and Dihing valleys, mahouts are also Adivasi, Nepali, Assamese, and occasionally Chakma. All these groups migrated from elsewhere. The Adivasis came from central India during the nineteenth century to work on the tea plantations of

Assam, which were rapidly expanding up the Brahmaputra Valley during the British colonial era. The Adivasis are sometimes called, simply, the "tea tribes" because of their association with tea harvesting. However, many of them farm other crops, and a few are mahouts. I once met a young Adivasi mahout at a sawmill camp in the Lohit Valley named Gudu. He was eighteen years old and fed his elephant bananas as we talked. Gudu came from a family of farmers, but the nearby farming areas had become crowded, and wages for agricultural work had declined.

By contrast, wages in the logging industry stayed strong, so he headed to the Lohit logging area. At first, he worked at a sawmill, where logs dragged in by elephants were cut up and then trucked out for eventual sale. Most of the sawmill workers in the area were young Adivasi men like himself. The Hkamti sawmill owner saw that Gudu had good rapport with the elephants bringing in the logs, so he offered Gudu a job as a mahout's assistant. Gudu thrived in the new position and was now in charge of this elephant eating the bananas. (The elephant had given me a ride to the mill some fifteen minutes earlier and nearly tossed me off.) His wages, he said, were significantly better than they would have been had he stayed on the farm. Furthermore, "I like the sense of adventure, of being out there in the forest with my elephant, who is really like a best friend who understands me in every way." Gudu added that his mother was unhappy about his chosen profession and wanted him to return to the farm.[24]

I encountered another Adivasi mahout, below the Lohit Valley, in Assam, in an area of huge tea plantations. The domesticated elephants here dated from the days when the tea plantations used elephants for draft labor and were interpenetrated by forest. Nowadays those forests are gone, and the industry is organized around motor transport. But many of the big tea estates still keep elephants as a mark of prestige, and they keep mahouts on the payrolls as well. The elephants have relatively little to do all day and have no forests in which to roam or mate, but they still have rivers and tree groves in which to spend their days.

This tea plantation mahout and his elephant had wandered up from the nearby river, to a cluster of shops alongside the main highway. Cavalierly, the elephant was reaching his great trunk into a shopkeeper's window for a loaf of bread. The shopkeeper jumped in his seat with surprise. The mahout looked on nonchalantly, arms crossed, from high on the elephant's neck. A boy stepped out of the shop with a box of crackers and fed them to the elephant. Then on the other side of the market lane, another shopkeeper said something with a scowl. The mahout took offense, leaped down from the elephant, and ran up to the shopkeeper with a menacing grin on his face. The shopkeeper was smaller, and the mahout had no trouble picking the poor man up and dragging him toward the elephant.

With the agility of a playground tyrant, the tea plantation mahout then turned the shopkeeper upside down, so that his feet were pointing upward. The elephant promptly wrapped his trunk around the unfortunate shopkeeper's ankles. At this point the victim said something that I took to mean, "I take it back!" He was released from his misery. This absurd scene gave me a sense of the power wielded by a man whose best friend weighs five tons. And yet at the forest camps up in the hills, I had never seen anything remotely like this display. This bullying behavior was, perhaps, what happened when an elephant and mahout pair functioned as mere status symbols for a powerful estate in the plains, rather than as work partners at a site in the forest.

DOES AN ELEPHANT care whether its mahout is a man or a woman, a Hkamti or a Kachin, an Adivasi or a Moran? Likely not. Do the social relations and distinctions among the humans at the camps and villages make no difference at all to the elephants, then? They likely do, primarily because many of these relations trace back to a village system or a camp system as the chief spatial principle organizing the elephants' lives. An elephant logging village is a planned, bureaucratically managed environment where an elephant is likely to cross paths with veterinarians or with professionals who have a broad sense of the methods in many regions. An elephant might perceive intervention from this "professional" world as negative if it senses that its mahout tenses up when the "man with the trousers" approaches with his report book. Or an elephant might be glad to get attention from trained veterinarians or from forestry managers who are planning a new village site on a broad river with an attractive current.

Similarly, a domesticated elephant might have good reason to prefer the camp system, which keeps it in constant proximity with wild elephants. Furthermore, the mix of tribal groups at the forest camps increases the likelihood that the elephant will change hands a few times during its life, thus passing through different forest areas and encountering different wild herds. That said, from the elephants' perspective, the camps may also have drawbacks. Tribal mahouts' training and daily treatment of elephants in the Trans-Patkai region tends to be harsher than in the government-run villages, where elephant officials have systematically pushed the mahouts to do training based on positive rewards rather than punishments.

Another drawback of the Trans-Patkai area—though the elephants are likely not directly aware of this problem—is that modern, weather-resistant roads are gradually snaking their way into the region, and will likely bring forces of agricultural and urban development with them. Signs of change are especially noticeable on the Indian side of the Trans-Patkai where, slowly yet surely, the government has been constructing expensive all-weather road infrastructure to link the Lohit and Dihing valleys with the motor traffic network in Assam. Large concrete viaducts, sometimes many miles long, are rising in the jungle. If completed, they will turn torrential monsoon river courses like the Sissiri into geographic features to be merely passed over rather than moved through. These road projects will not reach every village and inhabited monsoon island. But once the new infrastructure is completed, it will permanently alter the spatial organization of the region. Likely, the local political balance will tip away from forest-based economies. If this happens, it's not clear what will become of the elephants or who will protect them. Perhaps the Indian government can set up wildlife preserves. But the same state forces that built the expensive new roads might need to open previously forested areas to new development in order to generate the revenue needed to pay for the infrastructure.[25]

The Burmese state bureaucracy, by contrast, has a proven track record of directly managing elephant-based labor in the forest, through its unique system of teak-harvesting villages. But the future of the government elephant logging villages is also uncertain. As Burma's economy opens and becomes more susceptible to global market forces, the Burmese timber industry seems likely to become more mechanized. If elephants no longer contribute to the industry's profitability, then industry profits will likely stop flowing toward elephant welfare, instead going toward better machinery and improved hard infrastructure. In such a future, logging will not be able to support the human-elephant working relationship in the forest. As we'll see in the next two chapters, a different model, built on the use of elephants for transportation rather than for logging, may be more promising.

Chapter 8

PENCIL LINES
ON A MAP

THE WORLD'S LAST BUREAUCRATICALLY ADMINISTERED
system of elephant-based transportation is run by the Kachin Independence Army, or KIA, in the far north of Burma. Here dozens
of elephants link camps, villages, secret manufacturing sites, and
other strategic locations otherwise separated by seasonal flooding and roadless forest. As we've seen, the presence of "fugitive"
peoples avoiding powerful states helps explain the persistence of
elephant domestication in this part of the world. The KIA's elephant transport convoys illustrate this dynamic in an especially
pronounced way.

The KIA formed in response to the Burmese military takeover of
the country in the early 1960s. A quasi-government (the governing
counterpart is officially called the Kachin Independence Organization, or KIO), the KIA has controlled significant swaths of the
Kachin Hills for the past half century. As of the 2010s, its elephant
teams are still very active. Sending elephant convoys through the
jungle allows the group to move supplies beyond the view of the
Burmese army, or Tatmadaw, whose ground vehicles can travel
only on the region's sparse network of roads. I came to think of
these furtive routes, which elephants and rebels follow together in
the forest, as like so many erasable pencil lines on a map. While

the Tatmadaw's jeeps and trucks have to follow the map's inked-in permanent thoroughfares, the paths of elephant convoys are always flexible and movable, leaving hardly any trace of themselves.

The KIA's use of elephants for transportation, rather than for logging, is significant. As we've seen, elephant logging presents a serious limitation: by definition, it is destructive of forest cover. In order to be profitable, especially in the short term, logging has to be ecologically destructive. But elephants who carry cargo and passengers across rivers and forests do not present this problem.

This means the KIA has unique knowledge about how to organize environmentally friendly elephant work. In turn, its elephant system ought to be of great interest to governments throughout the Asian elephant's natural range: in India, Indonesia, Thailand, the rest of Burma, and so forth. These governments might bristle at the more subversive aspects of the Kachin militia's logistical network, but they all administer territory that suffers a paralyzing monsoon season, when roads become flooded or obstructed by mudslides. Indeed, the severity of monsoon is precisely what turns the Kachin forest into the KIA's political refuge, inaccessible to the Tatmadaw's motorized transport. Elephants' off-road abilities are strong regardless of what makes the roads impassable, be it weather or warfare. So why shouldn't governments throughout South and Southeast Asia institute their own departments of elephant-borne logistics?

Thus far, governmental authorities have overlooked the KIA's elephant system—and so, for that matter, has the international elephant conservation community. But knowledge about what exists in the present shapes our assumptions about what is possible in the future. I had a notion like this on my mind when I traveled to Myitkyina, the main city in Kachin State, in 2015. There I spoke with a KIA colonel, Nan, who had several decades of experience leading the KIA's elephant transport convoys. In part, I wanted to better understand this "half-wild" transport system that elephants and rebels have created together over the last six decades. Do the elephants have freedom in the forest each night? What cargo are they carrying? How have the secret elephant trails interlocked with the region's wider geopolitics? In addition to piecing together this picture of what the elephant transport teams have been doing, I hoped to gain a better sense of what they *could* be doing—that is, of their potential.

Warfare has caused much human suffering in Kachin State. In recent years, the conflict has accelerated, as the Tatmadaw has surged into the forest to bring more territory under its control. Between 2011 and 2018, over one hundred thousand people, mainly rural Kachins, have fled the violence and destruction, either to other countries or to displaced-persons camps inside Burma.[1] I owe a great debt to those who, despite the surrounding circumstances, kept me out of harm's way and found time to speak with me. The elephant culture of the Kachin Hills is one of many aspects of life here that deserves to last. Hopefully, the near future will bring the people of this region peace, justice, and survival.

"MY FAVORITE MAHOUT WAS a Hkamti, actually, not a Kachin," Colonel Nan, who led the KIA's elephant brigade in the Hukawng Valley during the 1980s, told me through our talented translator, Nkumgam. The three of us were having tea. The rain had let up outside, and the sun was momentarily peering in through the window.[2]

"His name was Mong Shwe," the colonel continued, "the apple of my eye. He was the most careful with the elephants and always knew what to do when they were sick. The elephants always had a good relationship with him. He's since passed away."

The colonel paused and drank his tea, reflecting on this part of his life.

"Are there still Hkamti mahouts in the KIA?" I asked.

"No, it's all Kachin now. The Hkamti mahouts today are all in civilian work. It's not like before. Some of the Hkamtis are very good mahouts, but our mahouts are good too. Not all the brigade mahouts are soldiers—some are civilian mahouts who help us during certain times of the year."

Nan had grown up in an area of southern Kachin State where there were relatively few elephants. Like Xuan Thieu of the Ho Chi Minh Trail, he had never worked with elephants before, when he suddenly found himself leading a rebel army's elephant brigade. In the early 1980s, the KIA's high command decided to expand its elephant-based transport operations through the Kachin forest country. One look at a map would explain why: Kachin State was the most heavily forested region of Burma and had relatively few year-round roads. Nan was assigned to the largest elephant brigade of all, which ranged in size from twenty to thirty elephants. This group's main area was in the Hukawng Valley, where the best mahouts were either Hkamtis or from a Kachin tribe called the Jinghpaws.

The Hkamtis and the Jinghpaws historically alternated between friendship and violence. Nan had likely been picked for the assignment because he was neither Jinghpaw nor Hkamti but hailed from a smaller and less powerful Kachin tribe in southern Kachin State. Furthermore, while the Hkamti mahouts in his brigade were Buddhist, and the Jinghpaws mostly Baptist, Nan was from a smaller Christian denomination. He was well positioned to serve as an arbiter, a neutral force in a potentially polarized situation. Certainly, the command hadn't sent him to the transport brigade for his elephant skills.

I had many questions but let the conversation pause so Nan could rest. We had more tea. Nkumgam, brilliant with languages but poor in geography, looked with some confusion at a map I'd brought, onto which Nan had been penciling in various routes taken by convoys of elephants carrying food and arms. We were in the main Myitkyina office of the KIA's governing counterpart, the KIO.

It felt odd to me that this office existed at all. It had been set up as part of a treaty between the KIO and the Burmese government.[3] But the treaty had collapsed, and the Tatmadaw and the rebels were currently fighting. I'd been stuck in Myitkyina for over a week, waiting for the fighting to subside.

Across the street was a large grassy area, the Manau park. Manau is an important Kachin cultural festival, and at the center of the park was a colorful performance stand built in front of six large decorated poles, each around thirty feet high. These high poles were painted in bright reds, yellows, and blues, and capped by a carving of a stylized hornbill or crossed swords. The aesthetic called to mind the totem poles of the Pacific Northwest. The park had been constructed recently, on a spot where an old river oxbow, long since filled in for paddy fields, met the Irrawaddy. Upstream was the leafy Shatapru neighborhood and a restaurant on the water specializing in delicious spiced satays and ginger sautéed with chilis and mountain herbs. Downstream was the city's main market area, which was shaded beneath hundreds of rainbow umbrellas. River fish were for sale, as were snails and periwinkles. A hunter was selling deer skulls and bear claws. Shan seamstresses were fitting and selling clothes.

Surrounding the market area were several large religious structures: a Buddhist monastery, a Baptist compound, a Roman Catholic church, a gated mosque, and a large Hindu temple overlooking the water. I was told that due to the fighting, the city's economy had stalled, but everywhere people seemed busy shopping for groceries, phones, and motorcycles. There were more women out in the streets than I'd seen in other cities in this part of the world— puttering along on scooters, going to work or school or running errands. Many of the men were somewhere else. There was clearly some additional input of wealth.

"There are three elephant groups," Nan continued. "One is with the Second Brigade, in the Hukawng Valley. Then there's the First, which is near the Chinese border, and the Fifth, which is to the south. There are maybe fifty or sixty elephants overall, I don't know the exact number these days. The Second always has the most elephants. At any given time, most of the elephants are around the Hukawng Valley and the Hpakant jade mines, or else they're near Laiza." Laiza was the Kachin Independence Organization's de facto capital, on the Chinese border.

The colonel explained the organization of the transport missions. Each mission usually consists of three or four elephants. A brigade has fifteen to thirty elephants total, but never assigns a large number of elephants to a single convoy, for fear of attracting attention. Occasionally a convoy has to cross a busy road, like the Ledo Road in the Hukawng Valley, and waits until nightfall to slip across, one elephant at a time.

Nan recalled some memorable brigade elephants from his youth. "One of my favorites was Lah Ong, a Kachin name. He'd been donated by a villager near Shadazup, at the entry to the Hukawng Valley, in 1965. He was sensitive to human words and always knew to be extra careful and diligent when he was told that the enemy was approaching. Even with a huge amount of ammunition on his back, he could be incredibly quiet while moving in the forest." My mind drifted to Pak Chan, the elephant who moved ammunition on the Ho Chi Minh Trail. "Lah Ong's prime was when I was brigade leader, in the 1980s, but he stayed with the brigade until he died, in 2009."

The dangers and challenges of the terrain were manifold: fast-moving rivers, steep slopes, landslides, mud, quicksand, mosquitoes, and leeches. "Some of the places we go in the independence army, the things we do, we really couldn't do it without the elephants. There are a lot of villages in the Hukawng Valley area and elsewhere that you can't get to by jeep or even on a dirt bike. And the number of inaccessible places like that only expands during the rainy season."

The brigade elephants carried an impressive array of cargo items: Nan mentioned clean water, tent supplies, rice, clothes, arms and ammunition, forest gems like jade, gold, and amber, medical supplies, papers, appliances such as radios, and construction materials. They gave rides to civilian passengers sometimes, from village to village. Nan remembered an incident where, wishing to be helpful, a brigade had tried to carry a sick villager on elephant-back toward Tanai, the one real town in the whole Hukawng Valley, so this man could find a clinic there. "The rocking back and forth of the elephant made him feel even sicker, so he had to get down," the colonel recalled. "We had to be careful about that—some people get motion sickness on elephants."

Like all the mahouts of the Trans-Patkai and the Burmese logging forests, the mahouts of the KIA brigades release their elephants into the forest each night. I asked Nan if it ever worried him, watching the brigade's logistical lifeline wander off into the jungle every evening. "What if an elephant ran away? Couldn't the brigade become stranded?"

The brigade mahouts tend to be more concerned about thieves than runaways, he explained. To discourage elephant thefts, the soldiers mark the elephants' ears with a small hole, or with a star on their rump. "But our elephants aren't so hard to track in the morning. They wear a long chain and a bell"—like those at the government logging camps. "I remember that sometimes, when we knew the Tatmadaw was nearby, we'd stuff the bells with mud and leaves to silence them. But"—he leaned back in his chair, holding his tea—

"at night it would sometimes happen that a wild herd would cross paths with our route. This is what really created the problems with losing elephants. Our elephants would follow the wild ones, in search of a mate. But even this wasn't the main problem, because they'd always come back. If they tried to join the wild herd, the herd would reject them." The bigger issue, he explained, was that the brigade's males would start fights with the wild males. "My mahouts' feeling was that it's good to let the males fight a little bit, because otherwise our own males would take out their aggression on us. But if the fight became too intense, we had to intervene."

Staying with the theme of mating, Nan turned to the issue of pregnancies. These could be inconvenient, he explained, because "a female who is well into her pregnancy can't do the brigade work." If she was a KIA elephant, she would go to the KIA's elephant camps in the forest, where soldier-mahouts would raise the calf. But if she was an elephant lent to the brigade by a civilian mahout (likely from Hpakant or the Hukawng Valley) for a short-term mission, the calf belonged to the mahout and would receive tutelage in the mahout's own village.

Musth presented another inconvenience. As in the logging camps, the KIA mahouts give extra time off in the forest to adult males showing the "black tears" of hormonal aggression. Brigade mahouts tried to anticipate periods of musth so that males who seemed due were not sent on sensitive transport missions.

I still had many questions for the colonel about KIA transport elephants, but he had office work to attend to. He finished his tea. We agreed to continue the discussion the next day over lunch. But that night the Tatmadaw shelled several Kachin villages in southern Kachin State, not far from where the colonel had grown up. He became busy and had no time to reminisce about elephants. Our follow-up meeting was delayed by several weeks.

THE WAR BETWEEN the Tatmadaw and the KIA is nearly six decades old, by some measures the longest-running conflict in the world today. But the origins of the conflict date to the time of British colonialism in Burma. During the nineteenth century the British won all three Anglo-Burmese wars and brought the populous valley sections of the country under their direct control. They recognized early on, however, that the Kachin Hills would be difficult to seize through military force. In the 1880s, a geographic scout on a British expedition to the Kachin Hills described the road as surrounded on all sides by shadowy mountain fastnesses, full of bandits and intimidating tribespeople. Here, wrote the scout, "any three might make a new Thermopylae"—a reference to the ancient Greek battle where a small group of Spartans reputedly held off a much larger invading army of Persians in a narrow mountain pass. The geographic report noted that many of the people of the Kachin Hills had elephants and appeared to "breed" them.[4] Such phrasing was typical of how British colonists described Burmese forest mahouts' practice of letting their elephants roam at night.

By the early twentieth century, British colonists had established friendly relations with the inhabitants of the Kachin Hills, mainly by ceding local authority and resources to tribal and clan leaders. The colonial government granted partial control of the region's lucrative jade mines to Kachin *duwas*, or chiefs.[5] British military and police had presence up the Irrawaddy to Myitkyina, but beyond this the only British military outpost was at Fort Hertz, in an area that was mostly Hkamti rather than Kachin. The main Kachin areas—the Hukawng Valley and a large hill range at the headwaters of the Irrawaddy called the Triangle—were left firmly in control of the Kachin elites.

Christian missionaries also reinforced friendly Anglo-Kachin relations during the colonial period, though the missionaries were mostly American. In the decades preceding World War II, then, Kachins were redefining themselves around experiences with the missionaries and with the English-speaking world—and against the dominant Burmese culture associated with the lower Irrawaddy Valley.[6] This trend all but ensured that, with the outbreak of war, the loyalties of the Kachin duwas were almost entirely with the British, not with the Japanese. In 1942 the leaders of Burma's major anticolonial, pro-independence faction sided with the Japanese, while the Kachins remained aligned with the British. This Anglo-Kachin coalition was essential for the elephant-mounted escapes at the Chaukan and Pangsau passes. Rungdot and Maggie were both Kachin elephants.

Other groups in Burma were unsettled in their loyalties. The Japanese relied on ethnic Burmese, Karen, and Mon mahouts for their elephant-based operations, which included logging, railroad construction, and the invasion of Manipur. But these mahouts changed sides as soon as the war's tide changed, as was the case in late 1944. Aung San (the father of Aung San Suu Kyi), one of the principal leaders of the Burmese independence movement, was able to shift the movement's allegiances just when the Allies' fortunes were beginning to turn. The switch and its impeccable timing reflected Aung San's political cunning and proved highly effective in positioning his own anticolonial faction as the natural heir to national power.[7]

In 1948 Burma achieved independence from the British Empire. This would prove a pivotal historical moment for Kachins. Some British statesmen proposed to the tribal leaders in Kachin State that the area remain a British protectorate rather than joining independent Burma. However, the new Burmese state's constitution offered good terms to ethnic minorities like the Kachins. In addition to establishing a parliamentary democratic system, the constitution declared that country's seven major ethnic minority areas could hold a referendum within a decade, to determine if they wanted to stay in the Burmese union or not. The excitement of independence was in the air, and just as Aung San had anticipated, the British Empire's panicked retreat out of the country in 1942 had cost it a tremendous amount of legitimacy. The Kachin leaders chose to join the union of Burma.[8]

In many ways, the 1950s were a golden age for Burma. In addition to having democratic elections, it was, during that time, the most economically developed country in all of Southeast Asia. Simmering beneath the surface, though, were intractable tensions, especially between the country's majority-Burmese ruling elites and the ethnic minority areas. Such tensions kept the country's fledgling parliamentary system in a perpetual state of dysfunction. Burma's hopeful but crisis-prone postwar period came to an end in 1962, with a coup and the installation of a military junta. The referendums on ethnic minority independence never took place.[9]

In response to the coup, numerous insurgencies broke out in the country's peripheral highlands, lasting in several cases through the 1980s, and in Kachin State's case to the present day. Several of these insurgencies, especially in the Shan Plateau, one of the world's major poppy-growing areas, were partially financed through the opium trade. Frequently, the central government's counteroperations were financed this way as well. But much of the financing for the Kachin insurgency came from jade. The jade, though mostly borne by truck, is essential for understanding why, to this day, the Kachin militants are so reliant upon their unique convoys of trained elephants.[10]

VIRTUALLY ALL the world's high-quality jade comes from Kachin State's Hpakant mining region, which lies at the headwaters of the Uyu River (and just a few hills over from Mong Cho's elephant camp). Hpakant jade is in great demand in China, where it holds enormous cultural value. Jade has nowhere near the same significance in the West as it does in China, and so for many Westerners, the scale and intensity of Chinese demand for Kachin jade, and the ways this demand shapes the region's geopolitics, may be hard to imagine. A 2015 study, reported on by the BBC and the *Guardian*, estimated that $30 billion worth of black-market jade flows from Kachin State into China annually. The number is astounding. For comparison, Burma's formally reported, non-black-market GDP in 2015 was $60 billion.[11]

The jade mines are geographically immense: mile after mile of once hilly, forested landscape has been turned inside out by great fleets of bulldozers and backhoes. The operation is at the scale of Chinese industrialism in the twenty-first century and stands in disorienting contrast to the traditional agrarian and forest-based livelihoods just a valley over. These mines are mostly owned and controlled by Burma's ruling military circles: generals and former generals and generals' family members and so on. Much of the jade wealth flows to the new Burmese capital of Naypyidaw. Some of the mines, however, are owned by Kachin people, and so a significant amount of wealth also flows toward Myitkyina, which explains why, in spite of the fighting, the city's economy has remained relatively strong.

Between 1994 and 2011, when the Tatmadaw and the KIA observed an official cease-fire, the Burmese and Kachin interests in the Hpakant jade mines coexisted uneasily. During the 2000s, though, the Burmese regime started asserting more control over Kachin State development projects financed by Chinese companies. These included proposed oil and gas pipelines that would link China to the Indian Ocean, partially by crossing through Kachin State. Most consequentially, the projects included a proposal to build a huge dam at the headwaters of the Irrawaddy River, at Myitsone.

This dam, if built, would flood a portion of the Triangle region, displacing a large number of Kachin villages. The Kachin Independence Organization (along with many Burmese people throughout the country) protested the project, and shortly thereafter the cease-fire between the Tatmadaw and the Kachin rebels fell apart.

As the cease-fire disintegrated and the Kachin conflict started anew, the ruling regime's powerful military families grasped for greater control over the lucrative jade mines. In 2014, after a Kachin mine owner found an extremely rare thirty-seven-ton slab of jade, the military temporarily closed off the entire mining valley and placed the Kachin owner in custody.[12] And yet despite such tactics, the central military is in a poor position to control the flow of jade out of these mines—mostly because the Kachin mine owners, unlike the Burmese generals, have elephants.

In 1996 an American specialist in rare gems, Richard Hughes, visited Hpakant and was impressed by the number of times elephants were required to drag his ride, a cargo truck, out of the mud.[13] The main road to Hpakant has been improved since then, but the severity of the monsoon conditions, and the unwillingness or inability of the military government to direct jade wealth toward infrastructure, has preserved the elephants' fundamental usefulness for transporting the gems to their eastern markets. Most of the gem tonnage still travels by truck, but the elephants' ability to dislodge trapped gem trucks and to carry the jade off-road makes them strategically important for embattled Kachin mine owners.[14]

Elephants carry other precious gems as well: amber from the Hukawng Valley and gold panned from Kachin mountain streams. These resources, as well as the elephants themselves, give Kachin elites clout in the region. These elephant-owning elites have unusually strong political and economic incentives against destroying forest cover. Thus, Kachin State remains the most heavily forested region in Burma and one of the most heavily forested zones in all of South and Southeast Asia, despite all these mining operations.

Both "civilian" elephants, like Mong Cho's tusker Neh Ong, and KIA elephants have hauled cargoes of the precious gems. To get from Hpakant to the big jade markets in Laiza, on the Chinese border, Colonel Nan said his convoys would pass by the plain of Indawgyi Lake and then walk through the mountain pass at Japi Bum. They then had to cross a railroad and highway corridor, which required caution and good timing to avoid being seen by a patrol. Then they'd enter the large Kaukkwe forest country, more or less following civilian elephant logging routes. But rather than turning southward toward Shan State, as Mong Cho might do in search of teak, the rebels' elephants would proceed eastward, swimming across the Irrawaddy River around Sinbo, sometimes with huge, valuable jade rocks strapped on their backs. They'd continue through the eastern hills to Laiza, where buyers from all over China, as one journalist has written, have "made the KIA one of the richest rebel armies in Burma."[15]

"IF YOU GO a different way from the jade mines," said Nan—that is, not southeast toward Laiza but northeast—"you can get to our elephant training camps." I had returned to see the colonel once the violence in the south of Kachin State had calmed down earlier in the week. On a coffee table in the common room of the Kachin Independence Organization's Myitkyina office, I had unfolded my map. Nan rattled off a number of village and river names for which the map showed no corresponding labels. Poor Nkumgam, the translator, clearly taxed by the geographic turn the conservation had taken, looked exhausted. As a geographer, I relished the details. The trails the brigade would use were sometimes cut in deliberately mazelike patterns, a device aimed at confusing the Burmese military. Such patterns rendered my map at this particular spot, between the Hpakant jade mines and the KIA elephant training camps, a confusing tangle of pencil scratches.

"From Hpakant we head toward the Hukawng Valley, usually along the Nam Jan Hka. We ford the Mogaung River and approach the Ledo Road. But rather than follow the Ledo Road toward the main part of the Hukawng Valley, we cross the road and go through some other hills toward the uppermost section of the Tanai River."

I knew the upper Tanai was a tiny valley that crept through the Kumon Mountains. The valley was well positioned but also very secluded: the epicenter of the great swirl of mountain ranges formed by the Kumons, the Patkais, and the Kachin Hills. Local Kachins sometimes called the Kumons the Maji Bum, "Mountains of Quiet Hunters." Other locals called them, simply, the "bad mountains."[16] This was heavily forested country, full of gibbons and macaques. The headquarters of the Second Brigade were usually located somewhere in this vicinity, nestled beneath the tree canopy, changing location two or three times per decade.

This small valley was also where the Second Brigade trained its newly caught elephants. Two Western journalists passed through here in the 1980s in separate voyages, both escorted by Kachin soldiers. Each saw the rebels' elephant training camps. Shelby Tucker, an American writer who was being escorted from Kachin State's eastern border west to the Indian frontier, noted at this spot that KIA mahouts, along with one khoonkie elephant, were training a baby. The small elephant was being marched up and down a sandbank, and the elephant trainers were singing lullabies to "allay the baby elephant's fears."[17] Bertil Lintner, a Swedish journalist who became a leading expert on Burma's armed ethnic conflicts, was escorted in the other direction, from India toward China. He had more time to spend with the rebel elephant trainers and kept his notes from the encounter. KIA fandis were mixing the inner part of a banana plant with water and salt—a treat for elephants in training. The fandis were Kachins. One of them explained to Lintner that historically the Kachin people didn't have elephants; they learned their elephant skills from the Hkamti Shans many generations ago. Originally, the Kachin fandi went on, the Kachins caught elephants using the pit method, but as their skills improved, they embraced the superior lasso method, or mela shekar.[18] The camp area was called Tanai Yang, which in Kachin means something like, "Clearing on the Tanai."

During our discussions in 2015, Nan confirmed for me that the militia was still doing elephant training around here, though likely not at the exact same spot. The camp would change locations periodically, not only for security purposes but also because the camp's swidden garden clearings needed to shift every few years.[19] In 2018, the KIA appeared to withdraw from the vicinity, due to a Tatmadaw assault there.[20]

During my travels in Kachin State, I happened upon a map showing two types of armed bases in the Hukawng Valley: the rebels' and the government's. The rebels' bases follow a roadless chain perpendicular to the Ledo Road, the Hukawng Valley's only thoroughfare for motor traffic. Some of the bases on this chain could possibly be linked by riverboat, but many of them would have to be linked by porters walking on foot—or by convoys of elephants. By contrast, the Tatmadaw's bases were all on the Ledo Road, linked by jeep or by truck.[21] This road is, of course, the one built by the Allied forces during World War II, to link British Assam with the Chinese resistance armies by way of the Pangsau Pass. After the war, the road became dilapidated, an ugly scar of mud, gravel, and tar slicing across the forestlands of the Hukawng Valley. The military's control of the road has enabled it to award lucrative sugar plantation contracts along the corridor. These plantations erase forest cover and spill into an area that, at least on paper, is supposed to be the Hukawng Valley Tiger Reserve.[22]

The experience of another journalist, an Indian, Rajeev Bhattacharyya, indicates where many of the KIA's elephant trainers have been catching their elephants in recent years. In 2011 Bhattacharyya was engaged in an intensive months-long project to meet with and interview the leader of a different rebel militia, the National Socialist Council of Nagaland. Though Nagaland is in India rather than in Burma, there's a substantial Naga population in the Burmese Patkais, between Homalin and Pangsau Pass. This Naga area is claimed, and mostly controlled, by Naga militants, who refer to the area as "Eastern Nagaland." Eastern Nagaland is very close to the KIA's westernmost territories. They meet in the isolated Taro Plain.

Escorted by Naga rebel soldiers, Bhattacharyya had spent five or six weeks hiking from India into Eastern Nagaland, hoping to meet with the Naga militants' head commander. One day in late December, while walking along the mountain trail, he and the Naga soldiers had to step aside for a "convoy of five elephants steered by olive-clad Kachin Independence Army mahouts." The men were chopping tree branches to clear the path ahead of them. Bhattacharyya noted that "the mid-sized elephants seemed suited to walking the narrow hill trails." These were the KIA's fandis, its elephant catchers. The Kachin and Naga militants had a friendly rapport, and the two groups shared a meal. "This place is swarming with elephants," one of the Kachins explained to the Indian journalist as they ate. The two rebel groups had an arrangement: the Kachin fandis were permitted to catch elephants in this area but had to split their haul with the Naga militia.[23]

Civilian fandis told me the same thing: that this particular stretch of the mountains has been a very good spot, in recent years, for catching wild elephants. The area is lush with bamboo, watering holes, and salt springs. Also, opium production in the area is quite lucrative, which tends to direct locals away from hunting and ivory poaching.[24]

In 1987 Bertil Lintner followed the route from this elephant-catching zone back toward the KIA elephant-training camps. He entered Burma through Eastern Nagaland with his wife, a Shan reporter named Hseng Noung, and their newborn baby, Ee Ying. They were traveling with a KIA escort. The militia leadership hoped that the journalists' trek across the region would make the Kachins' struggle better known to the outside world. The following year Shelby Tucker found himself with a similar escort, for largely the same reason.

On the way from the Eastern Nagaland Patkais to the upper Tanai, Lintner and his party followed a mountain stream called the Taka, which merges with the upper Chindwin River at the Taro Plain.[25] British and American forces retaking Burma in 1943 noted that Taro "is like a small closet adjacent to the long narrow room of the Hukawng and the Mogaung valleys. He who wishes to enter the long narrow room from its northern door must be sure no one is lurking in the closet."[26]

A dugout canoe was fetched for Lintner's party, and they drifted downstream, passing by rare species of waterfowl. They disembarked at Wan Phalang, a small Lisu village on the riverbank that appeared to survive by trading with gold panners in the nearby hills. The party then proceeded on foot (they had no elephants at this stage) across an especially difficult hill range, "a vast natural labyrinth of dense jungle streams and sharp ridges."[27] They slept in abandoned gold panners' huts. Partway through the trek across these hills, Lintner's health declined due to blood poisoning. The culprit was leeches. Wading across the streams in the hill region had exposed his legs to constant attack. A leech bite was becoming infected. Seeing his health worsen, the Kachin escorts determined that the party needed an elephant, to keep him out of the water.[28]

Tucker, though never injured like Lintner, faced similar problems with leeches in the forests of this region. In a single day, he later recalled, he had to remove 241 leeches. A friend traveling with Tucker, a Swede named Mats, found a leech in his nostril. Mats developed a blood poisoning ailment similar to Lintner's and was in similarly poor condition by the time he and Tucker limped into India.[29] Though passengers on elephant-back in these hills are not impervious to leeches (some of which drop from the trees), riding elephants does significantly reduce the severity of the problem and minimizes the likelihood of infection from trail-kicked dust.[30]

The KIA's elephant came to retrieve the injured Lintner at a riverside area where the rebels had set up a large secret fishing camp. Fish were caught from the river and then dried out and sold to miners in Hpakant, one valley over. Lintner marveled at the scale of the operation, just one among many covert industries the Kachin independence fighters had established under the cover of the forest canopy. From here the party proceeded toward Tanai Yang, following the narrow gorge of the secluded upper Tanai, where "hundreds of fish swirled around my mount's massive legs," Lintner recalled. At Tanai Yang, Lintner's foot finally began to heal.[31]

ONE ELDERLY Kachin mahout told me about another important branch of this clandestine network, from the area around Tanai Yang into India, by way of the Chaukan Pass. The elephant convoys retrieve supplies from a mountain hamlet on the Indian side of the mountainous border. This had been occurring, the mahout said, for many years, and it was still occurring during the period I was conducting my research.

I knew of this remote hamlet nestled in the Indian Patkais. Just a few thousand people lived there, mostly Lisus, growing dry rice and vegetables for subsistence, and cardamoms and ginger for cash. It was extremely isolated, with no all-year road or airfield. The Indian military did an occasional airdrop. A dirt jeep trail that went toward the village was unusable for many months due to rain and mud. For parts of the year, the only way to reach this remote outpost was on the back of an elephant. Indian mahouts from Miao brought regular supplies there this way: bags of rice, farm appliances, concrete blocks, iron rods, corrugated iron sheets, and so on.

But this Kachin mahout was telling me about transport elephants getting there from the other direction: from Burma. It was raining hard as we spoke together inside a cabin. His son, a schoolteacher, was there to translate. The old mahout said that the Chaukan Pass was still the main passageway across the border for riders of elephants—though other, even more isolated passes could be used as well. The Chaukan was especially useful to the Kachin soldiers during the wet summer months. When the rain came, leeches made the terrain totally inhospitable to foot patrols. Riding on pachyderms with thick-skinned, leech-resistant legs, the KIA mahouts dominated the Chaukan environs during monsoon time. As thunder echoed above, the mahout, his son, and I discussed the "great game" of Trans-Patkai geopolitics, and the organization (whose identity I've chosen to keep anonymous) that, according to the mahout, was bringing supplies to the elephant-borne rebels.[32]

Shelby Tucker gives us a good sense of what it must be like for the KIA's elephant brigade to approach this outpost along the difficult Chaukan paths. Tucker's elephant escort in 1989 brought him in this direction by following the Tawang Hka watercourse. "With their trunks," Tucker wrote of the elephants along the Tawang Hka, "they explored the always-tricky bottom before committing themselves, and whenever need arose they were superb swimmers."[33] But Tucker's elephant-mounted party didn't actually cross into India. He and his companion Mats parted ways with the Kachin soldiers prior to reaching the Indian border, and the two proceeded the rest of the way on foot. They made use, of course, of that same mountain pass, Chaukan, through which the railway party had fled in

1942, to be rescued by Rungdot and many other elephants in the foothills above Assam.

The history of elephant-mounted movements through the Chaukan Pass stretches even farther back in time. Centuries ago elephant convoys through the Chaukan linked the Hkamti Long kingdom of the Putao Plain in northern Burma with fledgling areas of Hkamti settlement along the Brahmaputra Valley in India.[34] Likely, the Hkamti flight from far northern Burma during the Kachin invasions there was aided by elephants through the same passage, as well as through the Pangsau Pass. For anyone without elephants, the pass was an unforgiving upland barrier. But for people with elephants, it was an intercultural bridge, escape hatch, smugglers' gate, and means of militant revolt, all rolled into one.

AN EASTERN ARC of the KIA's convoy network branches off from the training camps on the upper Tanai and crosses the Kumon range at Daru Pass.[35] Here in the summer months, air blowing from the Himalayas brings in icy mists, which patter fine crystalline hail against tents in the early morning. The route passes by swidden farms lined with coxcomb flowers. From these small hill farms, which shift in location every few years, people grow dry rice, maize, ginger, chilis, gourds, taro, coarse peas, mint, lemongrass, and other mountain-friendly crops. There are jungle deer here, mountain ox, and wild pigs. These animals are sometimes hunted, the meat then left to dry out on pikes in the sun or cooked over slow fires. Mixed with herbs and wild mushrooms, the hill food of the Kumon range can be mind-expanding for visitors.

Beyond the Kumons is the Triangle, and here the convoys pass over the two main feeder streams to the Irrawaddy: the Mali Hka and the N'mai Hka. The convoys then bend their way southward toward China, exiting the range of wild elephants, who find these eastern mountains along the border too high and cold. The convoy route continues along the international border, where the mahouts might cross paths with muleteers from Yunnan.[36] Hugging the frontier, the convoy reaches Laiza.

"So the routes make a kind of circle," I remarked.

Nan considered. "That's partly true, but it's misleading, because really the elephants can go anywhere, and the whole point of them is that the Burmese military can't predict where they'll be or where they'll go. A route might be used once and then never again." Even the mountain passes, he further explained, were not "single point" locations where the Tatmadaw could simply crouch and wait for a KIA convoy to approach. The passes were really fields of many different possible trails across the broad "saddle" of a mountain range. The trails could be many miles apart, separated by especially difficult and isolated jungle terrain. Furthermore, the annual monsoon storms tended to obliterate the previous year's configuration—as the railway party had discovered to its dismay when crossing through the Chaukan Pass in 1942.

Certainly, this wasn't a transport circle like Chicago's Loop or London's M25 highway. But it was, perhaps, a symbolic circle: a belt enveloping the official Kachin capital at Myitkyina, with branches going toward India, and an eastern terminus at the Kachin "alternative" capital, Laiza, with its jade markets serving buyers from China. During these interviews, Nan had been marking routes with his pencil on my map. The paper now showed a circular pattern. Beneath the penciled-in routes, the original published ink of the map showed a transportation infrastructure as conventionally conceived by a modern state: lines symbolizing the routes of railroads, highways, and country roads. Some of these inked-in lines were, I knew from personal experience, mere projection: the highways were sometimes just dirt tracks, and the back roads might not even be footpaths. But most of the inked routes referred to permanent thoroughfares that were used by motor vehicles for most of the year.

By contrast, the penciled lines, composing a ringlike shape, marked the projection of an alternative kind of power, hovering in the background of the "hard" network of railroads and highways. This alternative was hidden in the shadows of the jungle and rarely acknowledged on maps or in writing. And yet it connected the world's two most populous nations—India in the west and China in the east—and commanded the movement of significant resources: gems, arms, and timber. The penciled lines conveyed the possibility of clandestine connections between forest communities, and of such secret journalistic tours as those taken by Lintner and Tucker. Motor equipment and road-bound patrols attempting to follow the brigades found themselves blocked by spiraling forces of land, water, and air: the vortex of churning plates and jagged topography where the Patkais crash into the Himalayas; or the swirling veil of clouds and rainfall, which stir a muddy rebellion against the advance of the Ledo Road.

WHY DOESN'T the Tatmadaw use elephants? The Burmese state has, by far, the world's most sophisticated bureaucratic relationship with work elephants, employing thousands in the government-managed teak industry. Why not send some of those elephants to the Kachin Hills to do patrol work? Then the central military's patrols would no longer be confined to the region's sparse network of roads.

The main obstacle, for the Tatmadaw, is the practice of the morning elephant fetch. It's impossible for an outside power to set up local elephant patrols without having strong loyalties from a local group of mahouts . If the military brought in outside mahouts (say, ethnic Burmese or Karens from the south), they would have to fetch elephants every morning in unfamiliar, hostile forest terrain. If, on the other hand, the military attempted to coerce local mahouts into assisting in patrol work, the mahouts might use the morning fetch as an opportunity to desert. In either scenario, the government patrol would risk winding up stranded in the forest. Nor could the military solve the problem by simply keeping the elephants chained up at night, cutting the morning fetch out of the patrol scenario altogether. The elephants' daily feeding requirements are just too large: the soldiers on the patrol would have to work day and night to gather the hundreds of pounds of fodder per elephant.

In theory, local political, ethnolinguistic, or religious wedges could emerge among the Kachin Hill mahouts, which could become, at some future stage, substantial enough for the Tatmadaw to exploit. The Hkamti mahouts, who as Nan pointed out have drifted away from the KIA in recent years, are generally Buddhist, while the Kachins are generally Christian. But the Hkamti-Kachin relationship is intricate and complex: the two groups' histories are interwoven in ways that the present-day religious divide does not at all capture or reflect. At any rate, the Hkamti mahouts seem to want nothing to do with the central military, preferring to stick to "civilian" elephant work.

Other internal differences exist as well, such as language, but none of these differences has proven meaningful enough for the central military to manipulate for the purpose of creating its own local elephant corps. For the foreseeable future, then, the Kachin Independence Organization will likely remain the world's only governing body with an elephant-based system of transportation. As the last entity of its kind, the Kachin system presents a model for governments, and quasi-governments, throughout South and Southeast Asia that are looking for ways to incorporate elephants into human-inhabited landscapes. If elephants are to thrive by doing forest work that does not destroy forest cover, the insights of the KIA's elephant brigades will prove invaluable. Kachin mahouts and brigade leaders like Nan offer rare, irreplaceable knowledge about the elephants' capabilities and limits. During the rest of this century, the region's violence will hopefully fade. But usefulness of the elephants, for linking communities separated by jungle and monsoon conditions, need not fade as well.

Chapter 9

FLOOD RELIEF
ELEPHANT

I'LL SKETCH OUT ONE HOPEFUL SCENARIO FOR THE ASIAN elephants' future. This scenario begins, though, with a premise that is perhaps *not* so hopeful: that the species' future cannot be secured through tourism or through wildlife preserves. This grim assumption merits some explanation.

For elephant tourism parks to generate revenue, a tourist infrastructure has to be in place: roads, hotels, restaurants, and so on. All this development creates a significant pressure on forests. In 2015 I visited an elephant park designed for tourists in North Sumatra. From the point of view of the elephants, the conditions there were excellent. The park was located deep in the forest. Near the elephants' large leafy stockade flowed a wide, fast-moving river that the elephants happily walked along every day, both for exercise and to give tourists spectacular forest rides. But this park was a five-hour drive from the nearest city—a mostly industrial metropolis with very little tourist appeal of its own—along poor roads that passed by mile after mile of unattractive palm plantations. The park's issue wasn't so much its remoteness, perhaps, as its remoteness from other tourist sites. And due to its isolation, it was not drawing a sufficient number of visitors to expand its operation beyond a mere ten elephants.

An elephant park I visited in Thailand exemplified the opposite problem. Here the park was conveniently set in a city amid other key tourist attractions, which included museums, restaurants, markets, and ancient ruins. The city had a large railroad station and a major bus hub, with convenient connections to Bangkok. It was easy for visitors to get to the elephants, and the elephant park drew many people. The park was making plenty of money and was able to afford several dozen elephants. With more space, it could have had many more—but there was no forest. The same forces and conditions that had made these elephants accessible to tourists, and therefore so profitable, had negated virtually all this particular region's forestlands, leaving the elephants with nowhere to roam, nowhere to forage for fresh leaves and shrubs, and no wild herds with which to mate. The elephants mostly ate dried fodder, brought to them in barns: the same dietary situation as elephants living in zoos.

Some elephant tourism parks do manage to be a kind of "best of both worlds," drawing a substantial number of tourists to remote forest locations. A park located outside Chiang Mai, in northern Thailand, is a standard-setting example. But such parks aren't just rare—they *have* to be rare. It is the rarity of the experience that makes tourists willing to spend large amounts of time and money to get to such locales. And this is probably the most fundamental limitation of elephant tourism as a strategy of elephant conservation: the more elephants are in such parks, the smaller the revenue-generating capacity of each individual elephant becomes. Where "best of both worlds" parks exist, they are best understood as a reflection of the current rarity of elephants rather than as models for other parks—let alone as a basis for a future re-expansion of the species.

Elephant wildlife preserves funded primarily through the altruism of taxpayers and donors, rather than through tourism revenues, present a somewhat different, though comparable, set of problems.

Such wildlife preserves have been most successful in South India, which has a quarter of the world's remaining Asian elephant population but very little remaining tradition of training and utilizing elephants for work. Most of this region's elephants live in wildlife preserves—but the preserves exist in large part because the region as a whole has been intensively developed. Large tax revenues from both urban and agricultural economies, combined with a deeper aristocratic tradition, in India, of protecting elephant forests from encroaching farmlands, have created the economic and institutional resources necessary to sustain these preserves.

But the preserves are surrounded on all sides by deforested land and cannot possibly be expanded. The limitation of these wildlife preserves is the same as for well-managed elephant tourist parks. The preserves' existence, and size, reflects the extent to which local forces of deforestation proved willing to leave a few pockets of forest—of rareness—behind. Creating a comparable system of preserves in, say, the Trans-Patkai region would almost certainly require intensified urban and agricultural development, to create a taxpayer base willing to support the new parklands. Paradoxically, formal forest preservation would require deforestation.

By contrast, elephant-based logging is able to pay for the elephant caretakers' troubles (that is, the income of the mahouts) without depending upon an expansion of tourist infrastructure, or on adjacent urban and agricultural activities. Nor does it depend upon the elephants' rareness. Rather, the funding comes from economic activities that give the elephants periods of freedom in the forest. Of course, the logging industry requires periodic destruction of forestlands, but unlike urban development and irrigated mass-agriculture, logging—at least when well managed—does not replace forestlands permanently. Generally, harvested areas are left alone for many decades, to permit new saplings to take root and mature.

Nonetheless, an industry predicated on the destruction of scarce forestlands offers limited possibilities for conservation. Furthermore, as all-weather road networks proliferate, and as the global timber industry gradually converges around motorized methods, the logging industries of Burma and northeastern India may well abandon the timber-skidding elephant altogether.

BUT THERE IS, we know, another vital use for elephants: for transportation across flooded areas. We know this from following Burmay-Moti and Pradip across the Sissiri River near the village of Dambuk, observing the pair's provision of a monsoon-time "ferry" service for local travelers. We know it from following elephants like Maggie and Rungdot across many swollen mountain river courses in May and June 1942. We traced the path of the Kachin rebels' elephants across the Irrawaddy River and through forests where the roads were washed over.

In some areas, all-weather roads will make elephants redundant. In recent years, the Indian government has been building an all-weather highway to link the mountain valleys of Arunachal Pradesh, a project that will open many new areas to urban and agricultural development. But even when this project is completed, there will still be large swaths of the state that will be hard to reach during monsoon. The Indian government might be able to "all-weatherize" one or even several road corridors—but to do so with *every* road, in one of the most rain- and flood-prone areas on the planet, would be a Herculean feat. Thoroughfares would have to be carefully reengineered to permit the runoff of huge amounts of rainfall, elevated above seasonal high-water marks, and buttressed against mudslides. Public works at this scale would be unlike anything currently found in rural and agricultural areas of far wealthier countries than India.[1] As for the Burmese side of the Patkai

Mountains, roads here are still primitive compared with India. It appears elephants will remain essential to travelers in much of the Trans-Patkai during monsoon.

It should be stressed, here, that some of these communities that become especially isolated during the monsoon flooding do also have other means of flood-time transport at their disposal. In addition to mahouts and their elephants, the Arunachali village of Dambuk has a number of extremely skilled raftsmen, most of them ethnic Adis. On my last day in that remote village, during the monsoon season of 2017, both rivers surrounding the Dambuk environs—the Sissiri and Dibang—flooded. I could not get hold of a local mahout to get me across the water back to the "mainland." (I had a flight to catch in Dibrugarh.) The village's taxi service, which coordinates with the mahouts, had learned of a landslide on the Pasighat highway, meaning that with or without the elephant crossing, the trek to Pasighat would still be extremely slow going. The taxi men had determined to wait until later in the week to try to organize transport across the flooding Sissiri. With no fording work to do, the mahouts had all taken their elephants into the forest for the day, for logging or hunting.

I appeared to be trapped. But then some local boatmen offered to take me across the Dibang in their rubber whitewater raft. It was well past the point in the season when rafting would be considered the safe, normal way across. But these Adi boatmen had some experience racing in national whitewater rafting competitions. They were eager to show off their skills.

That crossing was far more dangerous than the elephant ride I'd been expecting. First we rode for twenty minutes on a tractor, with the rubber raft in tow, across a flooding swamp to the river's edge. Then we bushwhacked sharp thistles and creepers out of our way. Then came the frightening boat ride itself, down and across four white-capped river channels that were heaving with water runoff from the mountains. The channels were broken up by rocky shoals, where we portaged with the raft on our shoulders. It was pouring rain, and wave after wave splashed into the little vessel. By the end of this ordeal, which took about an hour overall, my luggage was soaked through. Nonetheless, the Adi boatmen had proved their mettle.

While spending time in Dambuk, I noted that the village also has a helicopter landing pad. It is generally used only by VIPs—elites from Itanagar, Arunachal Pradesh's capital city. But a number of people in Dambuk remarked to me that, really, during bad rainstorms, a helicopter is the most dangerous transport option of all. Riding an elephant or rubber raft is safer than navigating midair in conditions of high winds and poor visibility. In general, Dambuk residents preferred to get across by elephant.

Eastern Arunachal Pradesh has a history of employing elephants not just for routine fords during the rainy season, as at Dambuk's Sissiri crossing, but also during emergencies. In the early 1950s, Sadiya, the district capital for the Lohit and Dihing valleys, was destroyed by a huge earthquake and subsequent flooding. The earthquake, which measured 8.6 on the Richter scale, was so severe that it caused the Lohit River to shift in its course following the earthquake, deluging the town.[2] During the floods, the town's many elephants, which numbered in the hundreds, carried people and possessions out of the worst-affected areas and toward safety. The town ultimately washed away, replaced by the new course of the great river. In the years afterward, the former Sadiya elephants assisted in the construction of new district capital at Tezu, where the Mithong logging elephant Air Singh was born.[3]

A settlement dating to medieval times, Sadiya had been known as a "city of elephants." British colonists arriving there in the nineteenth century noted the festivals at Sadiya, where the local Hkamti and Kachin duwas would parade on elephant-back.[4] During the

1940s, the well-off tribal families in the town each had several elephants. Sadiya's immediate hinterlands were heavily forested, so elephants would roam these nearby forests at night and do transport work during the day. Logging was secondary, providing only seasonal income. Today the situation in the region is the inverse.[5]

Massive rural floods at the scale of the Sadiya disaster still occur throughout South and Southeast Asia, brought about by earthquakes, landslides, and abnormal monsoon rains. A shattered glacial ice-dam can swamp a valley, especially one with diminished ground absorbance due to deforestation. A large force of elephants could provide logistical relief during such crises. But one has to go all the way back to that Sadiya flood for the last time hundreds of elephants were systematically utilized in a large rescue and relief operation.

The Burmese government, despite its thousands of highly skilled elephants, does not mobilize its logging elephants into flooded rural areas. At most, the elephants might help move supplies in and out of the logging villages during monsoon, when main access roads become flooded (a constant occurrence). A logging village with fifty or sixty elephants might send just three or four elephants for this relatively minor task, leaving the remainder in the village area to drag timber for the day. Timber and forestry officials could send extra elephants to bring needed supplies to neighboring villages full of farmers and hunters who are also stranded by the monsoon storms. Currently, they don't. The KIA does send elephant brigades to help cut-off communities, but their monsoon-time logistical operations are obviously complicated by warfare with the Tatmadaw.

But what if countries developed official departments of flood-time logistics that were organized around the abilities of elephants? Such bureaucratic organizations, if developed, could employ large crews of trained elephants and mahouts, perhaps operating in the mode of the Kachin elephant convoys, or of lost elephant "hubs" like Sadiya. This would connect the elephants with the growing human need to live with large flooding events, while also keeping the work elephants located in the forest for much of the year.

The idea has its limits, to be sure, not least of which is that though elephants are dexterous and mobile in flooded areas unreachable by jeeps or boats, the composition of the floodwaters in certain areas can be hazardous to their welfare. This would be, unfortunately, especially true in most urban areas, where floodwaters often become intermixed with sewage, chemical pollutants, and dangerous debris. During flooding in Ayutthaya, Thailand, in 2011, elephants from a nearby major elephant park waded through flooded urban neighborhoods to high ground, carrying their mahouts and sometimes passengers or salvaged possessions. Photographs show them navigating skillfully along streets submerged in two or three feet of water—too deep for wheeled vehicles but too shallow for boats. But the water was brown with pollutants and full of metal debris, a clear hazard for the elephants.[6]

An even more dramatic example of elephants helping in flooded areas occurred in Banda Aceh, at the northern tip of the Indonesian island of Sumatra, in late 2004 and early 2005. This city, the one-time capital of the Aceh Sultanate and the current provincial capital of Sumatra's Aceh Province, was the major city closest to the epicenter of the 2004 Indian Ocean earthquake and tsunami, which killed a quarter-million people worldwide. In Banda Aceh the tsunami wave reached forty feet in height. A quarter of the city's population was killed.[7]

Banda Aceh's horrific destruction and the subsequent local, national, and international efforts at rebuilding the city is a vast and multifaceted story of suffering and resolve. The story of the eight elephants who were brought from the Acehnese forests to help in the disaster relief effort is just a small part of that larger story, but it ought to be told, and more widely known, not least because of how it showcases elephants' abilities and limitations during a massive human emergency. Early in my research, I knew about Banda Aceh's "tsunami elephants" only from a few newspaper articles from January 2005, which provided very little useful information.[8] I went to the city in 2015 to learn more from elephant experts there who were familiar with the episode.

The city was in far better shape than I expected. Many of its flooded areas had been rebuilt, and some of the worst-hit districts were left (for the time being) as development-free wetlands. Banda Aceh can be scenic, especially along its river harbor, which is lined by fine wooden fishing boats painted in bright reds and blues. Scents of fish and crab fill the air, and mallets clatter as boat hulls are finished or repaired. I wound up spending a long afternoon here speaking with a forest official, Wahdi Azmi, and an elephant veterinarian, Chris Stremmer, an immigrant from Germany. The three of us chatted in Wahdi's office, drinking Acehnese coffee and snacking on fried sundries.

A few days after the tsunami struck, one of the Acehnese elephant conservation officials, who had been stranded in the uplands during the flood, returned to the city to find that his home had washed away. He'd lost his wife and one of his children. This official was very close with his mahouts, many of whom had families who lived in the same destroyed residential neighborhood. Many of the mahouts had lost loved ones as well. The official and his mahouts went back to their elephant camp in the uplands and rounded up the best work elephants they had there, eight in all, to come back with them to the wreckage in Banda Aceh.[9]

Mostly the elephants hauled debris out of the way: torn-up beams from destroyed homes, smashed cars and motorcycles, twisted sheets of metal, and so on. With the debris removed, tsunami survivors could access the areas where their homes had once stood, to recover possessions or possibly locate the bodies of loved ones. The elephants were in great demand: wheeled relief vehicles couldn't access these areas, at least not during the initial weeks after the catastrophe. Photographs of the tsunami elephants taken by fascinated journalists convey the unique usefulness of the elephants in this ruined landscape. Everywhere the ground was covered in mud and rife with debris. Even a tank would have become bogged down, but the elephants were mobile.

Chris Stremmer arrived in the area shortly after the disaster, and as a veterinarian, he was alarmed at the condition of the elephants. Their feet and trunks were getting cut from sharp metal objects or broken glass or huge splinters of wood that were everywhere. The cuts were getting infected from the dirt and grime in the standing floodwater. The elephants also weren't receiving adequate nutrition, since they were no longer in the forest, and they weren't getting anywhere near enough fresh drinking water. Nonetheless, Chris recognized that for many of the people at the scene, who'd undergone such a terrible trauma, the presence of the elephants was both practically and emotionally significant. Despite his qualms about this use of the elephants, Chris decided to help over the subsequent months, mending the elephants' wounds, treating their infections, and organizing a steady supply of nutrients and fresh water from the major relief agencies camped nearby.

"It was fucking hard work," he remembered, "both for the elephants and for the mahouts. It was basically a war zone, and the elephants were in an area where elephants should not be." But the official who brought the elephants to the city was "just trying to *do* something, during such an awful time." The official (whom both Wahdi and Chris opted not to name) had started out as a mahout and wanted his mahouts and elephants near him for companionship. And the mahouts all wanted to be at the site of their former homes, where they'd last seen their family members. The mahouts kept themselves busy, and two and a half months later, all eight elephants returned to the Acehnese forest, all in reasonably good health. "It sounds absurd, I know," Chris remarked, "but for me it was actually a *good* time. I started building a close relationship with the mahouts and the elephants . . . and it was really full-dive-in, yeah? The kind of work I like to do."

Wahdi joined in the conversation and talked about the unusual history of elephant domestication in Sumatra. I knew some of this history from books and articles. Historically, Sumatra had domesticated elephants for only two or three centuries, during the period of the precolonial Aceh Sultanate. Under this regime, elephants were caught from the Sumatran forest and trained for logging, transport, parades, and occasionally warfare. In Java too, people had caught and trained elephants prior to the colonial period, but elephants disappeared from Java's dwindling forest interior during the eighteenth century (whereas elephants persisted on the more heavily forested island of Sumatra).

After the Sultanate period in Sumatra came Dutch colonial rule, during the nineteenth and early twentieth centuries. Elephant capture and taming in Sumatra ceased, partly because the Dutch, unlike the British in India and Burma, were uninterested in investing in elephant-centered methods of extracting forest resources.[10] However, the speed with which elephant culture disappeared from Sumatra also indicates that elephant domestication here, while it existed, had been organized primarily by the island's most powerful rulers, the Acehnese sultans. Once these figures were deposed or replaced by Dutch governors, there were no indigenous social structures to keep the local traditions of elephant domestication in place. By contrast, on the Asian mainland, elephant domestication was organized both by powerful kings and also by forest peoples and hill tribes. So even when local kings and emperors fell, traditions of elephant capture and domestication were sustained by groups on the margins of power, like the Hkamtis and the Morans.

All of Sumatra's domesticated elephants were released back into the forest and joined wild herds there, and from the early nineteenth through the late twentieth century, Sumatra's elephant population was entirely wild. This wild population, though, clashed with farmers who were expanding into Sumatra's interior. The problem became pronounced during the 1950s and 1960s, as the post-independence Indonesian government encouraged large migrations of Javanese to Sumatra, to relieve the island of Java of its long-standing overcrowding problems. In Sumatra, the Javanese primarily engaged in agricultural work. In turn, conflicts between farmers and wild elephants became more frequent, as elephants wandered through farmers' crops and farmers sometimes responded by killing the elephants.

During the 1980s, the Indonesian government tried a new strategy for reducing these farmer-elephant conflicts: turn the wild elephants, or at least a large number of them, into trained work elephants, whose movements could then be controlled. The Indonesian forestry department had in mind something like the Burmese forestry model, where elephants would be captured and trained to do logging work, which in turn would help pay for expanded forest and elephant conservation efforts. The forestry department hired mahouts from Thailand to teach locals how to capture and train elephants.[11] Given that the forestry model the Indonesian officials had in mind was the Burmese one, it likely would have been better to bring in Burmese mahouts, but Burma's political isolation during that period made this difficult.

Several hundred of Sumatra's three to four thousand elephants were captured this way, then sent to a network of new conservation camps to engage in logging. But the logging camps never proved especially profitable, as Sumatran lumber was susceptible to global market forces: economic protections were lacking, and the types of timber that proliferate in the Sumatran forests were relatively widely available. In the 1990s, forestry officials repurposed many of the caught elephants for tourism, either by building new elephant parks in the Sumatran forest or, in many cases, by sending caught elephants to the island of Bali, which has a higher concentration of tourists than anywhere in Sumatra. But this strategy also had limits. The camps in Bali generated plenty of revenue but didn't place elephants near sufficient forestlands. The camps in Sumatra had ample forestlands but couldn't draw enough tourists.

Perceiving the weaknesses of both the logging and the tourism strategies, Wahdi Azri and other officials initiated a third utilization for the caught elephants: for "patrol" work. Wahdi explained the concept: "In many areas the issue with farmer-elephant conflicts is that there's no 'buffer' between the two, and the farmer communities only see elephants as a negative in their lives. To address this issue, we move along the forest periphery with our patrol elephants, and when we hear of a farmer-elephant conflict, where a wild elephant has wandered onto a farmer's land, we go to that area and pressure the wild elephant back toward the forest. Sometimes we need to use sound cannons to do this, but usually what happens is that the moment the wild elephant sees our patrol elephants, it understands it has to go back in the other direction, toward the forest."

He continued: "The farming communities get used to the patrols and start to see them as a benefit to the community. Sometimes they get very attached to the patrol elephants, which is a completely different cultural mentality than a decade ago, when most local people just saw elephants as a nuisance."

"It happened recently," Chris cut in, "that a community in South Sumatra learned that their favorite patrol elephant was being sent to another area, to a park. And they became so enraged that they threatened to burn the park headquarters down if they didn't get their elephant back!" The German grinned.

Wahdi seemed a bit embarrassed by the story but clearly appreciated its implications. "The main problem with how the elephant domestication program was designed here in the 1980s and 1990s," he went on, "was that for the forest officials, it wasn't a 'trained work elephant' that had value. No, it was a 'caught elephant' that had value: the value of no longer presenting a nuisance to the farmers." This meant that this earlier generation of forestry officials had never entirely thought through the question of what to do with the elephants once they were caught. "The legacy of that mindset is still very much in the forestry department today," Wahdi explained. The patrols had much potential as a model, but they couldn't give all of Sumatra's caught elephants, of which there were many hundreds, something to do. "And if they don't have something to do, they don't receive good care," he added. Chris nodded in agreement.

I knew there was another major restraint in Sumatra's young, or "relaunched," tradition of elephant capture and mahoutship: in Sumatra they do not let their trained elephants roam the forest at night. That practice, so key to the elephant cultures in Burma and northeastern India, would require people who were willing to spend a large portion of their lives in the forest—and a government, or some other funding source, willing to pay for that kind of commitment. This limits the elephants' usefulness for logging and closes off the use of elephants for transportation during the monsoon season, a task which Sumatra's trained elephants don't do at all.

Hearing about these challenges within Sumatra's elephant conservation programs, I wondered whether the official who had brought the elephants to Banda Aceh after the tsunami was aware of this ongoing problem, of finding a "use" for the caught Sumatran elephants. Perhaps, in some way, he was trying to demonstrate a value that his fellow officials had not yet perceived: the elephants' value during floods. Banda Aceh was likely not the best place to demonstrate that worth, due to the dangerous conditions left in the tsunami's wake. But Banda Aceh wasn't the only tsunami-hit area where elephants aided relief efforts. In southern Thailand, elephants from some tourist parks were brought into destroyed sections of a beach area called Khao Lak. There the working conditions were better for the elephants than in Banda Aceh, as the scale of the wreckage was not as severe.[12]

THE REAL LIMITATION in deploying elephants for relief work in places like Banda Aceh is not so much that these places are cities as that, infrastructurally, they are not designed to flood "cleanly"— that is, to keep floodwaters unpolluted as they surge in. To some extent, this is a problem in all flood-prone cities. But it's far more severe in cities, which, due to poverty or age, can't easily engineer a hydraulic infrastructure that quarantines the sewage system during a flooding event. To expect relatively poor places like Banda Aceh to have such sophisticated infrastructure in place, when even many developed cities don't have anything like this, would be unrealistic and unreasonable. But what about wealthier cities within the Asian elephant's natural range? Singapore is a pocket of incredible wealth located at the southern tip of mainland Southeast Asia—but at this point the tiny city-state has almost no forestland, which is also true of the portion of Malaysia adjacent to Singapore.

What about Brunei? A small and lesser-known sovereign state on the northern coast of the island of Borneo, Brunei is within the Asian elephant's natural range. Since its major industry is offshore gas rather than agriculture, it has a generous amount of forest cover. Its towns become highly flood-prone during monsoon, as does its one major city, called Bandar Seri Begawan. The country's gas deposits have made the country extremely wealthy, not just by Southeast Asian standards: Brunei has one of the top five gross domestic products per capita on earth—ahead of those of the United States, Saudi Arabia, and Norway.

Brunei is so small that elephants from the Borneo interior rarely wander into its forests. Generally, the country doesn't even turn up on official lists of countries with wild Asian elephants. Yet the herds of Borneo elephants are present—if not literally within Brunei's borders, then certainly in the nearby Malaysian and Indonesian sections of Borneo's huge forest interior. The Borneo elephant, which is a subspecies of the Asian elephant, has a nebulous past. Some experts say that Borneo's elephants are actually the last remaining Javanese elephants, who were brought to Borneo by the Sultan of Sulu in the seventeenth century, prior to elephants' eventual disappearance from the island of Java.

An alternative theory is that Borneo's population of elephants is indigenous and goes back for millennia.[13] The elephants got there, this theory goes, the way they got to Java and Sumatra: some ten thousand years ago, all three of these islands were connected to the Asian mainland. During that epoch, Southeast Asia was not divided into a mainland half and a maritime half, as it is today, but rather constituted a huge and united subcontinental landmass that paleogeographers refer to as Sundaland. The southern half of Sundaland rapidly flooded during the melting of the Arctic ice sheet, which raised global sea levels. All that remains of southern Sundaland today is the Indonesian archipelago west of Lombok (at the so-called Wallace Line), in particular the three large islands of Java, Sumatra, and Borneo. Of course, it's plausible that both theories are right, that Javanese elephants transplanted to Borneo mated with indigenous Borneo elephants. All these animals are, after all, simply Asian elephants.

I visited Brunei in 2016, not to see elephants but to see Brunei's main city. Could this place *have* elephants, I wondered, even though it is a modern urban environment? Bandar Seri Begawan feels very much like two completely separate cities superimposed on top of each other. One is a kind of "pile dwelling" settlement. Residential neighborhoods built entirely on stilts sprawl into the city's main waterway, the Brunei River, linked by a labyrinthine network of wooden planks and gangways.

These districts exemplify a traditional Malayan urban form, the *kampong*, or water village, built partly in anticipation of periodic flooding. Bandar Seri Begawan has several of these water villages, the largest of which, Kampong Ayer, is effectively a man-made island on stilts in the middle of the river. People get from kampong to kampong on private boats or water taxis, which are well organized throughout the city. The kampong style of settlement, where many urban residents live over the water rather than in the city's plains and hills, keeps many of those plains and hills clear of development, so the city is heavily penetrated by lush forest.

The city's other layer feels much more like the Islamic petro-metropolises of the Persian Gulf. While some of Brunei's gas wealth has gone toward the kampong settlements, most of it has gone toward a more conventionally modern city. This other urban layer has wide streets, concrete apartment buildings, an office downtown (with a rather colorless shopping complex), and a distinctive neo-traditional gold-domed mosque. The city was a British imperial outpost during part of its history—called Brunei Town then—and this legacy shows up in the demographics of the city's workforce, which often hails from India, the U.K., Australia, and New Zealand. Workers come from nearby Malaysia and Indonesia as well. To a solitary visitor wandering Bandar's streets, the city feels a bit like a large American college town during the summer months when everything is a bit too quiet and one's only company is the chilly wealth on display in the surrounding institutional architecture. At the same time, Bandar Seri Begawan is very much its own place, with a unique and startling presence of nature in the heart of the city. During my visit, macaque monkeys were everywhere, sometimes lingering by street markets. Enduring the hot midday sun in one of the kampong districts, I spotted small crocodiles and a monitor lizard lurking in the water below.

Several forest corridors begin near the downtown area and wind their way toward the larger forest country beyond the city's edge. These corridors are full of bamboo and vines and creepers, as well as many macaques and the famous Borneo proboscis monkeys. To me, the fact that the city already had these urban forest corridors in place, virtually all them with a substantial amount of uninterrupted connectivity to the vast Borneo rainforest beyond, seemed extraordinary. Of course, the city has had the luxury to be developed in this way because of the offshore gas, which is environmentally damaging but not in ways that a wanderer here would perceive or experience directly. Given the spatial layout of the city, its wealth, its kampong-like structuring around the inevitability of annual flooding, and its proximity to the Borneo rainforest, I thought it incredible that the place didn't have a few domesticated elephants already.

It could. Trained work elephants here could assist in transport and logistics during the rainy season, moving passengers and supplies across flooded roads, both within the city and between the towns and villages that dot Brunei's forested hinterland. A Bruneian department of floodtime logistics could hire mahouts from the Trans-Patkai region or from central Burma—areas where mahouts still tend to be skilled at using their elephants during the rainy season. Over time, these skills might be picked up by Malay-speaking Bruneians, Malaysians, Indonesians, and other groups already in Brunei, just as the Kachins learned mahoutship skills from the Hkamtis. Administrative expertise could come from the Burmese forestry department, with its knowledge about setting up elephant villages, and from the Kachin Independence Army, with its knowledge about conducting elephant-based transportation during floodtime on a systematic basis.

The work elephants, too, would likely at first come from elsewhere. The elephants could spend much of the year in the rainforest beyond the limits of Bandar Seri Begawan, tended to by their mahouts. During the rainy season, they would come with their human attendants into the city, to do far safer work than elephants did in Banda Aceh in early 2005. If such a model were shown to be effective in Brunei, it might be replicated in other parts of South and Southeast Asia, as other regions urbanize and develop. Even some cities in China, within the Asian elephant's range dating from ancient times, could foster these kinds of government-managed elephant teams for floodtime logistics.

Using elephants in this way could open up exciting new possibilities in planning human-inhabited landscapes around "soft," flexible infrastructure. Rather than requiring every new development in flood-prone terrain to involve construction of huge new levees, concrete run-off channels, and expensive, hulking road viaducts, more watercourses could be left to meander naturally. Communities could live alongside these courses, following some version of the Sissiri river-crossing model: temporary bridges would cross the rivers during the dry season, barges would cross during transitional times of year, and elephants would cross during the wet season (when unpredictable channel shifts create problems for barges). Not only would such communities be well positioned to absorb the shock of major flooding events, they would be able to capitalize on the benefits (agricultural and aquacultural) of being set on riparian ecosystems with healthy, dynamic flooding cycles.

It's just a dream, of course. But elephants' usefulness in flooded areas, rural and urban, is real. Investing in elephants to help during floods is the kind of thing that could connect elephants' unique abilities to a set of human needs that is likely to grow in coming years—a linkage that could even, in turn, help reverse Asian elephants' population decline. Until now, the Asian elephants' principal working alliance has been with those who ride them in the forest. But this alliance could grow to include many other human beings as well.

CONCLUSION

THE PROSPECTS FOR THE ASIAN ELEPHANT ARE BLEAK.
Just twenty years ago, there were sixty thousand Asian elephants
on Earth, already a calamitously small number. Today the number seems closer to forty thousand. This drop has occurred despite
the efforts of a vigorous international conservation community and
despite the presence of relatively stable political conditions throughout South and Southeast Asia. In fact, elephants have done relatively
well in areas adjacent to zones of political instability (in particular
around Burma's Kachin State), while improved economic development throughout this part of the world has gone hand in hand with
dramatic rates of deforestation. In the section of the planet most
densely settled with humans, little room is left over for the planet's
second-largest land animal.

Any hopeful future for the species likely has to entail those who
know them best: the people who fetch elephants out of the forest
every morning and return them every night. Such people have the
most sophisticated understanding of how humans and elephants
can coexist within the same social and environmental setting. And
yet in the global community of professional conservationists, veterinarians, scientists, and development experts committed to protecting Asian elephants, virtually no one involved hails from mahouts'

camps or villages. The global elephant conservation community holds many conferences. Fandis like Miloswar and mahouts like Mong Cho ought to be involved in them. The conferences are usually held in major cities—London, Singapore, Bangkok, Bangalore—but sometimes they should be in Chowkham, Miao, or Tanai, places with lots of people who've spent long years living and working with elephants deep in the forest—catching them, training them, riding them, fetching them, finding that one has become pregnant, raising and training the calf, and so on. Their involvement would broaden and improve the professional conversation about what to do with these giants in an upcoming era when Asia's human population and agricultural output will surely continue to expand.

Also usually in attendance at these conferences are representatives from the forest and wildlife bureaucracies of the states that have large elephant populations. But people like Colonel Nan, who is in a quasi-governmental, militant independence organization, ought to be there as well. Indeed, the demographic and environmental situation of Asia in the twenty-first century may make the Kachin Independence Army's "elephant brigade" model, which organizes an elephant management bureaucracy around the imperative of transportation, even more valuable and instructive than the Burmese government's current "timber enterprise" model, which organizes elephant management around the goal of logging.

Asian elephants would likely also benefit from a correction of a few misperceptions that are still widespread among many people in parts of the world that do not naturally have elephants of their own—and this includes most of the developed or "first" world. An all-too-common perceptual conflation of Asian with African elephants, combined with frequent and visually graphic news reporting on ivory poaching in Africa, has left many people with the mistaken impression that the main problem afflicting elephants today is that they're receiving insufficient antipoaching protections from police. And that impression may be accurate for parts of Africa and may correctly comprehend a significant threat facing the African elephant species.

But the fact is that Africa has half a million elephants, while Asia has a tenth the number. Even if we grant that ivory poaching is a major problem and that better protections are needed, the main problem afflicting elephants in Asia is not ivory poaching but deforestation. The reason Asian elephants' numbers are so low compared with those of African elephants is that thus far, deforestation between the Indus and Yangtze rivers has been a vastly more intensive historical process than has deforestation between the Senegal and the Zambezi. This strongly suggests that whatever hope the Asian species has rests in the hands of those human communities with a proven, ongoing ability to base their livelihoods on elephant domestication practices that keep elephants situated within the forest.

This problem of the perception, or misperception, of ivory poaching gets to a much deeper issue, a moral one. To many outsiders interested in the welfare of the elephants, support for antipoaching measures, or for larger wildlife reserves, may seem morally very intuitive, offering a particular appeal to the conscience, whereas the capture and conscription of individual elephants is much more morally fraught. Even if one of the core aims of forest-based domestication, looked at in totally "utilitarian" terms, is to keep a larger percentage of Asian elephants situated within forest ranges, and to give them plenty of free roaming and mating time in the forest, the sheer *domination* of these elephants' lives—they are literally in chains, after all—may strike a morally distressing note for many outside observers, and for readers of this book, who want to see elephants free and in the wild.

I have attempted to complicate this picture of domination. The chains are breakable. Many elephants seem to have profound feelings of loyalty and protectiveness to their mahouts and their mahouts' comrades. The whole system of the nighttime release depends upon the elephants' not taking advantage of a constant opportunity to escape. The elephants might even, to some extent, be the ones innovating some of the work tasks that they perform, or aspects of those work tasks, as a kind of collective strategy of survival. What I would urge outsiders concerned for elephants' long-term welfare to consider is that the desire (an all-too-human desire) to gravitate toward holding the "pure" or "perfect" positions is *not* the same thing as Asian elephants' desire to survive in a human-dominated world. The elephants do not have the luxury to ignore Voltaire's old aphorism that the perfect is the enemy of the good.

The relationship between the elephants and their forest mahouts certainly contains problems and frustrations. Currently, mahouts have to fetch their elephants in the forest on a daily basis, sometimes for many years on end. This keeps the mahouts more or less permanently wedded to the forest, as long as they're attending to their elephant. For some mahouts, like Mong Cho, even visiting close family members in a nearby village occurs only on occasion. Camp and forest life, and the bond with the elephants, reign supreme.

This situation could perhaps be ameliorated by the introduction of recent technology. For instance, the elephants could wear light-weight GPS devices, allowing mahouts to find them even if they've wandered many miles away. During the off season, elephants could be given multiple days or even weeks in a row in the forest, with fetters loosened, and the mahout could get more time participating in village or town life. Perhaps an elephant could be given months—years, even!—in the forest, permitted to wander for a hundred miles or more, as the mahout watches the route on a computer screen and eventually "fetches" the elephant in a truck-pulled portable stable.

This GPS-enabled scenario would grant more personal freedom

and autonomy to both forest mahout and elephant, allowing them to live as more "regular" members of their respective species. Of course, overlong separations could pull the human and elephant apart. But perhaps carefully staggered, short "vacations" could improve the interspecies bond rather than undermine it.

UPSTREAM FROM the fording spot where Burmay-Moti and her mahout Pradip cross the Sissiri with their passengers and cargo, a concrete viaduct is under construction: the Trans-Arunachal Highway. Intended to follow the long, Himalaya-hugging arc of Arunachal Pradesh, and to help assert Indian sovereignty in territory still claimed by China, the highway must pass over many high viaducts to traverse the floodplains of Himalayan rivers draining toward the Brahmaputra: the Sissiri, the Dibang, the Siang, the Lohit, the Dihing, and others, all of which have a gigantic water discharge during monsoon and can become, in multiple cases, several miles wide. The viaducts have to be both higher and wider than the reach of the most severe floods, so as not to be submerged. The viaduct projects are attempting to overcome a daunting engineering challenge, and once completed, they may prove insufficient in the event of a major rivercourse-altering earthquake, of the type that struck in 1950 and forced the total abandonment of the town of Sadiya.[1]

These lumbering concrete viaducts are, of course, the sort of transportation infrastructure with which the modern world is very familiar. Their construction should not come as any great surprise. The greater surprise for most outside observers is, surely, the persistence of elephant-based transportation as the highest-value means of passage across the Sissiri during monsoon. And visiting this spot and watching Burmay-Moti and Pradip at work, I could not help but suppose that if the Indian state involved itself more in such elephant "ferries," at river-crossing points along the forest frontier, and less in throwing huge sums of money at concrete projects of questionable soundness or finishability, it could in fact project far greater control over the area than it is currently able to do. The predictable, prosaic insistence of the modern technocratic state on the great concrete highway may actually undermine control. Thus far the only form of state leverage the project has brought is the ability of government officials to give out payoffs to local tribal leaders.[2]

No doubt, many development projects in Arunachal and elsewhere in the region do require investment in the form of concrete and steel, but there are limits to what this kind of hard infrastructure can do. The landscape of Arunachal Pradesh, like the landscape of the Kachin Hills, is not the hard, arid earth of, say, southern California—that is, the sort of landscape where the distinction between land and water is more rigid and predictable, and where the automobile seems most to come into its own as a creature of transport. The Trans-Arunachal Highway project is an attempt, and one not yet proven effective, to harness modern building materials at a massive scale to erect a huge fiction that the landscape is something other than what it is. But the hydra-like advance of water, mud, and silt in the area during monsoon is sublime—thunderous forces conjured up by elemental gods. Ultimately, such power may prove to be too much for the new paved leviathan.

ONE AFTERNOON on the way to one of the hill ranges of central Burma, I passed through Naypyidaw, Burma's new capital city, built by the military government during the late 2000s and early '10s. It is the only major urban settlement in Burma far from any waterway. Billions of dollars have gone into the rapid construction of the sprawling new metropolis, and at every turn the place begs comparison with the previous capital, Yangon. While Yangon is forever suffering power outages, Naypyidaw's bright, tall lights are kept on through the night. Yangon's streets are full of crowds, food stands, and honking traffic jams of taxis and motorcycles, while Naypyidaw is planned around empty superhighways of absurd width (one is twenty lanes across, with hardly any traffic at all). Yangon's downtown is arranged on a tightly knit street grid similar to New York's. With its more sprawling fabric of curvilinear arterials and cul-de-sacs, Naypyidaw's analogous "model" could be Lake Havasu or Palm Springs.

Naypyidaw is a kind of bubble of gleaming first-world luxury in one of the poorest countries on earth. It hosted the World Economic Forum in June 2013, a few days after I passed through. The metropolis is equipped with high-end supermarkets (unused), sweeping office parks (mostly unused), and an army of landscapers and gardeners to keep the many highway medians looking trim and pristine. Precious little street life was anywhere to be found, except at an unplanned open-air market at the edge of town, used by the capital's workforce and by the inhabitants of Pyinmana, the district's preexisting town, which Naypyidaw has swallowed up and annexed. No one I spoke with cares for the new capital city; one person told me curtly, "It's a sore subject," and left it at that. Some told me the idea for the new capital came to one of the generals' astrologers in a dream. Another said that during the run-up to the U.S. invasion of Iraq, the Burmese regime's leading military officials convinced each other that they were next. Naypyidaw's position between the Bago Hills and the Karen Hills seemed easier to defend than Yangon, which faces the sea.

Later in my travels, I was in a hotel in Yangon, going through notes and photographs. I considered Naypyidaw's landscape of vacant superhighways alongside various scenes of transport by elephant: a logging village's well-trod elephant trails, the elephant convoys of the KIA winding their way through the forest, the elephant ford at the Sissiri River, the "relief" elephants who rescued refugees in the Patkai Mountains in 1942 and who cleared tsunami wreckage in Indonesia in 2005. I considered the elephants I had met in my travels or had come to know from mahouts' tales or records from history: Air Singh, Neh Ong, Maggie, Rungdot, Sokona, Pak Chan, and many others. Naypyidaw's planners intend the new capital, more exurb than city, as a vision of a "modern," newly opened Burma. But in the contrast between landscapes of mobility, the freshly hardened ribbons of asphalt appeared regressive and constricting. The animals and their riders seemed to be carving out unknown frontiers that were otherworldly and everywhere.

Acknowledgments

THIS BOOK WOULD HAVE BEEN IMPOSSIBLE HAD I NOT crossed paths with and received help and advice from dozens of people. Kushal Konwar helped me identify research sites. Ja Seng Mai Lahkyen and Naw Doh graciously provided me with conversational language lessons. Yingkying helped me get to the field, as did Marj Rosenblum. Richard Lair and Khyne U Mar shared their deep knowledge about elephants' care. Bertil Lintner, the Bisa family, Larry Brown, David Air, Shona Patel, Philippe Gautier, Prajna Chowta, Semh Sumhka, and Ewa Narkiewicz all provided invaluable leads and recollections. My research in Indonesia came together thanks to the help of Wahdi Azmi, Ika Nurhayani, Asri Wijayanti, Chris Stremmer, and Hasbi Azhar. Nikil Saval gave me the momentum I needed to get the project moving during its early stages. Mimi Sheller, Gijs Mom, Mandy Sadan, Bob Wilson, Joachim Schliesinger, Kishore Saval, James C. Scott, Mark Elvin, Kafui Attoh, Andrew Liu, Piers Locke, and Daniel Schlozman all offered important historical, anthropological, and theoretical input. So did the late Rob Mason—whom I shall miss terribly.

Frustratingly, much of the most significant and brilliant help I received was from people whom I cannot directly name, due to the sensitivity of some aspects of the research. The guides and translators whose names have been coded in the book as Sang, Kagung, Nkumgam, P., and J. all deserve special mention. In the field, I was grateful for their acumen, creativity, and friendship. I want to extend this gratitude to others as well, in particular to the person, who must go unnamed, who arranged for me to visit the logging village site in central Burma, and with whom I traveled to the Karenni Hills. And of course this gratitude extends to all the mahouts and mahouts' friends and family members who were kind enough to talk with me, share their time, food, and drink with me, and grant me some degree of entrance into the world of forest mahoutship and elephants.

Finally, I cannot imagine having launched this project without the love and support of members of my family—too many of whom I lost during the period when I was writing this book. Marc Shell, Susan Shell, Hanna Rose Shell, Jason Sanford, Yvette Sanford Shell, the late Murray and Sophie Meld, and the late Sophie Shell: thank you for your wisdom, solace, and encouragement.

Notes

Map Citations

The ancient range of the Asian elephant in Map A roughly shows information from Mark Elvin, *The Retreat of Elephants* (New Haven, CT: Yale University Press, 2004), esp. 10; and R. Olivier, "Distribution and Status of the Asian Elephant," *Oryx* 14, no. 4 (1978): 379–424. The ancient range of the African elephant in Map D roughly shows information from Deon Furstenburg, "Focus on the African Elephant—*Loxodonta Africana*," *South African Hunter* 05040 (2010): 46–49; and Nick A. Drake et al., "Ancient Watercourses and Biogeography of the Sahara Explain the Peopling of the Desert," *Proceedings of the National Academy of Sciences* 108, no. 2 (2011), esp. appendix fig. 11. Present ranges roughly show geographic information drawn from International Union for Conservation of Nature, *IUCN Red List of Threatened Species* (2008).

A Note about Interviews and Anonymization

Throughout this notes section, I denote most of my 2013–17 mahout interviews with a randomly assigned letter rather than with a specific time and place. This precaution became necessary to protect the identities of people who spoke with me about sensitive subjects. A letter-coded document with further information about each interview is kept privately.

INTRODUCTION

1. Walter Kollert and Przemyslaw Walotek, "Global Teak Trade in the Aftermath of Myanmar's Log Export Ban," *Food and Agriculture Organization of the United Nations—Planted Forests and Trees Working Paper Series* 49, no. 6 (2015).
2. Dambuk Interview 1, 2017.
3. Population estimates of Asian elephants, as well as of their numbers in domesticity (and of these, how many are doing which kinds of work), are highly imprecise. Richard Lair, *Gone Astray* (Bangkok: FAO Regional Office for Asia and the Pacific, 1997), estimated that, around the turn of the millennium, roughly a quarter of the world's Asian elephant population, then around 60,000, were in domesticity. Of these, roughly 9,000 were engaged in logging and transport work, as opposed to work in the tourism and festival sectors. During the subsequent two decades, the total species population has shrunk from roughly 60,000 to somewhere between 40,000 and 50,000 (according to the World Wildlife Fund and other agencies). If we assume the proportion of domesticated to wild elephants has grown during this subsequent period—which seems reasonable due to intensifying human pressure on wild herds—and widen the margin of error to account for a shift in the ratio of tourism and festival elephants to transport and logging elephants, then a very broad estimate would suggest that in the 2010s, somewhere between 7,000 and 11,000 domestic elephants are outside the tourism and festival sectors.
4. Some elephant researchers have gone so far as question the word *domesticated* as a descriptor of the situation of Asian elephants who do work alongside human beings. Words like *trained, captive, work* (as in "work elephants"), or simply *domestic* come up throughout the relevant literature, each term presenting its own semantic tradeoffs. In this book I use these words interchangeably, to describe a situation that no English adjective describes perfectly. See Lair, *Gone Astray,* 3–4; and Piers Locke, "The Anomalous Elephant: Terminological Dilemmas and the Incalcitrant Domestica-

tion Debate," *Gajah* 41 (2014): 12–19. Recognizing the exceptional nature of the Asian elephant, Jared Diamond omits them from his analysis of the global history of animal domestication on the grounds that "Asian work elephants are just wild elephants that were captured and tamed; they were not bred in captivity." Jared Diamond, *Guns, Germs and Steel: The Fates of Human Societies* (New York: W. W. Norton, 1997), 159.

5. Dogs (to continue the example) are similar to Asian elephants, and a range of other species, in that they have adjusted their behavior to strike up symbiotic relationships with humans. Indeed, dogs seem to have played an active role shaping the dog-human working relationship in prehistoric times. But to develop skills like sniffing for bombs, performing rescues, or aiding mobility of the blind—that is, cognitively demanding skills useful to humans in high-stakes situations—dogs required many additional generations of externally imposed mating selection. See Raymond Pierotti and Brandy Fogg, *The First Domestication: How Wolves and Humans Coevolved* (New Haven, CT: Yale University Press, 2017); and Rebecca Cassidy and Molly Mullin, eds., *Where the Wild Things Are Now: Domestication Reconsidered* (Oxford: Berg, 2007).

6. Victoria Taylor and Trevor Poole, "Captive Breeding and Infant Mortality in Asian Elephants: A Comparison Between Western Zoos and Three Eastern Elephant Centers," *Zoo-Biology* 17 (1998): 311–32; F. Kurt and Khyne U Mar, "Neonate Mortality in Captive Asian Elephants (Elephas maximus)," *International Journal of Mammalian Biology* 61 (1996): 155–64; and Interview U.

7. Ros Clubb et al., "Compromised Survivorship in Zoo Elephants," *Science* 322, no. 5908 (2008): 1649; and Interview U.

8. Elizabeth Kolbert, *The Sixth Extinction: An Unnatural History* (New York: Henry Holt, 2014).

9. See Piers Locke, "Explorations in Ethnoelephantology: Social, Historical, and Ecological Intersections Between Asian Elephants and Humans," *Environment and Society: Advances in Research* 4, no. 1 (2013): 79–97; Piers Locke and Jane Buckingham, eds., *Conflict, Negotiation, and Coexistence: Rethinking Human-Elephant Rela-*

tions in South Asia (Oxford: Oxford University Press, 2016); Maan Barua, "Bio-Geo-Graphy: Landscape, Dwelling, and the Political Ecology of Human-Elephant Relations," *Environment and Planning D: Society and Space* 32, no. 5 (2014): 915–34; and Jamie Lorimer, "Elephants as Companion Species: The Lively Biogeographies of Asian Elephant Conservation in Sri Lanka," *Transactions of the Institute of British Geographers* 35, no. 4 (2010): 491–506.

10. A notable exception is Nicolas Lainé, "Conduct and Collaboration in Human-Elephant Working Communities of Northeast India," in *Conflict, Negotiation, and Coexistence: Rethinking Human-Elephant Relations in South Asia,* ed. Piers Locke and Jane Buckingham (Oxford: Oxford University Press, 2016): 180–204. This study focuses on the logging mahouts of the Hkamti area of Arunachal Pradesh.

11. Interview X.

12. Throughout this book, I have altered or scrambled some names to preserve anonymity of interviewees who discussed sensitive subject matter. Similarly, each field interview is referred to by a randomly assigned letter, which does not reveal date or location.

CHAPTER 1: CATCHING ELEPHANTS

1. Interview fully anonymized.
2. Interview H.
3. Interviews N and P.
4. Some people in central Burma use a different term: *djaung pandu.* The words *fandi* and *pandu* appear to be related. Interview H.
5. Interview K.
6. U Toke Gale, *Burmese Timber Elephant* (Singapore: Toppan Printing Co., 1974), 88–98; Thomas Trautmann, *Elephants and Kings: An Environmental History* (Chicago: University of Chicago Press, 2015), 324; and Interview K.
7. Guy Tachard, *A Relation of the Voyage to Siam* (London: Printed for J. Robinson, at the Golden-Lyon in St. Pauls Church-Yard, 1688), 233.

8. Michael Charney, *Southeast Asian Warfare: 1300–1900* (Leiden: Brill, 2004), 139.

9. Interview U.

10. Gale, *Burmese Timber*, 98–103; Tappan Kamar Baruah, *The Singphos and Their Religion* (Shillong: Government of Arunachal Pradesh, 1977), 39; Richard Lair, *Gone Astray: The Care and Management of the Asian Elephant in Domesticity* (Bangkok: FAO Regional Office for Asia and the Pacific, 1997), 62; and Interviews G, J, K, P, U, V, and W.

11. Interviews J and K.

12. Interviews C, J, K, and P.

13. Interview fully anonymized.

14. Interview U.

15. Interview J.

16. Interview X.

17. C.W.A. Bruce, "Some Notes on the Indian Elephant," *Journal of the Bombay Natural History Society* 14 (1903): 151–55, esp. 152.

18. Interviews F and Y.

19. Interview T.

20. Gale, *Burmese Timber*, 35. Gale notes that during the work period, logging and transport elephants may require 1,000 to 1,200 pounds of fodder per day.

21. James Howard Williams, *Elephant Bill* (London: Rupert Hart-Davis, 1950), 56.

22. Interviews U and Y; Victoria Taylor and Trevor Poole, "Captive Breeding and Infant Mortality in Asian Elephants: A Comparison between Western Zoos and Three Eastern Elephant Centers," *Zoo-Biology* 17 (1998): 311–32; and F. Kurt and Khyne U Mar, "Neonate Mortality in Captive Asian Elephants (Elephas maximus)," *International Journal of Mammalian Biology* 61 (1996): 155–64.

23. Interviews C, P, and W.

24. Interview P.

25. Interview fully anonymized.

26. Interview W.

27. Interviews C and F.

CHAPTER 2: POWERS OF TRUNK AND MIND

1. Guy Tachard, *A Relation of the Voyage to Siam* (London: Printed for J. Robinson, at the Golden-Lyon in St. Pauls Church-Yard, 1688), 233.
2. Gary Marchant and Jeheskel Shoshani, "Head Muscles of *Loxodonta africana* and *Elephas maximas* with Comments on *Mammuthus primigenius* Muscles," *Quaternary International* 169 (2007): 186–91.
3. Interview B.
4. The Singphos are closely related to the Jinghpaws on the Burmese side of the Patkai Mountains; both are Kachin groups.
5. Interview F.
6. Interview Z.
7. Interview F.
8. U Toke Gale, *Burmese Timber Elephant* (Singapore: Toppan Printing Co., 1974), 129.
9. Gale, *Burmese Timber*, 129–30.
10. Dambuk Interview 3, 2017.
11. Dambuk Interview 1, 2017.
12. Dambuk Interview 2, 2017.
13. Interviews A, C, J, N, and Y.
14. Interviews G, N, and W.
15. Interview A.
16. Interview Y.
17. My 2013 central Burma field notes.
18. Interview W.
19. Interview Z.
20. Interview W.
21. Interview B.
22. Interview P.
23. Interview T.
24. James Howard Williams, *Elephant Bill* (London: Rupert Hart-Davis, 1950), 295–97.

CHAPTER 3: MUDDY EXODUS

1. Geoffrey Tyson, *Forgotten Frontier* (Calcutta: W.H. Targett & Co., 1945), 102; and Andrew Martin, *Flight by Elephant* (London: Fourth Estate, 2013), 59.

2. Raymond Bryant, *The Political Ecology of Forestry in Burma* (Honolulu: University of Hawaii Press, 1997), 22–32, 78–92.

3. Martin, *Flight*, 47–48.

4. Tyson, *Forgotten Frontier*, 103; Felicity Goodall, *Exodus Burma* (Stroud, UK: Spellmount, 2011), 217.

5. Martin, *Flight*, 49.

6. Williams, *Elephant Bill* [UK ed.], 267, 272.

7. Williams, *Elephant Bill* [UK ed.], 275–76.

8. Martin, *Flight*, 49.

9. Tyson, *Forgotten Frontier*, 102.

10. Martin, *Flight*, 99.

11. Francis Kingdon-Ward, *From China to Hkamti Long* (London: E. Arnold & Co., 1924), 264.

12. Goodall, *Exodus Burma*, 217–19.

13. Martin, *Flight*, 100–1.

14. Tyson, *Forgotten Frontier*, 102.

15. S. Farrant Russell, *Muddy Exodus* (London: Epworth Press, 1944), 39.

16. Russell, *Muddy Exodus*, 15.

17. Russell, *Muddy Exodus*, 8–9, 26–29.

18. Russell, *Muddy Exodus*, 28–29.

19. Russell, *Muddy Exodus*, 29.

20. R. H. Gribble, *Out of Burma Night* (Calcutta: Thacker Spink & Co., 1944), 145.

21. Jayantha Jayewardene, *The Elephant in Sri Lanka* (Colombo: Wildlife Heritage Trust of Sri Lanka, 1994), 25.

22. Russell, *Muddy Exodus*, 6.

23. Russell, *Muddy Exodus*, 15–17.

24. Gribble, *Burma Night*, 80; Russell, *Muddy Exodus*, 15.

25. Gribble, *Burma Night*, 80; Russell, *Muddy Exodus*, 24.

26. Russell, *Muddy Exodus*, 31–32.

27. Russell, *Muddy Exodus*, 35–41. In these passages, the account becomes somewhat geographically confusing. Russell does not clarify whether the incident with the rope occurred at the Tagap ford across the Namyung or at a different crossing point. It is possible that the path was interwoven with the river along its ravine and crossed the river in multiple places. It is also possible that Russell, unsure of his surroundings, identified more than one mountain channel as the Namyung. Gribble, *Burma Night*, notes that four mountain rivers all bunched together around Pangsau, and all four had to be crossed (83).

28. Russell, *Muddy Exodus*, 40–42.

29. Russell, *Muddy Exodus*, 39.

30. Russell, *Muddy Exodus*, 49.

31. Also in the SOS party was a local tracker named Goal, a member of the Miri tribe and evidently not one of the Nung porters. See Tyson, *Forgotten Frontier*, 108.

32. Tyson, *Forgotten Frontier*, 105–8.

33. Tyson, *Forgotten Frontier*, 108.

34. Tyson, *Forgotten Frontier*, 112–14.

35. Tyson, *Forgotten Frontier*, 119–22; Martin, *Flight*, 156.

36. Tyson, *Forgotten Frontier*, 116.

37. Tyson, *Forgotten Frontier*, 112. Martin, *Flight*, suggests the elephant in the footage might be another tusker whom Mackrell favored, Phuldot, and the mahout a man named Gohain (156–58). These two had been the lead duo during the convoy's ford of the Dihing River several days before.

38. Mackrell Film Collection, Centre of South Asian Studies, University of Cambridge, Cambridge, UK; and Interview V.

39. Tyson, *Forgotten Frontier*, 115–16.

40. Tyson, *Forgotten Frontier*, 116.

41. Tyson, *Forgotten Frontier*, 123–43; Goodall, *Exodus Burma*, 214–16.

42. Goodall, *Exodus Burma*, 224; and Nigel Pankhurst, "'Elephant Man' Who Staged Daring WW2 Rescues," *BBC News*, November 1, 2010.

43. Tyson, *Forgotten Frontier*, 114–15.

44. Interviews I, L, O, P, and V.

45. Interview V.

46. Interview V.

47. Martin, *Flight*, 80.

48. Williams, *Elephant Bill* [UK ed.], 158.

49. Martin, *Flight*, 254.

50. Gribble, *Burma Night*, 146.

51. James LeRoy Christian, *Burma* (London: Collins, 1945), 146. *Shan* here likely means Hkamti.

52. Ian Fellowes-Gordon, *Amiable Assassins* (London: Robert Hale, 1957), 26.

53. Williams, *Elephant Bill* [UK ed.], 237, 241–43, 248, 294–98.

54. Williams, *Elephant Bill* [UK ed.], 314–15.

55. Hugh Clarke, "Of Elephants and Men," in *The Burma-Thailand Railway: Memory and History,* ed. Gavan McCormack and Hank Nelson (St. Leonards, Australia: Allen and Unwin, 1993), 37–44, 40.

56. Japan's elephant-mounted invasion of Manipur is referred to in Williams, *Elephant Bill* [UK ed.], 316: "the Japanese crossed [into Manipur] with a column of 350 elephants. . . . The elephants were used over precipitous and impassable country, linking up with motor transport and bullock-carts when they reached roads once more. Their transport system was improvised ad hoc from all available means and, though it did not look smart, it functioned and moved fast."

57. Williams, *Elephant Bill* [UK ed.], 315.

58. U Toke Gale, *Burmese Timber Elephant* (Singapore: Toppan Printing Co., 1974), xi–xiv, 86.

59. Haruko Taya Cook and Theodore Cook, *Japan at War: An Oral History* (New York: W. W. Norton, 1992), 100–1. See also Kazuo Tamayama, *Railwaymen in the War: Tales by Japanese Railway Soldiers in Burma and Thailand, 1941–1947* (London: Palgrave Macmillan, 2005), 142–43.

60. Ian Denys Peek, *One Fourteenth of an Elephant: A Memoir of Life and Death on the Burma-Thailand Railway* (London: Doubleday, 2005).

61. Yin Chun, "The Taciturn Pachyderm: Lin Wang the Elephant Veteran," *Sinorama* 84, no. 10 (1995): 108–17.
62. Williams, *Elephant Bill* [UK ed.], 307.
63. Vicki Constantine Croke, *Elephant Company* (New York: Random House, 2015), 288.
64. Russell, *Muddy Exodus*, 54.
65. Gale, *Burmese Timber*, 85.
66. Richard Lair, *Gone Astray: The Care and Management of the Asian Elephant in Domesticity* (Bangkok: FAO Regional Office for Asia and the Pacific, 1997), 104; and Khyne U Mar, Mirkka Lahdenperä, Virpa Lummaa, "Causes and Correlates of Calf Mortality in Captive Asian Elephants," *PLoS One* 7, no. 3 (2012): e32355.
67. Williams, *Elephant Bill* [UK ed.], 290–91.
68. See Chapter 5.
69. Interviews I, L, O, and P.
70. Interviews R and U.

CHAPTER 4: A COUNTERPOINT IN AFRICA

1. The term *subspecies* refers to subtle regional differences within the African species, or for that matter within the Asian elephant species. There is no sharp divide between one subspecies and another within the same species. Nonetheless, biologists will often make a distinction between the African forest elephant (*Loxodonta africana cyclotis*) and the larger and better-known African bush elephant, also known as the African savanna elephant (*Loxodonta africana africana*). A similar differentiation can be made between the mainland Asian elephant (*Elephas maximus indicus*), the Sumatran Asian elephant (*Elephas maximus sumatranus*), and the relatively smaller Borneo Asian elephant (*Elephas maximus borneensis*).
2. The World Wildlife Fund's 2016 population estimate for African elephants was 400,000 to 500,000.
3. Raman Sukumar, *The Living Elephants: Evolutionary Ecology,*

Behavior, and Conservation (Oxford: Oxford University Press, 2003), 57–59.

4. For this argument, see Thomas Trautmann, *Elephants and Kings: An Environmental History* (Chicago: University of Chicago Press, 2015). For further discussion of Indian war elephants, see Sukumar, *Living Elephants*, 59–64; and John Kistler, *War Elephants* (Lincoln: University of Nebraska Press, 2007), 204–24.

5. Frank Snowden, *Before Color Prejudice: The Ancient View of Blacks* (Cambridge, MA: Harvard University Press, 1983), 32. Snowden highlights a statement by the Greek historian Arrian (A.D. second century) that "Ethiopians" (Meroites) were domesticating elephants prior to Alexander the Great. See also Sukumar, *Living Elephants*, 81; Richard Lobban, *Historical Dictionary of Ancient and Medieval Nubia* (Lanham, MD: Scarecrow Press, 2004), 155; and Howard Hayes Scullard, *The Elephant in the Greek and Roman World* (Ithaca, NY: Cornell University Press, 1974), 127.

6. H. A. Sayce, "Second Interim Report on the Excavations at Meroe," *Annals of Archaeology and Anthropology* 4 (1912): 53–65.

7. Sukumar, *Living Elephants*, 20–21.

8. Alexander had encountered combat elephants somewhat earlier, at the Battle of Gaugamela against the Persian emperor Darius in 331 B.C. However, due to poor cavalry strategy or bad luck, Darius's elephants were ineffective during this battle, leaving the Macedonian leader unimpressed. See Kistler, *War Elephants*, chaps. 6 and 7.

9. William Gowers, *The Elephant in East Central Africa* (Nairobi: Rowland Ward, 1953), 143.

10. Kistler, *War Elephants*, 34–42.

11. Paul Kosmin, *The Land of the Elephant Kings: Space, Territory and Ideology in the Seleucid Empire* (Cambridge, MA: Harvard University Press, 2014).

12. Sukumar, *Living Elephants*, 45.

13. Kistler, *War Elephants*, 97.

14. Kistler, *War Elephants*, 98.

15. Scullard, *Elephant in Greek*, 131; and Frank Snowden, *Blacks in*

Antiquity: Ethiopians in the Greco-Roman Experience (Cambridge MA: Harvard University Press, 1970), 296.

16. The classical geographers Hipparchus, Polybius, and Marinus of Tyre proposed the land bridge, but evidently without reference to elephants. See William Smith, *A Dictionary of Greek and Roman Geography* (London, J. Murray, 1873), 2:51. Earlier, Aristotle had put forward the idea of a connection between the "extremities" of Africa and India, based on the observation that both landmasses have elephants. See Simplicius of Cilicia, *On Aristotle's "On the Heavens" 2.10–14*, trans. Ian Mueller (London: Bloomsbury Academic, 2014), 94. The Sicilian cartographer Muhammed Al-Idrisi's *Tabula Rogeriana* world map of 1154, commissioned by the Norman king Roger II of Sicily, shows the conjectured land bridge stretching from East Africa to Southeast Asia, almost entirely enveloping the Indian Ocean except for a few narrow straits linking Indian with Chinese waters. The German cartographer Nicolaus Germanus's *Ptolemy* map of 1482 is a relatively late world map to show the hypothesized land bridge; other significant fifteenth-century world maps, such as the famous planisphere by the Venetian monk Fra Mauro, omit it.

17. Kistler, *War Elephants*, 71.

18. Gowers, *East Central Africa*, 144–45.

19. Gowers, *East Central Africa*, 146; and Kistler, *War Elephants*, 138–39.

20. Gowers, *East Central Africa*, 148–49; and Kistler, *War Elephants*, 133.

21. John Prevas, *Hannibal Crosses the Alps* (Staplehurst UK: Spellmount, 1998), 61.

22. Kistler, *War Elephants*, 111.

23. With all this said, the ultimate cause of Hannibal's failure to defeat Rome was certainly not the strategy of bringing elephants, but rather lack of support from the ruling class in Carthage. See Kistler, *War Elephants*, 126.

24. Kistler, *War Elephants*, 141–42, 149, 156–57; Scullard, *Elephant in Greek*, 178–85.

25. Rhoads Murphey, "The Decline of North Africa Since the Roman

Occupation: Climatic or Human?" *Annals of the Association of American Geographers* 41, no. 2 (1951): 116–32; Mauro Cremaschi, "Steps and Timing of the Desertification During Late Antiquity," in *Arid Lands in Roman Times*, ed. Mario Liverani (Florence: All'insegna del Giglio, 2003); Graeme Barker, "A Tale of Two Deserts: Contrasting Desertification Histories on Rome's Desert Frontiers," *World Archaeology* 33, no. 3 (2002): 488–507; Deon Furstenburg, "Focus on the African Elephant—*Loxodonta Africana*," *South African Hunter* 05040 (2010): 46–49; David Harland, *Killing Game: International Law and the African Elephant* (Santa Barbara, CA: Praeger, 1994), 25; and Sukumar, *Living Elephants*, 45, 88.

26. William Barker, "The Elephant in the Sudan," in *The Elephant in East Central Africa* (Nairobi: Rowland Ward, 1953), 69; Sylvia Sikes, *The Natural History of the African Elephant* (London: Weidenfield & Nicolson, 1971), 291; and Kistler, *War Elephants*, 177. See also A. Paul, *A History of the Beja Tribes of the Sudan* (London: F. Cass, 1971), 50 and map on 53.

27. J. L. Burckhardt, *Travels in Nubia* (London: J. Murray, 1819), 527–28; E. A. Wallis Budge, *History of Ethiopia, Nubia and Abyssinia* (London: Methuen, 1928), 66; and Lobban, *Historical Dictionary*, 65.

28. Barker, "Elephant in the Sudan," 69; and Lobban, *Historical Dictionary*, 65.

29. Kistler, *War Elephants*, highlights the likelihood that the Ethiopian army was using Kushite war elephants during the third or fourth century (171).

30. Richard Bulliet, *The Camel and the Wheel* (1975; rpt. New York: Columbia University Press, 1990), 111–40.

31. See John Campbell, *Travels in South Africa* (London: Black, Parry & Co., 1815), 297; John Campbell, *Travels in South Africa: Being a Narrative of a Second Journey* (London: Francis Westley, 1822), 240, 256–57, and 307–8; and William Desborough Cooley, "The Tribes Inhabiting the Highlands near Delagoa Bay," *Journal of the Royal Geographical Society* 3 (1833): 310–24. This article contains a folding map with the label "Mahalasely?" just north of Maputo

Bay (Delagoa Bay). Elizabeth Eldredge discusses possible trans-
lations of the term *Mahalaseela*—see "The Delagoa Bay Hinterland," in *Slavery in South Africa*, ed. Elizabeth Eldredge and Fred
Morton (Oxford: University of Natal Press, 1994), 162n93. Neil
Parsons suggests the Mahalaseela were one of the Tsonga tribes—
see "Prelude to *Difaqane*," in *The Mfecane Aftermath: Reconstruc-
tive Debates in Southern African History*," ed. Carolyn Hamilton
(Johannesburg: Witwatersrand Press, 2001), 346n69.

32. William Edward Oswell, *William Cotton Oswell, Hunter and
    Explorer . . .* (New York: Doubleday, 1900), 111.
33. William Desborough Cooley, *Claudius Ptolemy and the Nile* (Lon-
    don: John W. Parker & Son, 1854), 1.
34. Edith Sanders, "The Hamitic Hypothesis: Its Origins and Functions
    in Time Perspective," *Journal of African History* 10, no. 4 (1969):
    521–32; and Jean-Pierre Chrétien, *The Great Lakes of Africa: Two
    Thousand Years of History* (Cambridge, MA: Zone Books, 2003),
    12, 202, 207.
35. Jacob Shell, *Transportation and Revolt: Pigeons, Mules, Canals
    and the Vanishing Geographies of Subversive Mobility* (Cam-
    bridge, MA: MIT Press, 2015), 46–50.
36. Shell, *Transportation*, 47; Robert Brown, *The Story of Africa and
    Its Explorers* (London: Cassell, 1893), 2:67; and *Annual Cyclopae-
    dia and Register of Important Events* (New York: Appleton, 1885),
    5:294.
37. Robert Foran, *Transport in Many Lands* (London: Frederick
    Warne & Co., 1939), 39.
38. Scullard, *Elephant in Greek*, 62; and Sikes, *Natural History*, 296.
39. Murray Fowler and Susan Mikota, *Biology, Medicine, and Surgery
    of Elephants* (Ames, IA: Wiley-Blackwell, 2006), 19; and Jacques
    Van Heerden and Barend Louis Penzhorn, eds., *Symposium on
    African Elephant as a Game Ranch Animal* (South African Veteri-
    nary Association Wildlife Group, 1995), 71.
40. Sukumar, *Living Elephants*, 45.
41. Herold Wiens, *China's March Towards the Tropics* (Hamden, CT:
    Shoestring Press, 1954), 64–65, 184–86.

42. James C. Scott, *The Art of Not Being Governed: An Anarchist History of Southeast Asia* (New Haven, CT: Yale University Press, 2009).

43. Edmund Leach, *Political Systems of Highland Burma* (London: Athlone Press, 1964), 36; and Wiens, *China's March*, 184.

44. Francis Kingdon-Ward, *In Farthest Burma* (London: Seeley, 1921), 133–35.

45. Donald Seekins, *Historical Dictionary of Burma* (Lanham, MD: Scarecrow Press, 2006), 251; Wiens, *China's March*, 310.

46. Holt S. Hallett, *A Thousand Miles on an Elephant in the Shan States* (Edinburgh: W. Blackwood, 1890), 21.

47. "Karen Languages," *Encyclopedia Britannica* (1998).

48. Scott, *Art of Not*, 127–77.

49. Edmund Russell, *Evolutionary History: Uniting History and Biology to Understand Life on Earth* (Cambridge, UK: Cambridge University Press, 2011), p. 55.

50. Interview X.

51. Trautmann, *Elephants and Kings*.

52. Mark Elvin, *The Retreat of Elephants: An Environmental History of China* (New Haven, CT: Yale University Press, 2004), chap. 2; Wiens, *China's March*, 64.

53. Michael Charney, *Southeast Asian Warfare: 1300–1900* (Leiden: Brill, 2004), 144; Harry Miller, *Prince and Premier: A Biography of Tunku Abdul Rahman Putra Al-Haj* (London: Harrap, 1959), 19; J. W. Palmer, *The Golden Dagon, or, Up and Down the Irrawaddi* (New York: Dix, Edwards, & Co., 1856), 112; Grattan Geary, *Burma, After the Conquest* (London: Low, Marston, Searle, and Rivington, 1886), 29–31; and Shell, *Transportation*, 33–39.

CHAPTER 5: BREAKABLE CHAINS

1. Some description of the Karen guerrillas' elephants can be found in Jonathan Falla, *True Love and Bartholomew: Rebels on the Burmese Border* (Cambridge, UK: Cambridge University Press, 1991), esp. 131.

2. Holt S. Hallett, *A Thousand Miles on an Elephant in the Shan States* (Edinburgh: W. Blackwood, 1890), 52, 285, 312.

3. Interviews F, C, Z, and R.

4. Ho Chi Minh Trail (HCMT), *The Ho Chi Minh Trail* (Hanoi: Foreign Languages Publishing House, 1982), 118–31.

5. HCMT, *Ho Chi Minh Trail*, 118.

6. HCMT, *Ho Chi Minh Trail*, 119.

7. HCMT, *Ho Chi Minh Trail*, 123.

8. HCMT, *Ho Chi Minh Trail*, 125–29.

9. HCMT, *Ho Chi Minh Trail*, 130.

10. HCMT, *Ho Chi Minh Trail*, 106–7.

11. The Kamooks (Khamus) and Kamaits, both part of the larger Kha group, were charged with tending to elephants and logging in the Lao region; see Hallett, *Thousand Miles,* 21, a book written in 1890. Lair, *Gone Astray,* discusses the complexity of the modern designation "Khamu," who are also partially Lao (97). See also Joachim Schliesinger, *Elephants in Thailand* (Bangkok: White Lotus, 2010), 1:81. During the colonial period, certain Southeast Asian ethnic groups (especially Khamu and Karen) became associated with elephant driving as a means of livelihood; see Katherine Bowie, "Ethnic Heterogeneity and Elephants in 19th Century Lanna Statecraft," in *Civility and Savagery: Social Identity in Tai States,* ed. Andrew Turton (Richmond, UK: Curzon, 2012), 21 and 330–48.

12. Vu Hung, *The Story of a Mahout and His War Elephant* (Hanoi: Foreign Languages Publishing House, 1976), 43.

13. Hung, *Story of Mahout,* 89–93.

14. Hung, *Story of Mahout,* 54–58.

15. Hung, *Story of Mahout,* 59–62.

16. Many thanks to Jerome Palawng Awng Lat and Njawng Brang.

17. HCMT, *Ho Chi Minh Trail*, 131.

18. John Prados, *The Blood Road: The Ho Chi Minh Trail and the Vietnam War* (New York: Wiley, 1999), 221.

19. Robert Mason, *Chickenhawk* (New York: Viking, 1993), 339–40.

20. Richard Lair, *Gone Astray* (Bangkok: FAO Regional Office for Asia and the Pacific, 1997), 219.
21. Ingrid Suter, "ElefantAsia in the Lao PDR," *Gajah* 33 (2010): 53–57; Lair, *Gone Astray*, 94.
22. Interview U.

CHAPTER 6: STRANGE BEHAVIORS

1. U Toke Gale, *Burmese Timber Elephant* (Singapore: Toppan Printing Co., 1974), 76–78.
2. Interviews I, U, and Y.
3. Interviews F, G, U, and Y.
4. Interviews C and U.
5. Interview J.
6. Interview P.
7. Interview P.
8. Interview fully anonymized.
9. Interview U.
10. Interview X.
11. Interview O.
12. James Howard Williams, *Elephant Bill* (Garden City, NY: Doubleday, 1950), 181–82.
13. Interview fully anonymized.
14. Raghav Srivastava and Richa Tyagi, "Wildlife Corridors in India: Viable Legal Tools for Species Conservation?" *Environmental Law Review* 18, no. 3 (2016): 205–23. See also the discussion in Elephant Task Force, *Gajah: Securing the Future for Elephants in India* (New Delhi: Ministry of Environment and Forests, 2010); and Interview U.
15. Interviews G, J, P, and Y. See also Prajna Chowta and Philip Gautier's documentary *The Old Elephant Route* (Aane Mane Foundation and Les Films d'Ici, 2000).
16. Interviews N and W.

CHAPTER 7: CAMPS AND VILLAGES

1. Interviews A and H; and my 2013 central Burma field notes.
2. Interviews Y and P.
3. James Howard Williams, *Elephant Bill* (London: Rupert Hart-Davis, 1950), 213.
4. Prajna Chowta and Parbati Barua, both of India, are examples.
5. Interview H.
6. Interview X.
7. Interview A.
8. See Raymond Bryant, *The Political Ecology of Forestry in Burma* (Honolulu: University of Hawaii Press, 1997), 43–76. In the mid-nineteenth century, British colonial officials in India hoped to emulate Southeast Asian tribal methods of getting their tamed elephants to breed, though British records do not make clear which tribes' practices officials had in mind. See K. Sivara-makrishnan, *Modern Forests: Statemaking and Environmental Change in Colonial Eastern India* (Palo Alto, CA: Stanford University Press, 1999), 102. Griffith Evans refers to the elephants of the Karens, Laos, and Talines (Mons) of the Karen Hills as "bred" elephants, so it seems likely that it was these three groups' elephant domesticating practices that drew colonial officials' attention during the nineteenth century. See Griffith Evans, *Elephants and Their Diseases* (Rangoon: Government Printer and Stationery, 1910), 1–2. See also Jacob Shell, "Enigma of the Asian Elephant," *Annals of the American Association of Geographers* (forthcoming).
9. A map of approximate village locations can be found in U Tun Aung and U Thoung Nyunt, "The Care and Management of the Domesticated Asian Elephant in Myanmar," in *Giants on Our Hands* (Bangkok: FAO Regional Office for Asia and the Pacific, 2003), 89–102, 101. However, these locations have all likely shifted somewhat during the years since that study.
10. Interview X.
11. My 2016 central Burma field notes.

12. One of these surprise visits occurred while I was staying at a logging village in 2013.

13. Interviews H, X, and U.

14. Richard Lair, *Gone Astray* (Bangkok: FAO Regional Office for Asia and the Pacific, 1997), 199.

15. Interview U.

16. Interview H and X.

17. Interview Z.

18. Interview F.

19. Interviews E, J, U, and X; and my 2016 central Burma field notes.

20. R. M. Nath, *Background of Assamese Culture* (Guahati, 1978), 60; and S. L. Baruah, *A Comparative History of Assam* (New Delhi: Munshiram & Manorharlal, 1985), 222.

21. Edmund Leach, *Political Systems of Highland Burma* (London: Athlone Press, 1964), 36; and Francis Kingdon-Ward, *In Farthest Burma* (London: Seeley, 1921), 133–35.

22. James C. Scott, *The Art of Not Being Governed: An Anarchist History of Southeast Asia* (New Haven, CT: Yale University Press, 2009), 24, 210, 255.

23. Interview E.

24. Interview C.

25. Government of Arunachal Pradesh, *Note on the Trans-Arunachal Highway* (submitted to Secretary to Governor, March 13, 2008). This official document includes a map of the project's routing.

CHAPTER 8: PENCIL LINES ON A MAP

1. Peter Beaumont, "Myanmar Army Killing Civilians in Escalating Conflict in Kachin, Warns UN," *Guardian,* May 1, 2018.

2. These interviews occurred over two sessions, referred to herein as Interviews R and T.

3. Interview T.

4. "Indo-Burma-China Railway Connexion," *Saturday Review of Politics, Literature, Science and Art* 67 (1889): 680.

5. Khin Maung Nyunt, *Selected Writings of Dr. Khun Maung Nyunt* (Yangon: Myanmar Historical Commission, 2004), 36; and Alice Virginia Petar, *Jade* (Washington, DC: U.S. Department of the Interior, Bureau of Mines, 1936), 10.

6. Mandy Sadan, *Being and Becoming Kachin: Histories Beyond the State in the Borderlands of Burma* (Oxford, UK: Oxford University Press, 2013), 198–253.

7. Gustaaf Houtman, "Aung San's Lan-Zin, the Blue Print and the Japanese Occupation of Burma," in *Reconsidering the Japanese Military Occupation in Burma,* ed. Kei Nemoto (Tokyo: University of Foreign Studies, 2007), 179–227.

8. Shelby Tucker, *Among Insurgents: Walking through Burma* (London: Radcliffe Press, 2000), 167; Shelby Tucker, *Burma: Curse of Independence* (London: Pluto Press, 2001), 128; and Martin Smith, *Burma: Insurgency and the Politics of Ethnicity* (London: Zed Books, 1991), 48.

9. Smith, *Burma,* 176–97.

10. Bertil Lintner, *Land of Jade* (1990; rpt. Bangkok: Orchid Press, 2011), 164, 245; and Interview R.

11. Global Witness, *Jade: Myanmar's Big State Secret* (London: Global Witness, 2015); Jonah Fisher, "Myanmar Elite 'Profits from $31bn Jade Trade,'" *BBC News,* October 23, 2015; and "Myanmar's Military Elite and Drug Lords Run £20bn Jade Trade, Report Says," *Guardian,* October 23, 2015.

12. Nang Mya Nadi, "Military Secures Hpakant Area After 37-ton Jade Slab Found," *Democratic Voice of Burma,* February 20, 2014.

13. Richard Hughes et al., "Burmese Jade, the Inscrutable Gem," *Gems and Gemology* 36, no. 1 (2000): 2–27.

14. Interviews R and Y; and my Kachin field notes.

15. Lintner, *Land of Jade,* 246–47; and Interview R.

16. Interview T; and my Kachin field notes. A driver described the Kumons as "N'kai Bum" or "bad mountains."

17. Tucker, *Among Insurgents,* 196–97.

18. Bertil Linter, KIA elephant camp 1987 field notes (with many thanks to Lintner for sharing these with me).

19. Interviews R and T.

20. Lawi Weng, "Tatmadaw Says Kachin IDPs Cannot Stay in Tanai," *Irrawaddy,* April 19, 2018.

21. The map is an English-language topographic map of the Hukawng Valley, with an added text layer translating place names into Burmese script, and another layer showing central military and KIA base locations.

22. In reality, the Tiger Reserve is virtually bereft of tigers. Since its 2003 founding, it has functioned to facilitate development access to the Hukawng Valley for mining and sugar plantation companies with connections to the country's military regime. See Francis Wade, "Is the World's Largest Tiger Reserve a Front for Burma's Cronies?" *Asian Correspondent*, November 22, 2012.

23. Rajeev Bhattacharyya, *Rendezvous with Rebels: Journey to Meet India's Most Wanted Man* (New Delhi: HarperCollins India, 2014), 80–87.

24. Interviews C, J, G, and P.

25. Lintner, *Land of Jade*, 147.

26. Charles Romanus and Riley Sutherland, *China-Burma-India Theater: Stillwell's Command Problems* (Washington, DC: Center of Military History, 1987), 39.

27. Lintner, *Land of Jade*, 148.

28. Lintner, *Land of Jade*, 153.

29. Tucker, *Among Insurgents*, 258.

30. Interviews P and R.

31. Lintner, *Land of Jade*, 154, 180.

32. Interview fully anonymized.

33. Tucker, *Among Insurgents*, 236.

34. Interview P.

35. Interview R; Lintner, *Land of Jade,* 155; and Tucker, *Among Insurgents*, xxviii.

36. Tucker, *Among Insurgents*, 106–12.

CHAPTER 9: FLOOD RELIEF ELEPHANT

1. Dambuk interview 3, 2017.
2. See Francis Kingdon-Ward, "The Great Assam Earthquake of 1950," *Geographical Journal* 119, no. 2 (1953): 169–82; and Francis Kingdon-Ward, "Aftermath of the Great Assam Earthquake of 1950," *Geographical Journal* 121, no. 3 (1955): 290–303.
3. Interview P.
4. S. D. Goswami and A. M. Saikia, "The Sadiya Trade Fair," in *Cross-border Trade of North-east India: The Arunachal Perspective,* ed. S. Dutta (London: Greenwich Millennium, 2002), 129–37.
5. Interviews B and P.
6. Interview M. See for instance Paula Bronstein's photo in Moni Basu, "Thailand Flooding: Fear Brings People Together," *CNN Online*, August 14, 2011.
7. Helen Gibbons and Guy Gelfenbaum, "Astonishing Wave Heights Among the Findings of an International Tsunami Survey Team on Sumatra," *Sound Waves: USGS Newsletter*, March 2005; and Shannon Doocy et al., "Tsunami Mortality in Aceh Province, Indonesia," *Bulletin of the World Health Organization* 85, no. 4 (2007): 273–78.
8. See Jacob Shell, "When Roads Cannot Be Used: The Use of Trained Elephants for Emergency Logistics, Off-Road Conveyance and Political Revolt in South and Southeast Asia," *Transfers: Interdisciplinary Journal of Mobility Studies* 5, no. 2 (2015): 62–80, 66–67.
9. Interview M.
10. Richard Lair, *Gone Astray: The Care and Management of the Asian Elephant in Domesticity* (Bangkok: FAO Regional Office for Asia and the Pacific, 1997), 73–74.
11. Lair, *Gone Astray*, 79; and Interview M.
12. James Brooke, "Thais Use Heavy Equipment: Elephants Help Recover Bodies," *New York Times*, January 7, 2005.
13. Rajan Sukumar, *The Asian Elephant: Ecology and Management* (Cambridge, UK: Cambridge University Press, 1992), 28.

CONCLUSION

1. For instance, the 1950 Assam-Tibet earthquake measured 8.6 on the Richter scale and caused the Lohit River to completely change its course, forcing the permanent abandonment of the district capital at Sadiya. See Francis Kingdon-Ward, "Aftermath of the Great Assam Earthquake of 1950," *Geographical Journal* 121, no. 3 (1955): 290–303.
2. Dambuk interviews, 2017.

Index

Note: Page numbers in *italics* refer to maps. Page numbers after 218 refer to Notes.